DATE DUE

IVAN TURGENEV

IVAN TURGENEV

IVAN TURGENEV

BY

J. A. T. LLOYD, 1870-1956

John Arthur Thomas

"My one desire for my tomb is that they shall engrave upon it what
my book has accomplished for the emancipation of the serfs."

Ivan Turgenev

KENNIKAT PRESS
Port Washington, N. Y./London

4/73   CX N   # 4104

IVAN TURGENEV

First published in 1942
Reissued in 1972 by Kennikat Press
Library of Congress Catalog Card No: 78-160769
ISBN 0-8046-1591-8

Manufactured by Taylor Publishing Company   Dallas, Texas

IVAN TURGENEV

CHRONOLOGY

1818	Born at Orel.
1835	Entered the University of St. Petersburg.
1838	Visited Europe for the first time.
1841	Returned to Russia.
1843	Met Bielinski and Pauline Garcia.
1847	Followed the Viardots to Europe.
1848	First visit to France.
1850	Death of Madame Turgenev.
1852	Published "Annals of a Sportsman."
1856	Left Russia to live in Europe.
1859	Published "Liza."
1859	Published "On the Eve."
1862	Published "Fathers and Sons."
1863	First appearance at Magny dinners.
1864	Settled in Baden-Baden.
1866	Met Flaubert.
1867	Published "Smoke."
1871	Commencement of Parisian period.
1877	Published "Virgin Soil."
1879	Visit to Moscow for the inauguration of the statue of Pushkin.
1882	Reconciled with Young Russia.
1883	Died in Paris.

HIS WORKS

The Annals of a Sportsman.
Rudin.
Liza.
On the Eve.
Fathers and Sons.
Smoke.
Virgin Soil.
Dream Tales and Prose Poems.
The Torrents of Spring.
First Love.
The Diary of a Superfluous Man.
A Lear of the Steppes.
Mumu, etc.
A Desperate Character, etc.
The Jew, etc.

CONTENTS

ILLUSTRATIONS

CHAPTER I

THE TROÏKA

Q UITE recently a distinguished Englishman puzzled the British public by maintaining that there is nothing new in the massed *furor Teutonicus*. Down the centuries, indeed, its brutishness has always found a suitable focus for the worshipper of Wotan as for the devotee of Nietzsche. The figureheads may change through the generations but the German remains the same. He remains the German of Tacitus, changeless as the earth itself. And this changelessness has found recognition in a long series of thinkers of his own race from Goethe to Schopenhauer and from Heine to Nietzsche.

In very much the same sense, the Russian has remained changeless in the midst of overwhelming change. New labels apply to him with as little significance as to the German. From the days of the Tartar yoke to that other yoke of Peter the Great, through the long despotisms of reaction to that alien despotism inaugurated by Lenin, the Russian has remained the Russian. Perhaps even his detachment from the particular nature of his State has made this inner changelessness peculiarly clear. For, as Kluchevsky has noted, the Russian attitude towards the Russian state was that of a servant rather than of a child of the household.

If the German was, is, and always has been exactly what Tacitus claimed him to be—close to the earth—the Russian, in spite of the long Tartar yoke, has always beaten against barriers. It was not for nothing that the cosmopolite Ivan Turgenev alluded to his compatriots as *des gens de l'humanité*.

Right through the topsy-turvydom of the present century, alike through wars and through revolutions, the Russians manifest exactly the same qualities that they exhibit in the pages of every one of their great writers from Pushkin, Gogol and Lermontov, to Dostoevsky, Tolstoy and Turgenev. And when Turgenev himself, as though anticipating Gorki with a long gallery of innovators whose doctrines were in an outer sense to make those of Bazarov pale, presents a Russian of the future the most casual Western reader detects that he is only a Russian of the old sort dressed up in a new fashion. This fact is particularly evident in the work of Chekhov who used to exclaim, with the humility of one great artist towards another, that he was not so good as Turgenev.

Still, the background of Turgenev was immeasurably different in certain externals from the background of any creative Russian writer of this century and, to comprehend him in his own setting, one must at least try to estimate the tempo of his period in relation to his race and his family. The river of Russian national life flowed then with what seems to us now an incredible leisureliness but it was the life of the same Russian people. Russians reacted then to liberty and to danger exactly as they do to-day. They lived with a certain fatalism and they died with a certain indifference. Above all, then as now, they behaved in a way that they were noted for through the centuries—they took the field easily. For the rest, Turgenev's Russian no less than Gorki's was *capable de tout*. And perhaps Turgenev realized, no less than Dostoevsky, that if the Russian embraced atheism he would do it with a passion that would turn it into a sort of religion.

Superficially the Russian has undergone, more than any other European, the process of Americanization. Superficially he has become modernized, to the exclusion of every cult and faith of the past. But he has not shaken off that past. The Russia of the twentieth century has not become crystallized in the sense that Turgenev was to find Western Europe crystallized. Even the Russian proletariat has refused to be wholly severed from the peasant background from which it has sprung. Neither soldier nor technician has become a robot. The speed car has not banished the glamour of the troïka. But one cannot forget that it was in the Russia of the troïka that Turgenev lived and worked.

The Russian novelists of the nineteenth century have an importance, denied at that period to any other country. Turgenev claimed for Gogol, the Father of the Russian novel, a historic significance. It certainly never occurred to him that this claim might be justly urged for himself, yet he undoubtedly sustained and deepened that historic significance. He with Tolstoy and Dostoevsky became, like Gogol before them, the suppressed historians of their race.

Suppressed historians through the medium of fiction have already begun to appear in twentieth-century literature, but in the nineteenth they were peculiar to Russia. The gibes against the reality of our English Constitutional History ring out on the lips of the ignorant as flippantly by the Thames as by the Moskova, but in Russia Constitutional History may be said to have been, and to be, simply non-existent. Generation after generation tyranny disdained explanation, disdained the processes of evolutionary freedom and demanded always the frozen silence of acceptance. The one voice that could pierce, however cautiously and indirectly, this proclaimed silence was that of the Russian novelist.

Driving through the steppes in 1812, Madame de Staël detected the great fact that, though nothing national found utterance in Russia, there yet was something national to utter which one day would assuredly find expression through those who realized "what is most intimate and real in their own souls." Gogol was then a child of three; six years later Ivan Turgenev was to be born at Orel; three years after that Feodor Mikhailovich Dostoevsky was to be born at Moscow. Then seven years later, in 1828, Count Tolstoy saw the light of Yasnaya Polyana. These four great novelists, each after his fashion, became not merely portrayers of Russian manners and customs; not merely exhorters to Russians on conduct and character; not merely analysts of human passion; not merely idealists viewing from Hegelian heights their groping and grovelling compatriots. These suppressed historians were themselves the expression of Russia's age-long repression. They and they only could insinuate the truth of what lurked behind the imperial façade of their country. They and they only could speak out where others dared not whisper.

Inevitably the Western development of the novel, from romanticism to realism and from realism to naturalism and from naturalism to symbolism and from symbolism to those individual reactions to individual emotional experiences, meant little or nothing to the Russian writer of the last century. His struggle for freedom of expression was wholly different from that of Western novelists. The historical novel, in the sense of Sir Walter Scott, was as foreign to him as was, for instance, the powerful animalism of Zola. Eroticism, essentially personal and subjective, could be no *motif* for a suppressed historian who, like Tacitus himself, must indicate very quietly the reek and rankness of a roughly scented corruption.

So Chichikov's journey in *Dead Souls* cannot be compared with Mr Pickwick's journey though both of them, oddly enough, set out in the same year, 1837, to re-discover their respective countries. The humour of Gogol could not blend with the sombre steppes as Dickens' humour blends gently and kindly with our English countryside. And though Mr Pickwick became grave enough, when forced to penetrate below the respectable surface of institutions, he had never to confront the accumulated festerings of a systemized tyranny. It was for Chichikov, the purchaser of dead serfs on which he may raise money at a Russian bank, to expose cautiously and by inference—as in the manner of Tacitus —these festerings of wounds that no one dreamed of healing. Gogol's hero is not squeamish, but even on this journey, Dantesque in spite of its very humour, there are pauses and hesitations. One such stab of self-consciousness occurs when Chichikov reads a bald list of dead serfs that have passed into his possession. With a start he realizes that these were once actually human beings, people like himself. They had never been things; yet all their lives and now, even after death, they had been bought and sold. It is the horror of this insensate commerce that the humorous Gogol flashed across the world through the novel entitled *Dead Souls*.

On such a journey the forgiving irony of Cervantes, the picaresque gaiety of Le Sage, the healthy English laughter of Dickens would be alike incongruous. On such a journey the Russian tang was needed in a *motif* exactly suited to this untaught Russian realism which meant the revelation of reality so far as one was permitted to reveal it. The bargainer for corpses was little likely to idealize the slave owners who haggled with him so ravenously. But on the surface *Dead Souls* is just a picture of the Russians in Russian colours, pity for the oppressed being never declaimed in the manner of Hugo but only insinuated as by mere accident. For to Gogol Imperial Russia was something far more than the oppressor of Russians. Realist though he was, he never shook off his mystic belief in the rôle of that Russia, "which can exist without any one of us, but without which no one of us can exist." And in this very book, *Dead Souls*, he expresses his fundamental faith:

"Is it not thus like the bold troïka which cannot be overtaken, that thou art dashing along, oh! Russia, my country. The roads smoke beneath thee, the bridges thunder; all is left, all will be left behind thee. . . . Yes, on the troïka flies inspired by God! Oh Russia, whither art thou dashing? Reply! But she replies not; the horses' bells break into a wondrous sound; the shattered air becomes a tempest and the thunder growls; Russia flies past everything else on earth; and other peoples, kingdoms, and empires gaze askance as they stand aside to make way for her."

That troïka thundered on to an abyss from which it is little likely to emerge. But there was another troïka of whose existence Gogol perhaps did not dream though he himself was its actual driver: In the middle trots the moral reformer Tolstoy, to the left gallops the spiritual mystic of Russian realism, Dostoevsky; to the right the artist who interpreted Russia to western Europe in terms of the west. All three continued the historic tradition of the founder of Russian realism; each interpretation was complementary and necessary. Gogol himself, through *The Revisor*, had cut with his terrible laughter right into the rich flesh of the octopus, while in *Dead Souls* he had presented on a huge canvas the stagnant ruin that it meant for those who swarmed and writhed under its tentacles. Tolstoy through *My Confession* claimed to have found light from those who, in the opinion of the whole world were most steeped in darkness, while in *Resurrection* he lit up the path of individual redemption through association not with the oppressors in their strength but with the last and least of the oppressed. Dostoevsky through *The Idiot* divined the spiritual Russian yet to be, while in *The Brothers Karamazov* against a background of animalism in conflict with an atavistic mysticism he claimed for his race—not through Imperial Russia but through the Russians—a new and strange proselytizing force. Turgenev, through the *Annals of a Sportsman* accomplished for the Russian serf what the author of *Uncle Tom's Cabin* accomplished for the American slave, while in *Virgin Soil* he showed himself a prophet whose prophecy can be tested by the actual facts of the Russian peasant's attitude towards the new masters of Moscow.

Dostoevsky wandered through the world enduring an odyssey of physical hardship and spiritual torture until, through self-knowledge, he became at once the inquisitor and the confessor of his compatriots. Tolstoy from Yasnaya Polyana focussed the attention of the whole world on the Russian people and became, as it were, a national host for western Europeans. But it was left to Turgenev to become, in an intellectual sense the Russian guest of Europe, who alone interpreted to Europeans, in their own manner, the genius of his country.

Tolstoy emitted the light of eastern wisdom from Yasnaya Polyana. Turgenev brought the light of western knowledge to Spaskoë. The morass of Russian life, first revealed by Gogol, was lit up as by irregular flashes of lightning probing its most stagnant depths by the author of *The*

Brothers Karamazov. But it was Turgenev and Turgenev alone who brought to this same background of Russia, the calm white light of meditative and forgiving irony.

It was, then, an event of no small significance to the Russian people when on October 28th, 1818, Ivan Turgenev entered the world of ruthlessly organized Russian slavery. For without him there would have been, throughout the whole nineteenth century, no suppressed historian to speak to Europe in Europe's own language for the Russian people who were not things but men.

CHAPTER II

A NEST OF NOBLES

THE author of *Liza* was himself born into "a nest of nobles." This fact is of no small importance not only to literature, but to the history of human freedom. Turgenev's western bias was intensified, not always agreeably, by the environment of childhood. His education was widely cosmopolitan. Fräulein, Miss and Mamzelle, each in turn perplexed him with foreign tongues and foreign manners. In other ways, his home training was Spartan and years afterwards he was to describe himself, with that physical insistence of memory which made him, in spite of so many conflicting tendencies, the realist he was, as "drinking with a kind of bitter pleasure the salt water of his tears." Still, even in those early days, he would forsake foreign influences to steep himself in the inspiration of the national poetry. These moments he was to recall with his nostalgic charm and in *Punine and Babourine* he has sketched an old serf of Spaskoë reading aloud from a big book to his young master who has just escaped from the French governess.

The boy treasures every word of this strange new lesson from the steppes and there, in the quiet garden, he absorbs the old traditions of his race from which these foreign preceptors were endeavouring to tear him away. In this same garden he was to breathe in those impressions of Russian country life with which he was to charm the capitals of Europe. At Spaskoë too, he learned to become a sportsman and commenced those wandering habits which lend the vividness of actuality to *The Annals of a Sportsman*. Even in boyhood, his love of nature became a passion and he has told us that on many a quiet evening he would steal out alone into this garden of so many perfumed memories to embrace—a lime tree. This garden of Spaskoë appears again and again in the novels; for Turgenev retained in manhood, with the very gusto of childhood's wonder, its long drowsy secrets of summer days.

In childhood he became conscious of loneliness, and spied upon as he was himself he became in his turn a watcher of human souls. For on the very threshold of life disillusion was to be forced upon him through those nearest to him. His own home implanted in him that irony with which he was afterwards to veil the cold finality of his pessimism. He had observed his own home with a too penetrating scrutiny; he had tasted of the tree of knowledge very early in that garden of Spaskoë. It is no wonder that in his manhood he was to exclaim: "But as for marriage, what a cruel irony!" For soon it was not only from the experiences of others that he divined those secrets of life and death which blend fugitively in a passing passion. It was not only with lime trees that he began to keep appointments in this garden of secrets. Only too soon he was to wait breathlessly, listening for footsteps on the fine sand. It was not only the naïve fresh love of early youth that was to tinge his novels with remembered regret. Passion came to him early and it was among the raspberry bushes of the garden of Spaskoë that a young serf girl looked into his eyes when he could speak no word. Perhaps it was she who came to him on a breathless summer day and, master though he was, seized him by the hair uttering the one word "Come." Her name was Claudie, and forty years later the great novelist felt those fingers playing between the white locks as he recalled lingeringly *ce doux empoignement* of that once blond hair. But neither Claudie nor any other serf girl nor any woman in the world taught him faith in love and he ceased early to believe in the protection of Providence. "It is here in this same garden," he wrote in 1868 from Spaskoë, "that I witnessed, when quite a child, a contest between an adder and a toad, which made me for the first time doubtful of a benign Providence."

Such was the atmosphere of his early home which he has recaptured in so many masterpieces. This atmosphere, like the art of Turgenev, is simple only on the surface. It is

pervaded by the curious and difficult personality of the
novelist's mother. In Madame Turgenev one is confronted
by the very symbol of the serf-owning past. Even if *The
Annals of a Sportsman, Punine and Babourine* and *Mumu* had
never been written, one could still realize from a portrait
of Madame Turgenev what the Russian landowners of that
period really were in their relations to the human lives that
they owned from the cradle to the grave. She was the incarnation of the old ruling caste for whom tyranny was as
necessary as oxygen to the lungs. But tyranny does not
always breed tyrants and it was with a sense of outrage that
the boy Turgenev watched until the moment arrived when,
through a single quietly written book, he was able to
challenge Russian absolutism before the eyes of the whole
world. He himself had experienced the dull complacent
tyranny; he could sympathize with its victims as probably
no other writer, up to that date, had been able to sympathize. The hero of *Dead Souls* had been startled by a list
of serfs who had died without having ever owned an hour
of life. With a more conscious tenderness for "anonymous
Russia" Turgenev projects upon this and that delicate
canvas, one victim after another of his mother's household.
He knew them so well and he knew to the core the châtelaine of Spaskoë who had given him life without implanting
in him the inheritance of tyranny.

One other person may be claimed to have known Turgenev's home and its ruler almost equally well. In 1838 a
child was brought into this strange household to become the
adopted daughter of Madame Turgenev. In 1851, a year
after the death of his mother, the novelist wrote specifically
to Madame Viardot on the subject of this Varya who was
afterwards to reveal to the world the intimate family life
of his old home. In this letter he speaks of "this young girl,
whom my mother adopted, a regular Madame Lafarge,
false, ill-natured, cunning and without heart. It would be
impossible to tell you all the mischief that this little viper
has done." In the same letter Turgenev alludes to Varya as
a girl of seventeen though she herself maintains that in 1838

she was only a few days old. Be this as it may, she has left a documented and by no means an ill-natured record of the châtelaine of Spaskoë. Moreover, Turgenev has urged on her behalf that her education under his mother's roof was detestable as indeed her narrative very clearly proves. Such as she was, Varya was undoubtedly in a position to describe objectively the environment from which Ivan Turgenev sought to escape—the background of the family which was also the background of the old Russia.

The tyrannical mother of Ivan Turgenev had been in her youth the victim of tyranny. Her stepfather, Somov, hated and ill-treated her until she reached her seventeenth year, when he began to persecute her in a different way. Then it was that she fled half-dressed from his house and took refuge with her uncle, Ivan Lutovinov, who lived on his property, Spaskoë. The girl's mother demanded that she should be sent back, but her uncle refused to give her up, and she lived in his house until his death, when at the age of thirty, she inherited his vast fortune, including the property of Spaskoë. Soon afterwards she married Sergei Nikolaevich Turgenev and they lived together at Spaskoë in a manner typical of the old Russia. The châtelaine had her own chapel and her own theatre, the actors being drawn from the serfs who also provided her with an orchestra. Her rule in the family as on the estate was absolute, but she had difficulties with her husband as well as with her two sons, Nicholas and Ivan.

Of Turgenev's father, who had died before she entered the house, Varya knew little or nothing. But she alludes to the fact that he was exceptionally good-looking and tells us of a certain German princess who remarked to the châtelaine of Spaskoë: "Ah, you are the wife of Turgenev . . . I have not forgotten him . . . After the Emperor Alexander I, he was the handsomest man that I have ever seen." Towards his son Ivan this Adonis appears to have been the very essence of despotism. Once, when the boy came in tears to kiss his father's hand he was met with these words: "You are a pretty youngster. . . . So young still and yet committing so many wicked deeds." This observation frightened the boy: "I thought all through the night without being able to discover what were these wicked deeds with which they reproached me."

When Turgenev's father died his uncle, Nicholas managed the property for the widow and life for the little adopted daughter, Varya, became almost a duplicate of what it had been in the novelist's own childhood. There was the same throng of foreign instructors and the same iron discipline from the mistress of the house. "Nobody had the right," observes Varya, "to maintain in her presence an idea that contradicted her own." Life at Spaskoë, in short, was wholly in accordance with the essentials of tyranny that underlie those graceful pictures of reality in *The Annals of a Sportsman*. At the time of Varya's first memoirs, the household consisted of Madame Turgenev, her brother-in-law Nicholas, her two sons Nicholas and Ivan, a niece and last, but by no means least, the little feminine Astyanax herself. The châtelaine remained what she had always been; now, as always she disdained to conceal the iron hand under a velvet glove. Nobody contradicted her, but sometimes her favourite son Ivan would permit himself very gently to insinuate his thoughts. In Madame Turgenev's private journal, dated 1839, there is an entry which sheds an interesting sidelight on the softer side of this tyrant: "*C'est que Jean, c'est mon soleil à moi; je ne vois que lui et lorsqu'il s'éclipse, je ne vois plus clair. Je ne sais plus ou j'en suis. Le cœur d'une mère ne se trompe jamais, et vous savez, Jean, que mon instinct est plus sûr que ma raison.*" This journal is said to have been bequeathed by his mother to Ivan Turgenev, but Varya states that in 1849 it was burnt in the garden before her eyes. "Is it in virtue," she asks, "of the fatal law of heredity that Ivan Turgenev in his turn refused to publish his own journal, and following the example of his mother burnt it at Bougival in a garden?" Like her son's journal in a lesser degree, this personal record of a Russian slave-owner is a loss, particularly for those who might wish to

see the old Russia as Turgenev saw it hour by hour in his
old home.

Madame Turgenev after her fashion was really fond of
Ivan, and on his visits to Spaskoë would force herself to be
kind to the serfs so as to bring a smile to the lips of her son.
Varya speaks of these visits of Ivan as patches of sunlight
in the monotony of her life, and it is difficult to believe, in
spite of the novelist's verdict on her character, that she is
writing with duplicity. She tells us that Ivan delighted in
making himself a child in order to play with her, that he
was studying Greek at the time, and that he even instructed
her in the famous "*Bre-ke-ks-keks-koaks-koaks*" of Aristophanes.

The household consisted of forty servants, without count-
ing a number of small boys always at the beck and call of
Madame Turgenev. Russian was used only with the servants and Turgenev's adopted sister remarks: "As for us,
the members of the family, we were accustomed to read,
to write, to think, and even to pray to God in French."
Madame Turgenev was in the habit of striking her dependents and this method of discipline was applied to her
favourite son who one day related to Varya this little
incident of his childhood: He had been whipped as usual
without understanding why and when he asked the reason,
his mother answered, "You ought to know yourself, and
if you don't know divine it, divine it." The following day
Ivan declared once more that he did not know why he had
been punished. To this his mother responded by more
chastisement and the promise of a whipping every day until
her son should confess his fault. Thoroughly bewildered, the
boy resolved to escape and would have fled the next night
had he not been intercepted by his old tutor who asked him
the reason for this strange behaviour. The boy replied:
"Because I am beaten, without knowing what it is for."
The old man was amazed: "You don't know why you
are punished?" he asked. "I swear to you that I do
not," came the reply. The worthy old man promised that
this senseless punishment should cease and he actually

succeeded in persuading Madame Turgenev to abandon it.

Despot though she was, Madame Turgenev never forgot the hard days of her own youth. On one occasion she took Varya to see her mother's property and they explored together the dim old house which she had such bitter cause to remember. On coming out of the drawing-room they passed into a corridor where Varya was surprised to see a door barricaded by planks: "I went up to it and placed my hand on the old brass latch which stuck out between the planks, when Madame Turgenev seized my hand and cried out: 'Don't touch it, don't touch it; these rooms are accursed.' Never shall I forget her accent, nor the expression of her face, such fear and hatred and fury were written in it." Madame Turgenev dragged Varya away from these apartments of her stepfather from whom she had escaped, half dressed, in the days of her own humiliated youth.

Madame Turgenev's attitude towards literature was characteristic. In 1841, Ivan returned from abroad bringing with him to Spaskoë a little volume with a blue cover; it had created no sensation in the outer world, but it was an object of some curiosity in this unlettered household. Varya hung on the young author's lightest words as indeed did all the others, with the exception of the châtelaine herself. Ivan was inclined to lay down the law and he laid it down against kvass, which was banished from the table as a plebeian beverage, much to the regret of one of the governesses. Kvass was at all events a safe topic of conversation, but it was difficult to discuss literature in the presence of Madame Turgenev. None the less Ivan spoke with enthusiasm of Pushkin, expressing incidentally that he himself would never write anything of value in all his life.

"As for me," replied his mother disdainfully, "I don't understand how the idea of becoming a writer ever came to you. Is that the business of a noble? You confess yourself that you will never be a Pushkin. . . . I understand writing in verse. . . . But to be a writer . . . a writer! . . . do you know what it is to be a writer? I am going to tell you. . . . A writer or a quill-driver, it's all one; both scratch paper for money. A noble ought to serve the Tsar and make a career and a name in the army, and not by scratching paper." She was not, however, wholly inimical to the arts and when Liszt came that very year to Moscow she accompanied her son to the concert. She was unable to walk at the time and as, owing to an oversight, the customary means of conveying her had been neglected Ivan took her in his arms and carried her up the steep steps of the concert hall. Five years later Madame Viardot came to Moscow, and, in spite of her disapproval of Ivan's rapture, Madame Turgenev went to hear her. "*Il faut avouer pourtant*," she admitted grudgingly, "*que cette maudite bohémienne chante fort bien!*"

An interesting member of this barbaric household was Porphyre Kartashev who accompanied Ivan to the University of Berlin in the capacity of a kind of superior valet. This serf had learned German and had studied medicine at a Russian University. His skill was much in demand all over the district. None the less, as a serf, Porphyre could attend no sick bed without the authority of his ignorant owner. In vain Ivan implored his mother to emancipate his friend. She urged that he was very well treated as he was and that he received four times as much wages as the other servants. Porphyre's actual position was soon to be put to an acid test. At the age of ten Varya had an attack of typhoid and Madame Turgenev wished to send for other doctors. Porphyre, however, who had commenced to treat her insisted that the case should be left to him. The Russian doctor's owner looked him in the eyes as she answered briefly: "Remember that if you do not cure her you will go to Siberia." Porphyre willingly accepted the risk and luckily for him Varya responded to his treatment.

A tyrant towards her serfs, towards the inmates of her household, towards her favourite son, this arrogantly irresponsible woman upon whom such enormous responsibility rested was a veritable juggernaut towards her elder son. Nicholas had aroused her fury by insisting on a love match with a certain Mademoiselle Schwartz. Ivan himself, in spite of his theory in regard to marriage, was more than once on the verge of the same phase of recklessness, but apart from this there was little resemblance between the brothers. "Just as Ivan Turgenev," comments his adopted sister, "was Russian in appearance, so his brother was English. When I read the romance of *Jane Eyre* I could not represent Rochester to myself, except with the features of Nicholas Turgenev." The elder brother, according to the same authority, was fond of teasing, was a master of foreign languages, had a strong voice in contrast to Ivan's high-pitched one, and was far less anxious than his younger brother to be of service to his fellows. In Madame Turgenev's journal, under the heading "*A mon fils Nicholas*" there was a significant note of warning against the trammels of passion. But, so far as Mademoiselle Schwartz was concerned, this tyrannical mother failed to coerce her elder son. At Petersburg she learned that Nicholas had become a father. She expressed the wish to see the children, but instead of inviting them to her house, she gave orders that they should be led up and down in front of her windows; her will was as usual obeyed. For some time she watched impassively and then observed that the elder child resembled his father when he was the same age. And that was all she had to say about her grandchildren. She insisted, indeed, that the union was illegal and in order to coax Nicholas to break this marriage bond she offered him the management of the Spaskoë property, at the same time promising him large sums of money. To all this Nicholas replied that he could not break his marriage tie and abandon his family.

At last, in 1849, Madame Turgenev gave her consent to the marriage just at the time when her son's home was plunged in the depths of misery, his three children having died during the space of a single winter. "One might say," Nicholas remarked long afterwards to Varya, "that it was the malediction of my mother which brought about the death of my children." This observation recalled to Varya a repellent scene, only too typical of the châtelaine. For some reason or other she had asked Nicholas for portraits of his children. When the box containing them arrived she ordered her major-domo, Polyakov, to open it at once, but before he had taken out the first portrait she told him to give the box to her and leave the room. Some minutes later she called Polyakov's wife Agatha who came in hurriedly to find the three portraits torn to pieces on the floor. "Pick that up," said her mistress, "and take care that no trace of it remains on the carpet." In that same winter her three grandchildren died.

Independence of character was a quality intolerable to Madame Turgenev. It always produced outbreaks to which a special term was applied by those in her immediate vicinity: "We used to say to each other under our breath, *'Madame cherche chicane'*." One day, Madame Turgenev *"chercha chicane"* on the subject of her major-domo, Simeon Sabolev. The incident is worth citing not only because it lights up this quietly terrible interior, but because it proves how faithfully in *The Annals of a Sportsman*, Turgenev reproduces scenes of actual life. Sobolev was a man of thirty, dark and with the manners of an extremely distinguished lackey. His duties brought him frequently in contact with his owner who would consult him about the affairs of the house. He was a favourite of hers until, in an evil moment, *"Madame chercha chicane."*

In this case a glass of water was sufficient excuse. Madame Turgenev complained that it was always of the wrong temperature. Once she threw the water in his face; the major-domo retired with the carafe, returned with it a few minutes later and poured the water into another glass. This time, Madame Turgenev found it satisfactory and told him so. To her astonishment the serf answered her. Standing in front of an ikon, he exclaimed: "I swear before this sacred image that I have not changed the water. . . . That which Madame has just drunk is the same as the other." Madame Turgenev ordered him out of the room at once and when he was next seen the distinguished major-domo was paying the penalty for speaking as though he were a man and not a thing: "Instead of the elegant dress coat, he was wearing a miserable grey cloth kaftan and held a broom in his hand. An order from his mistress had made him forfeit his position as major-domo for that of sweeper of the yard. He remained for four years in this new employment, until he was replaced by the mute, the master of Mumu." Yet, for all her strong will, this tyrant was thwarted in every relation of life. Her youth had been hideously warped; she had been married only for her money. Her married life had been brief and unhappy. She was obeyed by neither of her sons. Nicholas married against her will; Ivan became a writer in spite of her contempt for those who scratched paper for money. This scratching, incidentally, meant very little money for Ivan in the early days and his long quarrel with his mother spelt out for him the misery of poverty.

None the less on the 28th October 1845, Ivan's birthday was duly celebrated at Spaskoë, with all the barbaric plenty typical of a nest of nobles. There were on this occasion in the dining-hall roast geese, roast pigs and pâtés, while fish, cut into small pieces were spread on long tables flanked at each end by decanters of vodka. In the women's apartments the same dishes were to be found in addition to the samovar and bottles of red wine. The serfs' table was laid in the library which served as the quarters of the intendant of the house. At the entrance of the long gallery a huge armchair was always placed for the châtelaine who on these occasions would seat herself solemnly while each of the servants kissed her hand in turn. After this each would approach the table, take a glass of wine and bow low before his owner as he drank it.

On this particular day, however, there were obvious signs of "*chicane.*" Still, the day passed without any actual outbreak and everybody thought that the storm was, for the time being, averted. They had reckoned without the tenacity of Madame Turgenev who was the last person in the world to allow herself to be thwarted in chicane. That same evening, after the festivities, Madame Turgenev pretended to be dying. She sent for her confessor and, placing the portrait of her son Ivan in front of her, she exclaimed, "*Adieu,* Ivan! *Adieu,* Nicholas! *Adieu,* my children." After this, her forty servants and all the men employed about the house from the intendant to the cashier, were ordered to say good-bye to her. When they had filed out of the room their owner declared that she felt better and asked for tea. The next morning the following significant "order" appeared: "I give orders that to-morrow morning the disobedient servants, Nicholas Jakovlev, Ivan Petrov and Egor Kondratev shall sweep the court in front of my windows." These were the serfs who had failed to appear at her bedside, probably for the very good reason that they were drunk. "Good-for-nothings! drunkards!" commented Madame Turgenev, "they rejoiced at the death of their mistress!" On another occasion, the châtelaine declared that she was too ill to permit the Easter fête of Spaskoë to take place.

The art of Turgenev springs as naturally from life as flowers from the earth. Spaskoë was a hard soil and nowhere perhaps, not even in *The Annals of a Sportsman,* does its oppression strike at one so poignantly as in the story entitled, *Mumu.* It is a page of actual autobiography, an endictment not only against the tyrannical background of his own home, but against the background of the national life. Once, it seems, Madame Turgenev while driving through her domain chanced to notice a colossus at work in the fields. Struck by his huge stature, she stopped the carriage and ordered him to be brought before her. He proved to be a deaf mute, but in spite of this, she had him enrolled then and there among the number of her personal attendants. His name was Andrei and a little later he was taken by his owner to Moscow. Here the town life disheartened the giant, but, through his love of a little dog called Mumu, the poor deaf mute became gradually reconciled to his strange environment. The dog, however, annoyed their common owner and he was compelled to destroy Mumu by the order of Madame Turgenev.

In the story Andrei deserts his mistress after this final

act of tyranny. In actual life, however, the deaf mute bore it as he bore everything else. Some time after the death of Mumu, a person who had incurred Madame Turgenev's displeasure offered Andrei a blue cretonne blouse which he refused with emphatic gestures. His mistress was very pleased on hearing of this incident and early the following morning, while she was still in bed, she ordered in her customary Homeric way a dozen serf girls to make the deaf mute presentable so that he might appear at her bedside. Laughing, as the maidens of Nausicaa might have laughed, the serf girls vied with one another in decking out for the occasion this Slav Odysseus of the steppes. In the meantime, Varya was asked for a piece of blue ribbon and a sum of ten roubles was requisitioned from the intendant. With a gift in each hand the châtelaine smiled kindly at Andrei who began to mutter hoarsely to show his pleasure and gratitude. And as he went out from her presence, the dumb slave struck his breast heavily to express his undying fidelity to the woman who had grudged him even his Mumu.

But, Madame Turgenev had at least the courage of her qualities and when cholera broke out in the village she showed not the faintest trace of fear. When it had diminished she went to confession and, with all her old arrogance intensified, she insisted upon confessing in the presence of all her little court in spite of the fact that this publicity was against the rules of the Orthodox Church. No serf owner in *The Annals of a Sportsman* was more despotic than the mother of its author. Her major-domo Polyakov was suspected of having kept the news of her son Nicholas's marriage a secret. So enraged was she at this that she was on the point of hurling a heavy crutch at his head, when her brother-in-law's entrance checked her, thus probably saving Polyakov's life. The next day he was banished to a distant estate and was reduced from the position of major-domo to that of a simple copyist. His wife Agatha, who was *enceinte* at the time, pleaded in vain for her husband. A year later, however, the châtelaine did repent of this particular act of tyranny; she not only restored Polyakov in Biblical fashion to his old position, but actually asked Agatha to forgive her. Madame Turgenev was not without flashes of generosity, but the abstraction of liberty was to her simply incomprehensible. Her serfs were well treated and that was enough, she would urge when Ivan championed their cause. But even in these gloomy days he prophesied that the day of freedom would assuredly dawn for Russia as well as for Spaskoë.

He also championed his unhappy brother whom Madame Turgenev had deprived of all means of existence. To every demand she replied by an offer of property, but always declined to have the transfer legalized. She appears to have found considerable amusement in this comedy of giving without parting with anything. "I pity my brother," Ivan protested. "Why have you made him so wretched? You gave him authority to marry, you made him leave the service and come here with his family, while at Petersburg he was earning his living . . . and since he has arrived you torture him . . . you torment him ceaselessly."

His mother replied by a burst of anger against Nicholas and then the conversation turned on the detested calling of Ivan, who had informed her that his works were beginning to be criticized. "*Comment!*" she exclaimed, "*toi un noble, un Turgenev, on ose te critiquer!*" But in spite of these constant altercations Ivan's visits were very welcome in this rich, gloomy household. They were of little solace to him, however, and even a woman whom he had loved in his boyhood could bring him no distraction. "For a woman close on forty," commented his mother, "she is really not so bad. She has put herself to all this trouble for you and you have shown yourself scarcely grateful."

"It is true," replied Ivan without irony, "but at the time that I loved her I was still almost a child. What did I not suffer then! . . . I remember that when she passed close to me, my heart seemed ready to leap out of my breast. . . . But that very happy time has passed! Now I understand that love no more. . . . I have no longer that ardour of youth; it was made up of that love which was content with

a glance, with a flower that fell from her hair. It was enough
for me to pick up that flower; I was happy and I asked for
nothing more." Thus to Madame Turgenev of all people
in the world Ivan explained the delicate secret that he has
interpreted in *Torrents of Spring* and *First Love*.

During the last years of his mother's life, Ivan was so
poor that, on arriving from abroad, he was unable to offer
a bottle of wine to his friends and was reduced to borrowing
half a rouble from Porphyre Kartashev to pay for the
conveyance that had brought him from the station. But it
was his habit to plead for his brother Nicholas rather than
for himself and finally, setting aside the long dissimulation
of experience, he blurts out to his mother the naked truth:
"You do not wish to understand that we are no longer
children, and that your attitude towards us is outrageous.
You are afraid of giving us anything because you fear to lose
your dominance over us! We have always been respectful
sons to you, and you are unwilling to have confidence in
us. . . . You believe in no one, you believe in nothing. . . .
You believe only in your own power! And what does this
power give you! The right to martyrize everybody." His
astonished mother burst out with the exclamation: "I am
no scoundrel!" Her son answered deliberately, "No, you
are not a scoundrel. I understand neither what you are,
nor what goes on in your house. Think of it, examine things
for yourself." And when his mother asked of what she ought
to think and to whom she had done wrong, her son summed
up, as it were, the whole life of that mouldering Russia,
which at this very time he was preparing in his own way to
ransom: "To whom have you done wrong? But is there a
single one happy among those who surround you? Remember Polyakov, remember Agatha. All those whom you
persecuted, exiled, they might all have been able to love
you . . . and you have made them miserable. . . . As for
me, I would willingly give half my life not to know it and
not to be compelled to tell it to you. . . . Yes, all tremble
before you and yet they all might have been able to
love you." At this time Nicholas was living in a house in

the neighbourhood, but after this scene the brothers made preparations to move to Turgenevo, their father's property.

What their mother's attitude had become towards them may be judged by the fury she showed, when, on arriving at Spaskoë from Moscow, she learned that her two sons had been at her house the day before. "How did you dare to allow them to enter?" she called out to Polyakov. And when he answered that he could not refuse "our masters admission," she lashed him across the face.

But the end was very near now; the brothers continued to live at Turgenevo which was only a few miles from Spaskoë. Their mother, however, soon started again for Moscow, leaving behind her Varya and a companion who were to rejoin her as soon as the town house was in order. When Varya arrived at Moscow she found the old tyrant somewhat softened and she took down at her dictation the following letter: "My dear children, Nicholas and Ivan, I order you to give liberty after my death to Polyakov and all his family in addition to a reward of one thousand roubles; the same liberty shall be given to my doctor Porphyre with the reward of five hundred roubles." She signed this letter with her own hand: "Your Mother who loves you, Varvara Turgeneva."

On the 28th October, Varya reminded her adopted mother that it was Ivan's birthday; the châtelaine's eyes filled with tears. The struggle in the heart of this dying woman had become terrible and, towards the very last, she scrawled in trembling writing, her innermost secret: "*Ma mère! mes enfants! pardonnez-moi. Et vous, Seigneur, pardonnez-moi aussi, car l'orgueil, ce péché mortel, fut toujours mon péché.*" When death was actually at hand, she saw her elder son and the following day, the 16th November, 1850, she died without seeing Ivan, who arrived too late. To what extent she had realized the suffering that she had brought upon others can only be guessed; but Agatha at least forgave her dead mistress. "Yes," she sobbed out, "I had a great deal to endure from the late Madame Turgenev, but for all that I was very fond of her. She was a real mistress."

She was dead, this veritable symbol of the old Russian despotism; less than two years afterwards her own son Ivan proclaimed this tyranny so poignantly that it shocked the very tyrants themselves. It was his own mother who had taught him to perform the miracle which gave him the right to exclaim: "My one desire for my tomb is that they shall engrave upon it what my book has accomplished for the emancipation of the serfs." Because of this stupendous achievement no incident of this barbaric household is beneath the notice of him who would penetrate below the surface of the old Russian life. The childhood of Turgenev is significant because by it and through it one can judge both from above and from below the tragically prolonged childhood of the Russian people. It was an evil bringing up for a delicate and sensitive boy, but only through such a training could Turgenev ever have realized the death in life of those anonymous ones who were destined to remain things in a world intended for men. Whatever the great novelist's opinion of his adopted sister may have become, her record bears the impress of fact. She herself was a victim of the hideous system and for that reason she should not be judged harshly. Youth becomes warped in such an atmosphere, but its very oppressiveness taught Ivan to withdraw into his own inner dream. This he preserved always inviolate and inviolable like some flower delicately pure in spite of the poisonous swamp that gave it life. The very scenes of tyranny throughout *The Annals of a Sportsman* are permeated by this inner dream and it is not too much to say that Spaskoë is as significant from the standpoint of art as Yasnaya Polyana from the standpoint of moral purpose.

Certainly in the garden of Spaskoë everything was not naïve and simple, even when one had stolen away from the external life controlled by Madame Turgenev. In a love story of boyhood the novelist has caught the atmosphere of suspicion, disillusion and inner, as distinct from outer, oppression by which his youth was poisoned at its very source. His father is here, and his mother, but in this record she is in the background. Once, when he was asked which was the favourite of his books Turgenev replied: "*First Love*. It is a true story which happened just as I have related it and whose central figure is my own father." Just as *The Annals of a Sportsman* records with that intense lucidity which disdains the attitudes and altitudes of verbal pathos the whole outer life of Madame Turgenev's régime, so this love story of reality reveals the heart of its author for whom love, in spite of all his irony, retained always something of mystery and wonder and sombre regret.

CHAPTER III

FIRST LOVE

ALL his life Turgenev was pursued by the penetrating charm of *la femme russe*. At the famous "Dinners of the hissed authors" in Paris, he would speak in his high-pitched voice which even in French retained something of the Slav sing-song of a *couleur toute particulière* in love. Persistently he sought it and his magic failed him only when his heart failed to respond to the charm of the Russian girl; even when the presentiment of nearing the beginning of the end had seized him, he has admitted that for him the explanation of existence remained what it had been all his life. "I believe," he said, to the younger de Goncourt, "that I can find the explanation of that in the fact of my inability, now absolute, to love." But until that moment of ultimate disillusion the novelist was faithful to his inner dream of *la femme russe*, of whom he said at one of the Magny dinners: "*Aucune autre ne peut aimer d'un amour aussi absolu, aussi désinteressé. Elle aime le peuple, et ell va dans ses rangs sans phrases; elle va et elle le sert; elle s'enfouit dans un village; ell oublie sa propre personne, se refuse toute affection personnelle, et même la maternité.*"

It is by no accident, then, that in one novel after another the purifying love of a young girl redeems and sustains each stricken, will-less hero in turn. And though in after years it was the spell of the mondaine that held the man, the genius of the artist responded unerringly to the Russian girl and to her alone. In Russia, in Baden, in Paris, they come to him these heroines who are like no others in modern literature. To him and to him alone they whisper their shy secrets, the frozen secrets of the steppes. The cosmopolitan analyst of emotional experience looses the last vestige of his hesitating, often morose, irony in the presence of these courageous and exquisite beings who are translating through his lips the hopes and dreams of their race. Never with Turgenev does a heroine fail her lover in the moment of danger. Never is it the woman who falters on the eve of action. Everything that he denied to his heroes he granted abundantly to these blonde daughters of Russia for whom love itself is but a part of a larger sacrifice.

But the love stories of Turgenev are devoid of sentimentality in the English sense. The Russians are by temperament disdainful of the mild concessions and hedgings and compromises of this looking-glass passion. They reject its pale promises, its insignificant rewards and, above all, its theory of comfortable seemliness as the goal of conduct. With Russian novelists, as with the Ancients—their only equals in the portrayal of fatality—love is rarely dissociated from suffering. But in this again the three great Russian realists of the last century differ profoundly in their presentation of life. To Tolstoy, the fugitive blaze of a young girl's love was almost always the starting point on the *via dolorosa* of maternity. To Dostoevsky, it was essentially an abnormal excitation of the brain, painful whether it descended to the depths of atavism or ascended to the most lonely spiritual heights. But Turgenev, in this as in all else, remained first and last an artist who clung consistently to his delicately merciful analysis of that *couleur toute particulière* of human love.

None the less, his own first love was as it were poisoned, like so many other aspirations, in the difficult atmosphere of Spaskoë. For, in spite of the drowsy beauty of the Russian summers which he was to communicate to alien peoples, there lurked in that garden of experience an atmosphere of knowledge too quickly grasped, of emotion forced painfully upon immaturity. Long before *Fathers and Sons* was written, Turgenev had watched closely the elder generation in its relations to the rising one. Nor was it only the fight between an adder and a toad that had made the young Russian doubtful of a merciful providence.

For all that, the record of *First Love* reproduces with extraordinary freshness, that illusion which for Turgenev was the first and the last. Nowhere, even in his own works, do we seem to be made the confidents of a personal secret more surely than in this short novel in which youth stammers out its first tumultuous discovery as though to itself. It is the story of Turgenev at sixteen, when the unforgettable garden had begun to disclose vistas beyond those of boyish adventure. It is no wonder that again and again in his letters he reverts to this garden, to the lime trees and the raspberry bushes and the sanded paths; for it was here that he saw for the first time the young girl who was to haunt him with a permeating regret at which, through the after years, he never dared to mock. But the scrutiny of youth is not always blurred even by the exaltation of first love. Turgenev does not rhapsodize over his Zenaïda, but brings her before us simply with her "bright mobile face" and her "big grey eyes." One catches the gleam of those white even teeth; one notes the eyebrows ironically arched. And like this boy one finds oneself staring at her as though she were the only woman in all the world and as though this garden of Spaskoë were the garden of Eden, the garden of life.

Of plot in the ordinary sense there is scarcely any. An inflammable youth is brought into contact with the cool beautiful girl, five years older than himself and one feels oneself a boy of sixteen again, a participant in the action which is as simple and as complex as that of life. Vladimir's heart beats when he sees her from his garden for the first time. Yes, it is as simple as that. She will be there again reading a book, and she will smile and he will take off his cap. It is like a game of "consequences"; and yet from the very first instant one divines the low rustling of fatality. And from the first instant one is conscious not merely of reading a novel, nor of weighing an interpretation of life but of actually watching the expansion of youth as one may watch the unfolding of a flower. Here there is not even that concealment of art which is admittedly the summit of artistic expression. The characters obey no plot, but what there is of plot obeys instinctively the essentials of character. This, of course, is the very essence of Turgenev's art, but

what is extraordinary in this re-living of adolescence is the
sureness with which he reproduces the naïve watchfulness
of youth. All his life, he has told us, it was his habit to be
watchful in moments of agitation and Vladimir, even in this
first blaze of incomprehensible passion, watches carefully
Zenaïda while she prepares to enrole him among the
number of her victims. He notes the "surly little pigs' eyes"
of the servant, who admits him to the house and when he
kisses Zenaïda's hand, he is conscious of the tip of her nail
against his lips. And he recalls not merely the detail—the
shell of remembrance—but every minute physical thrill of
this intoxication of youth which manhood can only regret,
but never repeat: "I remember our two heads being all at
once in a warm, half transparent, fragrant darkness, the
soft, close brightness of her eyes in the dark, and the burning
breath from her parted lips, and the gleam of her teeth and
the ends of her hair tickling me and setting me on fire. I
was silent."

The girl herself is a veritable Calypso, at once cool and
wayward, before the coming of Odysseus. She not only
plays with hearts, but analyses their beating when suddenly,
like Calypso herself, she becomes changed. "Good God!"
the boy whispers to himself, "she is in love." Nobody in the
whole world knows just what this means better than poor
Vladimir. A little later, Malevsky whom he distrusts deeply
says to him: "You remember in the garden by night at the
fountain, that's where there's need to look out."

Already there have been hints of someone in the background, someone who can bring the love light to those grey
eyes, once so restless and so mocking. The garden has lost
already its first freshness. The boy knows that love is not
to all what it is to him. He divines that there is in it something different, something baneful, and that it is just to this
and not to his own innocent young love that his idol responds. Between them all they have destroyed his beautiful
dream. The freshness of youth has been torn from him
never to return quite in the same way. Knife in hand, he
follows the path that "coiled like a snake" to watch for his

enemy. At last he hears somebody coming: "Flashes of red were whirling before my eyes; my hair stood up on my head in my fear and fury. . . . The footsteps were coming straight towards me; I bent—I craned forward to meet him: . . . A man came into view. . . . My God! it was my father!"

With an English or French novelist this scene would have passed into a "tableau" either of romanticism or cynicism; with Turgenev it is nothing of the sort. It is the laws of heredity and environment that assert themselves instead of the professional wire pulling of the adroit entertainer. The scene closes neither in an emotional harangue nor in a derisive note of exclamation. Othello slips back into the self-conscious school boy from which he had momentarily emerged. Yet, so essentially part of life is this love story of reality, there is no sense whatever of anti-climax. Precisely as Vladimir is interested in Zenaïda's passion, as in something fatal that comes upon one suddenly from outside, so he is interested in this fellow victim whom Malesky has betrayed by an anonymous letter to the boy's mother. Here again we are not gratified by any traditional scene of high-flown vengeance. Vladimir's father merely remarks, a little more icily than usual, to Count Malevsky in the presence of a footman: "A few days ago your Excellency was shown the door in our house; and now I am not going to enter into any kind of explanation, but I have the honour to announce that if ever you visit me again I shall throw you out of the window. I don't like your handwriting." It is all very decorous and well bred, but even in his torment Vladimir preserves curiosity as to what is going on beneath the surface. He himself had arrived at the experience of love, but there was something else associated with it and of that, too, he was shortly to learn.

Standing outside the window of a mean house in a poor quarter of a town, Vladimir caught a glimpse of this something which he was never to forget: "Suddenly before my very eyes the impossible happened. My father suddenly raised the whip with which he had been flicking the dust from his coat and I heard a sharp swish on that arm, bare to the elbow. I could scarcely restrain myself from crying out, while Zenaïda shuddered, looked without a word at my father and slowly raising her arm to her lips kissed the streak of red. My father flung away the whip, and running quickly up the steps, dashed into the house . . . Zenaïda turned round and with outstretched arms and downcast head, moved away from the window."

But even now the boy does not judge conventionally on the English pattern. It is not the brutality, but the suffering of the scene that is registered on his brain—the suffering of passion experienced by these two beings who are so near to him, and yet so infinitely remote. The laughter-loving girl who had brought a new spell into his garden of secrets, she who had ruled her adorers amused by the pain that she could never share, has kissed the weal on her naked arm, because she loves the man who has struck the blow. How can he judge her? How can he judge his father, a victim punished by his own brutality. Vladimir can judge nobody, but in front of that window he has scanned yet another page of that mysterious book of life whose pages for so many remain always uncut. Yet through this recognition of the self-renunciation of passion, Turgenev, without rhetoric and without special pleading, has brought back to Zenaïda something of that lost aureole of youth's first imaginative worship. And when, two years later, Vladimir calls to see her only to learn that she is dead, one experiences physically that sense of intimate personal loss which is Turgenev's incommunicable secret. Like Vladimir, one can repeat only, "She is dead" and like him one feels that with her has passed the incarnation of love blending with passion and regret permeated by desire—the wonder of young life broken on the altar of its real meaning. Like Vladimir, one muses on "those dear features, those eyes, those curls—in the narrow box" as though one were realizing death for the first time. Like Vladimir, one sees suddenly in perspective the whispered promises of youth that can never be kept. And again, like Vladimir, one grasps dumbly that this is matter neither for reproach nor appeal and in the depths of one's being one understands why he "felt aghast for Zenaïda, and longed to pray for her, for my father, yes and for myself."

Others have sought to recapture the illusive fragrance of early passion. Others have shown the good love over-shadowed by the evil. But it would be difficult to find any parallel to the very magic of regret which Turgenev has infused into this story of his youth, which was to remain the story of his heart.

"All my biography," he confessed once, "is in my work," and, in this short novel he has recaptured, as though the book were written during the experience itself, all that lost charm of the days when love was content with so little because so little meant so much. It is significant, too, because it completes the picture of his home at Spaskoë. In the background of this spoilt romance one sees only too clearly the jealous elderly woman dissatisfied with life and incapable of tasting happiness except through the tyranny that denies happiness to others. One seems to be listening to hidden quarrels, half-strangled insults, inuendoes of suspicion, whispers of hate. And through it all, cold and impassive on the surface, but like a hawk in his pursuit of the swallows of pleasure there is the elder Turgenev whose only counsel to his son is : "Take for your-self what you can, and don't be ruled by others; to belong to oneself—the whole savour of life lies in that."

Le beau Serge was at least faithful to his principles and Madame Turgenev had real grievances against her husband. One of these according to rumour, was a young girl who became the mother of Porphyre Kartashev, the serf doctor for whose emancipation Ivan was to plead so uselessly.

It is more than a century ago that Turgenev experi-enced the love story of Zenaïda. The attitude of his country has changed towards such experiences. In the Russian novel of to-day such love as Vladimir's for Zen-aïda or of Vladimir's father for Zenaïda would be alike dismissed contemptuously as bourgeois passion. And Ivan Turgenev's early pleadings with his mother on behalf of the serfs would be dismissed with equal contempt as so much bourgeois pathos. In the one case, as in the other, what Turgenev offered in his youth would seem to modern Moscow but a drop from the ocean of what remained ungiven. What he was afterwards to give, that too was not enough. Still, there was something in what Ivan Turgenev communicated from the very first, which neither Moscow nor any other capital can kill. It was poetry. And until you can kill youth itself poetry will assuredly steal back to the human heart.

Steeped in poetry, this boy felt himself chained rather than attached to this curious moral group. For the inmates of Spaskoë it must have been an extraordinary group-consciousness, and whatever share in it Ivan accepted was inevitably tinged with that corrosive irony which, in spite of all his kindliness, was to cling to him to the very last. Everything in his home repelled him. He was regarded coldly and superciliously by his father. His mother ill-treated him in childhood and neither gave him her confidence nor succeeded in winning his. The boy's education was foreign and artificial. The language of his race was banished from this Russian home, which was supported by Russian slavery. Other boys might have accepted all this as so much routine, but Turgenev's eyes were always inquisitive. Everything that he detected in his elders' manner of living seemed to him false in origin and cruel in practice, and he never lived to change his mind. He began in those days to learn the reality on which all his romances were based. One will no more understand *Smoke*, without having studied the boyhood of Ivan Turgenev, than one will understand *Anna Karenina*, without having studied the ampler and more roughly candid record of Count Tolstoy's early days. But this unsympathetic environment did much for Ivan Turgenev. It taught him to preserve watchfully and jealously his inner life; from this emerged masterpieces. It taught him to preserve his deep sense of injustice. The expression of this was eventually to be of incalculable importance to the whole life of Russia.

When the days of foreign governesses and tutors had slipped by, Ivan was sent to a boarding school kept by a German in Moscow, after which he went to the Institut Lazarev in the same city. Here also he found the Russian language ignored, but he became an enthusiast for Zagoskin, one of whose works was actually read aloud in the original by one of the teachers. "I knew him by heart," Turgenev writes, "one day I fell on a pupil who interrupted the reading, with my fists clenched." In 1832, he left the Institut Lazarev in order to prepare for the University of Moscow. Already he had absorbed far more than book knowledge and in respects other than such knowledge he was prepared for those Moscow days which were to live again in the annals of Rudin. But it was neither the boarding school kept by a German, nor the Institut Lazarev, nor the University of Moscow, nor that of Petersburg, nor that of Berlin which really fashioned and moulded the author of *The Annals of a Sportsman*; it was the garden of Spaskoë.

CHAPTER IV

SAMOVAR NIGHTS

O N entering the University of Moscow, Turgenev came immediately under the spell of German philosophy and particularly under that of Hegel. Every young Russian of that period seems to have been a philosopher in the making, but the youthful followers of Hegel had their full share of the uncomplicated turbulence of youth. There were frequent disturbances in the lecture rooms: "We arrive at the class . . . uproar! The professor arrives and bows all round. He takes a book and reads. The uproar begins again. He goes out! Uproar! Uproar! Uproar!"

For all that, the spirit of liberty, of camaraderie, the impetus of general ideas came like a breath of emancipation to this lonely boy. And there were samovar nights when young people indulged in Russian talks prolonged until the morning, discussions of Goethe and Schiller, the objective and the subjective, discussions on the freedom of life and the glory of devoting oneself to the study of its actual meaning. "What," exclaimed Belinsky to Turgenev some years afterwards during one of those typical philosophical wrangles which had already lasted six hours, "we do not know yet if God exists, and you wish to dine!" Certainly, from the practical standpoint there was little to be gained from these Moscow nights which were to be repeated later on among Turgenev's compatriots in Berlin. But at least they were a spiritual antidote to the isolation of Spaskoë. Repeatedly in his novels he was to revert to these Russian talks on everything that to the true bourgeois means so little—from philosophy to music, from pantheism to nihilism, from the emancipation of the soul in one sense to the emancipation of the soul in another. But these young people were not disciples of Hegel for nothing; their attitude was curiously conservative. They accepted reality uncondition-

43

ally, disdaining for that reason all violent upheavals, especially the French revolution. In 1835, "*le beau* Serge" was cut off from the life whose savour he had persisted in relishing to the very last, in spite of the ceaselessly repeated vetos of his wife who had always kept her fortune ruthlessly in her own hands. The same year Madame Turgenev withdrew with her two sons to Petersburg. Nicholas entered the School of Artillery and Ivan entered the University of St Petersburg. Here for the first time he was seized by definite literary aspirations and he commenced those early efforts in verse, which were to bring upon him Madame Viardot's mot, "*Mauvais rimeur, bon tireur.*" Here, too, he was to catch a glimpse of Pushkin, his favourite poet. He was just leaving a drawing-room and the future novelist had only time to note "his white teeth, and his alert and awakened eyes." On a later occasion he encountered the poet at a concert: "He was standing near the door; his arms were folded across his broad chest, and he was glancing around with a dissatisfied air. I remember his small black face, his negro lips, his great white teeth, his drooping whiskers, his passionate eyes, without eyebrows, under a high forehead, and his woolly hair. . . . He cast a furtive look at me, the casualness with which I had fixed my eyes on him had displeased the poet. He shrugged his shoulders with annoyance and changed his place. A few days afterwards I saw him in his coffin."

No less a person than the great Gogol was one of the examiners at the University of St Petersburg, but the students seemed not to have realized who he was until after he had left. Turgenev never met him at the University and it was not until within a few months of Gogol's death that he paid him a visit. The author of *Dead Souls*, died in Moscow in 1852, the very year in which *The Annals of a Sportsman* appeared. Turgenev has left us a characteristic impression of the founder of the Russian novel: "I sat down near him on a large divan and began to examine closely all his features: his hair, which hung straight down the temples as among the Cossacks, still preserved its early colour, but had become scanty. His retreating forehead, smooth and white, indicated a high intelligence. In his small brown eyes there sparkled from time to time gaiety, yes, gaiety and not irony. But the glance was fatigued. His long pointed nose gave his physiognomy the cunning look of a fox. His lips, soft and protruding under the short moustache, were no more advantageous to his face; in the indecisive lines of the mouth one divined the dark side of his character. When he talked his lips rose disagreeably and disclosed a row of bad teeth. His small chin was concealed in the folds of a huge cravat of black velvet. His face and every movement of his body recalled the professor of a provincial college. At sight of him one could not help exclaiming: 'A spiritual being, strange and sick!'"

Gogol was fond of reading aloud from his famous comedy *Revizor* and Turgenev has drawn an interesting comparison between his manner of reading, and that of his famous English contemporary: "Dickens when he reads from his works acts them at the same time: his reading is dramatic, theatrical; he brings together in his own person several celebrated actors and makes us laugh and weep in turn. Gogol, on the contrary, impressed me by the simplicity and sobriety of his manner, and by a sincerity, at once serious and naïve, which seems to ignore the presence, or absence, of spectators. Gogol thought only of entering upon rôles which seemed to be new for him. He endeavoured to give only his own impression; the effect was remarkable, particularly in comic and humorous scenes. One could not help bursting into a good healthy laugh, while the author of all this gaiety continued to impress himself always more and more with the spirit of his rôle. Sometimes, however, about his lips and eyes there trembled the sly laugh of the master."

It is indeed a pity that Turgenev did not come under the literary influence of his great forerunner while at the University of Petersburg. As it was, that University left slighter impressions on Ivan, than did the University of the older capital. At Petersburg, however, Turgenev developed that love of mystification which was one of the most incongruous oddities in his sombre and ironical temperament. When examined by one of the professors on the subject of Trial by Ordeal, the future novelist after enumerating the different historical tests added the original one of the calf's tail. The professor asked for details and the undergraduate explained that the calf's tail was greased and then placed in the hand of the accused. The beast was struck with a stick and if its tail did not slip through the hands of the accused at the first blow, he was declared innocent. When asked for references, Turgenev cited numerous examples of this variation of Trial by Ordeal. But he was eventually exposed on a point of chronology. In after years, his mystifications became more inventive and also more personal. He would declare himself the hero of all sorts of incidents and accidents, from the capture of a woman's heart to an affair of a runaway horse. In such moods nothing was sacred to him. He would invent a quite imaginary game-bag and invite his friends to dine on its contents. But apart from these trivialities and from his first excursions into verse, Turgenev did little to distinguish himself at this University and was only too glad to leave the capital to continue his studies abroad. In 1838, at the age of twenty, he started on the steamer, *Nicholas I*, the first of a series of roamings through Western Europe that was to continue, with brief pauses, almost to the end of his life. And like all the other visits this first excursion had for its object the study of "men and things, more especially men." The crossing, incidentally, very nearly proved tragic for while occupied at a game of cards the young student was startled by the cry of "Fire." According to malevolent tradition, Turgenev dashed on deck, hustled women and children and cried out at the top of his high-pitched voice, which came so oddly from this giant body, "Save me! I am the only son of a rich widow." The suggestion of cowardice stung the novelist and years afterwards, while taking part in some private theatricals he exclaimed with all his individual irony, "save me! I am the only son of a rich widow." Only three months before his death, he was to revert to the same theme in a sketch entitled *Fire at Sea*, which he dictated in French. It is a minute description of what actually took place on the *Nicholas I*, and he makes it quite clear that on that occasion he, as a boy of nineteen, apart from his first quite natural spasm of terror, behaved with coolness and courage. In the first moment of that terror it appears that he did offer a sailor a sum of money to save him, but he denies implicitly having ever used the words, "I am the only son of a rich widow." Afterwards, the sailor approached him with a reminder about the reward of ten thousand roubles: "But as I was not quite sure of his identity, and as besides he had done nothing whatever for me, I offered him a thaler which he accepted gratefully." Turgenev had not been guilty of cowardice, but in this sketch, written so close to the end, he notes an incident which, in spite of all the horror of a fire at sea, he had observed with all his characteristic intensity of scrutiny: "I perceived in the middle of a group of passengers, a general of tall stature, his clothes literally soaked with water, who stood motionless against a bench which he had detached from a boat. I learned that in the first moment of terror he had brutally pushed back a woman who wanted to pass in front of him, so as to leap from the vessel in one of the first embarcations which had foundered. Seized by a steward, who had flung him back on the ship, the old soldier became ashamed of his momentary cowardice and took an oath that except the captain, he would be the last to leave the vessel. He was a tall man, pale, with a red scar on his forehead, and he kept casting around him contrite and resigned glances as though he were asking for pardon."

In no one of his novels does Turgenev show more minuteness of observation than in this sketch which links the very end of his life to the end of his boyhood. He had noted, this boy of nineteen, every phase and facet of stupefying fear by which so many of his fellow passengers were paralysed. And after so many years of sombre experience there came to him, as from yesterday, the shrill cries of women as

47

they leaped desperately from the burning ship. Boy as he was, he had already acquired the extraordinary receptivity that made this blond giant as it were a sensitive plate for the registration of the deepest and the most fugitive impressions. "You know," he once abserved to Gorsky, "that even in the most palpitating moments I cannot cease from observing other people." Certainly, no one paralysed by fear could have observed as Turgenev observed on that exploited occasion, when he was supposed to have cried out, "Save me! I am the only son of a rich widow: ten thousand roubles to him who will save me."

His boyhood may be said to have closed when he came on board the *Nicholas I*, with Porphyre (the reputed offspring of *le beau* Serge), who was accompanying him to the University of Berlin. The immediate supervision of Madame Turgenev was over and with the sea breeze Ivan must have breathed in the spirit of comparative independence. On the surface he was to develop and even to change, to come first under German influence, then under French and finally, again on the surface, to transform himself into an unfettered cosmopolitan. But beneath the surface he was to remain to the very last curiously the same.

In his mature years, Count Tolstoy was to write: "Let not anyone reproach me, saying that the illusions of my youth are as childish as were those of my childhood and of my boyhood. I am convinced that if it be my fate to live to a great age, I shall be found, when I am an old man, to have just the same impossible childish illusions as at present." And even when, in the crisis of his so-called "conversion" Tolstoy was to accept a definite line of demarcation between the old life and the new, the sensation produced upon him was oddly familiar: "It was strange, but this feeling of the glow of life was no new sensation; it was old enough for I had been led away by it in the earlier part of my life. I returned, as it were, to the past, to childhood, and to my youth."

In precisely the same way, the wholly different Turgenev was curiously bound to the impressions of his youth. The novelist was to develop upon the same lines upon which the boy of nineteen had become what he was. That boy had already espoused the emancipation of the serfs; the novelist was to write the book that brought about the emancipation. The boy was already embued with the generous dreams of idealism; in spite of the after-fatigue and disillusion the novelist was repeatedly to revert to those Moscow nights with all the old enthusiasm undimmed.

The boy had already tasted the bitter sweetness of first love; the novelist was to translate it into the imperishable language of art with a freshness that won back the very scent of that loved Russian garden. The boy had noted the equivocal relations that existed between his own parents; the man was to remain faithful to his gloomy expostulation. "But, as for marriage what a cruel irony!" The boy had become already distrustful of any merciful Providence hovering protectingly over the children of earth; the man was to sum up the philosophy of his life in the one word, *Smoke*. The boy had arrived intuitively at the idea of nature as *la grande Indifférente*; the man was to show human lives falling into decay and renewing themselves like the seasons as they pass. The boy had grasped that ordinary folk in spite of the atmosphere of cold indifference around them, are good and kind; the novelist was to detect in the tears of nature's suppliants the only warmth upon her altar.

This boy of nineteen was to emerge into the cosmopolitan of whom it was said that, "to dine with Turgenev, was to dine with Europe." He was to become not only one of the world's greatest novelists, but also a Slav Petronius in the world of art. He was to translate into terms of art every one of those half formed aspirations of his early youth. He was to wander through the world, just as the boy had wandered through the garden. But underneath the sophisticated irony and the confirmed pessimism of the psychologist there remained with him always something of the old childlike dreamer who had absorbed all the secrets, good and bad alike, of the garden of Spaskoë.

Childhood, indeed, remained the inspiration of Turgenev

no less than of Count Tolstoy. The author of *Anna Karenina* in spite of his relish of life, reverted again and again to childhood in his early gropings after that spiritual experience which was to haunt him from first to last. Turgenev who was to view life as a pageant that became only too tawdry the closer one came to it, reverted to early youth in search of the moments when the savour was fresh and untainted. Tolstoy, almost from the very beginning viewed life as an enigma which, in its apparent meaninglessness does conceal a deep spiritual significance and in search of this significance he reverted to youth. Turgenev sought from youth no such explanation any more than from old age.

Tolstoy's record of youth is the autobiography of a moral reformer, a register of moral conduct which, starting in the nursery of his old home was to become to no small extent the moral standard of the civilized world. The early youth of Turgenev is essentially that of a sensitive artist content to portray what life means to him indirectly in terms of art. It was for Count Tolstoy to confess, so far as he was capable of confession, the innermost secrets of his early strivings; it was for Ivan Turgenev to reveal the background of Russian life through that interior of Spaskoë and, above all, to interpret that lonely boy who wandered through the garden where love was waiting for him to teach him life.

It was no Freudean complex that tied him invisibly to an environment from which consciously he was eager to escape; he was in every fibre of his being a part of that old Russia which was so soon to pass for ever. For, in spite of Turgenev's western bias the more he saturated himself with foreign influences, the more he steeped himself in foreign atmospheres, the more essentially national he became. It is by no accident that those of his novels which were hailed by the critics as really Russian were precisely those which were written abroad. There was no danger, then, that Ivan Turgenev on board the *Nicholas I* would ever be really Germanized by the University of Berlin.

CHAPTER V

THE OATH OF HANNIBAL

Turgenev was delighted with Germany, first with Lubeck and then with Berlin. He was well received at the University and lost no time in renewing the inspiration of Hegel; but he now came under the influence of Goethe and he read Faust so often that he knew the first part by heart. He even improvized for himself a Gretchen and together with Porphyre took his plunge, not too deeply, into the lighter side of student life. There was a brief love affair with a *couturière*, and there was even rat hunting with a spirited terrier. But for the most part his compatriots— far more serious students than they appear, for instance, in *Smoke*—disdained such trivialities and Turgenev was quickly caught up into the old atmosphere of endless discussions amid the fumes of tobacco just as in Moscow.

Certainly he had come to the West to see "men and things, more especially men," but he was never unmindful of those voiceless slaves at home in Russia. Doubtless, it was an old ambition to tear from the West its coveted secret of freedom. At all events we hear of an oath of Hannibal, sworn in the dawn after one of those samovar nights, on behalf of the Russian serfs. "They must be taught," exclaimed Stankevich, "they must be dragged from their darkness. Let us all swear, my friends, to consecrate our forces to that object." Only a few years later in Petersburg a little group of Fourierists, under the presidency of Durov, met to discuss the same subject. "Our people," said Dostoevsky on that occasion, "will not follow the tracks of European revolutionaries." To this observation someone replied: "And if there are no other means than revolution to free the peasants, what must be done then?" Dostoevsky answered: "In that case, Revolution." This unpremeditated reply, given on the spur of the moment, was wholly opposed not only to the professed political theories of Dostoevsky, but also to his disposition and temperament. None the less, it spelt out for him first condemnation to death and then eight years of Siberia. No such danger attached to that oath of Hannibal, sworn on German soil, but it is interesting to note that Stankevich, who died soon afterwards, left his fortune to provide schools for his own part of Russia, while Turgenev himself, apart from his all-important book, was to interest himself in the education of the Russian people.

Russian discussions, German philosophy, German poetry and the more familiar distractions of youth were not the only influences at work on Turgenev. He experienced the charm of new aspects of nature. He travelled not only in Germany, but through Switzerland and Italy. But even at this period he preferred, curiously enough, not the grandeur of the Alps, but that serenity and quietude of nature which he caught from the long grassy stretches of his homeland, from those flat landscapes, birch woods, fields of rye and drowsy meadows fringed by lakes and sluggish rivulets. "I had no wish," he observed once, speaking of these early travels, "that Nature should impose herself upon me." So, in his reminiscences of travel, as well as in his novels, it is now neither world-famed scenery nor world-famed cities that captivate him, but rather glimpses of forest and plain and little corners of towns to which he is linked by the spell of memory that brings pleasure to regret. At Frankfurt, for instance, there was one such well imagined corner, that garden in which a young girl was sorting cherries, while a youth watched her as though in all Frankfurt, in all Germany, in all the world, there were no other women. Very well he remembered that spot for he himself was that youth and some thirty years later he was to tell, as it were, in a sequel to *First Love*, the story of a personal romance.

The memory of *Spring Torrents* was as close to Turgenev as that even of *First Love*. One day Pavlovsky expressed his appreciation of this book and Turgenev was delighted. "The whole of that story," he said, "is true. I have lived it and felt it personally. It is my own history. Madame Polozov is an incarnation of the princess Trubetzkoi whom I knew very well. In her time she made a great deal of sensation in Paris and she is still remembered there. Pantaleone lived at her house. He occupied there an intermediate position between that of a friend and that of a servitor. The Italian family, too, is taken from life. But I have changed the details and I have transposed, for I cannot photograph blindly. For example, the princess was a native of Bohemia by birth; I have drawn the type of a Russian grande dame of plebeian extraction. As for Pantaleone, I have placed him in the Italian family. . . . I wrote this romance with real pleasure and I love it as I love all my works written in this spirit." *Spring Torrents*, indeed, no less than *First Love* is autobiographical in the deepest sense.

Sanin at twenty-one is Ivan Turgenev; the love torrent that burst upon him at Frankfurt is a personal memory. This portrait of Sanin, sketched impassively thirty years afterwards, is the portrait of the novelist who retained always something of his youth: "In the first place he was very very good-looking. A handsome, graceful figure, agreeable, rather unformed features, kindly bluish eyes, golden hair, a clear white and red skin, and, above all, that peculiar, naïvely cheerful, confiding, open, at the first glance somewhat foolish expression, by which in former days one could recognize directly the children of steady-going noble families, 'sons of their fathers,' fine young landowners, born and reared in our open, half-wild country parts,—a hesitating gait, a voice with a lisp, a smile like a child's, the minute you looked at him . . . lastly, freshness, health, softness, softness, softness—there you have the whole of Sanin. And secondly, he was not stupid and had picked up a fair amount of knowledge. Fresh he had remained, for all his foreign tour; the disturbing emotions in which the greater part of the young people of that day were tempest-tossed were very little known to him."

For Sanin there is neither yesterday nor to-morrow. He "lives like a plant" and has no notion that there is any other way of living. Chance brings him to a little confectioner's shop at Frankfurt, where there is a wonderful Italian girl, Gemma, and an old Italian, half servant and half friend of the family, who had once sung in Grand Opera. Besides them, there is Gemma's mother and Gemma's brother, Emile. Suddenly as by enchantment this little world, hidden "under the water" becomes Sanin's world. He is infinitely contented with it as he chats about Russia over chocolate and angel cake, while Pantaleone, the poor old ex-baritone, dances attendance in the background. Sanin had intended to leave Frankfurt in a few hours, but now he wishes to stay near Gemma who has, incidentally, a German fiancé of whom she rarely speaks. He, indeed, and every one else, is remote from this little world where Pantaleone talks of famous singers and Sanin explains that houses in Russia are not built of ice. Life goes by like a dream, while wasps and bees and drowsy beetles in the little garden outside reproduce the very atmosphere of Spaskoë. In this atmosphere one can see love expanding literally like a plant before one's eyes. Sanin is hardly conscious of it so naturally does it flow like the torrents of spring without rage and without menace. But presently outside a commonplace café a drunken German officer drags the beautiful growth into full consciousness. He accosts Gemma and snatches up her rose; it is not her fiancé, who is present at the table, but Sanin who regains the rose and rebukes the German's insolence. A duel follows, a duel in the Turgenevean manner, without romance, with the doctor yawning on the grass, while the devoted Pantaleone discusses the preliminaries with the other second. It is almost a burlesque duel, but to the Italian girl the Russian has become the hero of all dreams, the conqueror at once of the rose and the sword. There remains only the third symbol—the ring—and Sanin with the torrent of spring in his heart, is only too eager for that.

Before such a torrent the German fiancé must stand aside. Gemma must marry Sanin, but first he must sell his property in Russia. Everything is simple, and as though providentially he meets at Frankfurt an old schoolfellow, Ippolit Polozov, who suggests that his rich wife might purchas. the property. So Sanin drives away with his old schoolfellow to discuss the sale with Maria Nikolaevna, the unknown quantity in this delicate equation of human destinies. She proves to be a half-gipsy who possesses exactly that exotic beauty, at once daring and subtle, which works such havoc in those almost naïve love stories of Ivan Turgenev. She introduces immediately the repetition of the old *motif*; the good love is poisoned by the bad. The spell of the flesh destroys that other spell of freshness and youth. Sanin's romance is poisoned in Frankfurt just as Vladimir's romance had been poisoned in Spaskoë. He sends a lying letter of excuse to Gemma and becomes the third figure in a dreary *ménage à trois*. The very memory of it, after the lapse of so many years of experience, festers afresh: "The life in Paris, and all the humiliations, all the loathsome tortures of the slave who dare not be jealous or complain and who is cast aside at last like a worn-out garment. . . . Then the going home to his own country, the poisoned, the devastated life, the petty interests and the petty cares, bitter and fruitless regret, and as bitter and fruitless apathy, a punishment not apparent, but of every minute, continuous, like some trivial but incurable disease, the payment, farthing by farthing, of the debt which can never be settled. . . ." That is what the loss of Gemma meant for Sanin, but what did the loss of Sanin mean for the Italian. Years afterwards he learned that she had gone to the United States, wrote to her and received a letter saying that she was happily married. She also enclosed the photograph of her eldest child, a beautiful young Gemma.

So close is this story to actual autobiography that its author was dissatisfied with it as a work of art. Writing to Madame Commandille in a letter dated August, 1873, Turgenev says: "Your criticism of *Eaux de Printemps*, is perfectly sound; as for the second part, it is neither properly worked out nor even necessary, I let myself be carried away by reminiscences."

German influence never penetrated very deeply into the character of Turgenev, but remained in Berlin very much what it had been in Moscow. But in Berlin he met among his compatriots a man who undoubtedly produced a lasting impression upon him. For it was while he was studying philosophy that Turgenev lived in the same house as the famous anarchist, Michael Bakunin. As Bakunin was eight years older than Turgenev he acted rather as his mentor, particularly in regard to that *courturière*, who provided a well remembered incident, or even episode, in the Berlin days. Bakunin himself was to appear as Dmitri Rudin, though undoubtedly there is a great deal of Turgenev himself in this will-less hero of the forties. "But," as Stepniak wrote towards the end of the last century, "it may be truly said that every educated Russian of our time has a bit of Dmitri Rudin in him." The historic agitator, however, has been presented to English readers without the alloy of subjectivity. In a novel entitled, *Aut Caesar Aut Nihil*, Bakunin appears in all his external shabbiness, a morose man, solitary and dominated by one passion—the despair of the disinherited. When talking to an English woman in French, this passion leaps suddenly to the surface: "Ah, down there! Dear lady, we know little of what goes on 'down there'! And it is we who are ignorant, we who are dull, stupid, blind, cruel. From our heights we overlook those 'down there'; they are ants, grubs, worms, moths. . . . So far off, so low down, so small, dark and insignificant. Such swarming millions; mere moths dancing in the sunbeams; mere fluttering futilities! 'Down there!'"

Instantly one sees the inner man, *tout net* as it were, just as one has already seen his clothes. Mellin as he is called in this English novel is crystallized in an inner as well as in an outer sense. He is like ice towards the young English girl who offers to dedicate her life to him and the cause he represents. It is a clear picture of Bakunin as he appeared to English eyes; it is also a clear picture of the sort of approach by which the nihilists of Bakunin's period sought to reach those "down there." Right up to Kerensky, that approach seems to have been in order, but it was not the kind of approach that ever really reached them. It was the unrhetorical *drops* of Lenin that penetrated to the proletariat, though it does not seem that these drops have stirred the Russian peasant who remains instinctively and even systematically opposed to organized system. However that may be, the light from Lenin's tomb is certainly remote from the nihilist Bakunin in his English dress.

But Bakunin in the pages of Rudin is in no sense a crystallized character after the Western fashion. The novel is steeped in Turgenev's reminiscences of the Berlin student days and most of them are put into the mouth, not of Rudin, but of Lezhnyov, a man of about thirty who wears an old greatcoat of grey linen and a forage cap of the same material. He has a "broad and colourless face," small "light grey eyes" and an almost white moustache. He is apparently one of those faded Turgenevean characters, but after listening to Dmitri Rudin he fires up, like Turgenev himself, with something of the old enthusiasm of those samovar nights in Berlin.

The plot of the novel, as usual with Turgenev, is almost perfunctory. A middle-aged man, wholly disillusioned, but a brilliant talker, bursts in upon the Oblomov-like torpor of a Russian country house. Everybody becomes dazzled by his intoxication with general ideas and when he has stopped talking his little audience begins to discuss the things that matter with an eagerness unknown to them before. Only the daughter of the house, who has been listening most intently remains silent in the background. Her name is Natalya and a little later Rudin begins to read Goethe's *Faust* to her, or Hoffman or Novalis. But best of all she likes to listen to him when he talks to her on love. Lezhnyov, who had himself been dazzled by Dmitri Rudin, is furious at this new phase: "He is playing a dangerous game—not dangerous to him of course; he does not risk a farthing, not a straw on it—but others stake their souls." Still, he admits even now how much he owed to Rudin in those Berlin days as well as to a certain Pokorsky and he goes on to sketch one of those samovar nights which meant more to Turgenev than all the German philosophers. It is a sketch that reveals the novelist at this period—the period of Sanin—more surely than pages of exposition and comment:

"Imagine a party of five or six lads gathered together, one tallow candle burning. The tea was dreadful stuff, and the cake was stale, very stale; but you should have seen our faces, you should have heard our talk! Eyes were sparkling with enthusiasm, cheeks flushed, and hearts beating while we talked of God, and truth, of the future of humanity and poetry. . . . Often what we said was absurd, and we were in ecstasies over nonsense, but what of that? . . . Pokorsky sat with crossed legs, his pale cheek on his hand, and his eyes seemed to shed light. Rudin stood in the middle of the room and spoke, spoke splendidly, for all the world like the young Demosthenes by the resounding sea; our poet Subotin of the dishevelled locks would now and then throw out some abrupt exclamation as though in his sleep while Scheller, a student forty years old, the son of a German pastor who had the reputation among us of a profound thinker, thanks to his eternal inviolable silence, held his peace with more rapt solemnity than usual; even the lively Schitov, the Aristophanes of our reunions, was subdued and did no more than smile, while two or three novices listened with reverent transports. . . . And the night seemed to fly by on wings."

This is actual autobiography and very similar passages of autobiography are to be found in the works of Tolstoy and Dostoevsky; they, too, in their different ways had sworn the oath of Hannibal, but it was only Turgenev who set out to the West in order to learn its secret of liberty.

Yet in this novel Lezhnyov, becoming more and more the mere mouthpiece of Turgenev, utters words that might have been taken almost verbatim from Dostoevsky's letters: "Rudin's misfortune is that he does not understand Russia, and that certainly is a great misfortune. Russia can do without every one of us, but not one of us can do without her.

Woe to him who thinks he can, and woe twofold to him who actually does do without her! Cosmopolitanism is all twaddle, the cosmopolitan is a nonentity—worse than a nonentity: without nationality is no art, nor truth, nor life, nor anything."

Lezhnyov is bitter enough towards his old comrade, he says that there is ice in Rudin's blood. But he claims that this is no fault of his and insists that though Rudin lives at the expense of others, it is not as a parasite, but rather as a child. And so even he, who knew the man to the core, drinks to the health of Dmitri Rudin and in doing so drinks to his own youth and the samovar nights and the oath of Hannibal and all that spelt out happiness for Sanin in Berlin. It is, indeed, frank autobiography and even the *couturière* finds a place in it; incidentally, Rudin himself appears as the perplexing hero of the little affair. Rudin, it seems, did not make love to her but bewildered her by discussing nature and Hegel with a more than Hegelian calm towards what she had to offer. None the less, the Frenchwoman consented to come for a row with Rudin and dressed in her best for the occasion. The Russian, however, was more difficult than ever. He patted the *couturière* on the head, looked up at the sky and informed her repeatedly that he felt towards her as a father towards his child. Her disillusion drew comedy from the Hegelian altitudes.

But for Natalya disillusion was to become tragic rather than comic. Rudin had played so flexibly on heart strings singularly responsive. Natalya had drunk in his words, as though they were literally a draught of new life, as to her indeed they were. She cannot comprehend that this man's heart is not warm and living, like her own. She cannot separate words from life. She does not understand that they can be sometimes at the very best beautiful dead things, ruthless, complete in themselves and isolated from life. How was she to guess that it is Rudin's torment to clothe an ideal with words alone, and to pass on with other words to other causes? How could she grasp that he was in reality a victim who half divined his own petrifying secret: "A strange almost farcical fate is mine. I would devote myself—eagerly, wholly—to some cause; and I cannot devote myself. I shall end by sacrificing myself to some folly or other in which I shall not even believe." This presentiment was only too true, but Natalya must suffer first.

The idyll is discovered quickly enough. Natalya's mother has no intention of allowing her to marry a Bohemian derelict merely because he talks cleverly in a drawing-room and she tells her daughter so quite plainly. In her turn, Natalya informs Rudin of her mother's decision with all the proud confidence of youth in her heart. As for her, she will follow Rudin the wanderer to the last winding of his destiny. It is for him to lead the way. Let him declare at once what they two, who love each other, must do. But the very word "do" robs Rudin even of the solace of words. "What must we do?" he repeats stupidly, "of course, submit."

At last she understands. It has been all a clatter of words that has drawn to the surface the very depths of a nature essentially silent and drawn in upon itself. Natalya knows Rudin now and she is deeply sorry for him because he is so utterly different, not merely from her dream of him, but from his own dream of himself. It is as though she had sought to warm herself before a reflected fire. It is as though she had answered the love words of an echo that rang from she knew not whose lips. And so Natalya turns away from Rudin, as so many have turned away from him and will yet turn away from him again.

It is for Rudin to wander alone over distance and over thought, from place to place and from ideal to ideal. His life was typical of that *nature errante de l'homme russe*, which was to drive Ivan Turganev constantly over Europe. Dmitri Rudin was to continue his wanderings but, in his own strange way and in spite of his inherent want of will, he was to remain consistent in his very inconsistency. There was something noble about Rudin to which Lezhnyov capitulates in the end, maintaining that he was not on a small scale. At all events Rudin has no instinct for soft places but continues easily his self-sought Odyssey of hardship. Dazzled as he is by his own rhetoric, he never uses it as a parasite would use it. He has nothing in common with parasites though parasites are the first to condemn him. Pigasov, for example, says of Rudin: "If he begins to attack himself, he humbles himself into the dust: come, one thinks, he will never dare to face the light of day after that. Not a bit of it! It only cheers him up, as if he treated himself to a glass of grog." That is the verdict of Pigasov, but he was a man who accepted bribes.

For his part, Turgenev refuses to label Rudin, refuses to show him *tout net* either for good or for evil as Mellin is shown in the English novel. The baffled shabby figure still preserves the glamour of those samovar nights, reviving all those breathless declamations on the meaning of life, love, beauty, passion, art, on everything in short, except avarice, selfishness, exclusion and every phase of that withered and withering pride which dwarfs for ever the human soul. Of these things at least Rudin was wholly innocent. Fantastic to the very end, he dies as he had prophesied for a cause in which he does not believe. On the summit of a barricade, in a narrow alley of the Faubourg St Antoine—already abandoned by its defenders—there appeared on the 26th July, 1848, carrying a red flag in one hand and a blunt sabre in the other, "a tall man in an old overcoat, with a red sash, and a straw hat on his grey dishevelled hair." To his retreating comrades this forlorn and doomed figure was known as *le Polonais*, but he was a Russian and his name was Dmitri Rudin.

At first glance, there seems little enough of Rudin in the Sanin of those Berlin days, but under the surface there survived in the great Russian novelist to the very end exactly that uncalculating simplicity of Gemma's lover, who "lived like a plant" and that uncalculating simplicity which left Rudin alone on that deserted barricade. Sanin and Rudin have this much at least in common: Each possessed the capacity to respond to forlorn hopes and lost causes and with all their faults and their weaknesses each possessed an utter detachment from interested motives. Turgenev could scarcely understand that form of worldliness and very seldom describes it. His heroes never wish to get on and accumulate money any more than did those students of the Berlin days whom he never forgot. And when, in 1841, he returned to Russia he was to keep, in his own fashion, that oath of Hannibal sworn at dawn in the staid German capital around a Russian samovar. And this oath is significant not only for its fulfilment in the book that brought freedom to the Russian slave. In another masterpiece Turgenev was to prove himself a singularly penetrating watcher of his compatriots. In *Virgin Soil*, he has detected that *vis inertiae* of the peasant which has proved in the days that pass, the most formidable obstacle to the new masters of Russia. Turgenev cannot be dismissed as a bourgeois artist who painted the old Russia in charming colours; he was in his way a prophet who foresaw the future by right of his comprehension of the present. *Virgin Soil* is as prophetic as Dostoevsky's *Demons* and is a much more accurate divination of the future than, for example, Maxim Gorki's *La Mère*, written so many years afterwards. Nor can Turgenev be dismissed as an artist who, in spite of his own prejudice against cosmopolitanism, became himself a cosmopolitan. In the West he never lost the nostalgia of his Russian home just as in Russia he never forgot that oath of Hannibal, sworn in the name of freedom and kept by him who became in very truth, the emancipator of the serfs.

CHAPTER VI

THE DAUGHTER

O<small>N</small> his return to Russia, Turgenev appeared to his compatriots in Moscow far more under German influence than he was in reality. He was still undoubtedly an advocate of Hegel and he nearly succeeded in becoming a professor at the University of Moscow. His candidature, however, was discussed by the authorities in such a dilatory fashion that he left abruptly for Petersburg, where in 1843, he entered the office of the Minister of the Interior. But his bureaucratic ambitions were of the very mildest and the change to Petersburg meant for him personally little more than the substitution of George Sand for Hegel as a spiritual inspiration. He began to write verse and comedies; he associated with all the young writers of the period and especially with the established critic Belinsky. His love of mystification seems to have developed at this period; one hears of him boasting not only of a phantom game-bag, but of a phantom French cook. "Come to dinner on Sunday," he urged Belinsky and other friends, "and you will see what an artist I have unearthed." The distrustful critic accepted after making a memorandum of the invitation in Turgenev's own notebook. The guests arrived only to find what had been described as a splendid villa a mere hovel. As for the host, he was not at home, but was discovered by his guests in the house of a neighbouring pope. A dinner was improvized without the assistance of any French chef. "It is true," Turgenev admitted in face of actual facts, "but come next Sunday, you will see!"

Underneath all this buffoonery there was the genuine desire to be hospitable, but Turgenev's mother held the purse strings and he was on strained terms with her. She still loathed the career of letters to which Ivan clung so obstinately and when he came to Spaskoë for his holidays, she would harp incessantly on two things: a suitable career and a suitable marriage. Ivan would have neither the one nor the other. He preferred men of letters to tchinovniks and made no secret of his preference. "As for marrying," he exclaimed, "the church of Spaskoë will be seen dancing the trepak on its two crosses before that." If he had only remained a bureaucrat his mother might have forgiven him a little dabbling in poetry, for she had a vague respect for Pushkin. But in 1845, he sent in his resignation and then supplies from Spaskoë were cut off ruthlessly.

For all that, this period was one of happiness for Ivan Turgenev who celebrated his mother's decision by composing a comedy entitled, *The Morning of a Prodigal*. This was the year in which Dostoevsky had found fame so suddenly by the manuscript of *Poor Folk*, which had led to his introduction to Belinsky as "a new Gogol." The young author was introduced everywhere after this and naturally enough was presented to Turgenev with whom at first he was delighted. "Ah, my brother," Dostoevsky wrote after this first meeting, "what a man!" He goes on to analyse the rival whom he is afterwards to hate: "He has a real talent, he is a poet, an aristocrat, good-looking, rich, intelligent, well-read, he is twenty-five years old—I do not know what nature has been able to refuse him! Finally, he possesses a character that is absolutely honourable, formed in a good school, and a perfect disposition."

But soon afterwards there was an unhappy misunderstanding which destroyed the future relations between these two great Russian writers. It occurred at a card party given by Turgenev; Belinsky, Ogarev and Hertzen were among the guests. The author of *Poor Folk* was expected and just as he came into the room one of the players happened to make a foolish mistake which was greeted by a general outburst of laughter. Dostoevsky grew pale and without uttering a word left the room immediately. No notice was taken of this, as everybody expected that he would return. As he failed to do so, Turgenev went out to see what had become of him. He was informed by the servant that this strange guest had been walking up and down in front of the house bareheaded for the last hour. Turgenev rushed out of the house and asked Dostoevsky the meaning of this extraordinary behaviour. "My God!" exclaimed his guest, "it is intolerable! Wherever I go, everybody mocks me. I had scarcely put foot in your house when you and your guests overwhelmed me with your ridicule. Are you not ashamed of it?" Turgenev endeavoured to convince him that no one had had the slightest intention of making fun of him, but his efforts were useless. Dostoevsky refused to listen to reason, returned to the hall for his hat and overcoat and then left the house without being reconciled to his bewildered host.

Turgenev's relations with Tolstoy were difficult in the extreme, but with Dostoevsky they became impossible. To Dostoevsky's generous, but irritable nature the personality of Turgenev became a perpetual irritant. The younger author fostered an ever deepening grudge against the man whom he had first hailed so rapturously. On the eve of his return from Siberia, he protested in a letter to his brother Michael, against the discrepancy between the payment for his work and the payment for Turgenev's: "I know very well that I write worse than Turgenev, but my work is not as bad as all that, and besides, I hope to write as well as he does. Why then, when I am in so great need, should I receive one hundred roubles, and Turgenev, who owns two thousand souls, receive four hundred roubles? Necessity compels me to hurry and to write in order to procure money and consequently to spoil my work inevitably." This not unnatural resentment was to pass into a different phase; Dostoevsky was to disparage the work that he had once so genuinely admired. He ridiculed, for example, *The Execution of Troppmann* and greeted *Lear of the Steppes* with the gloating comment: "He is failing; he is becoming paler and paler."

On his side, Turgenev wrote in reference to Dostoevsky's *Adolescent:* "On receipt of the last number of *Les Annales de la Patrie*, I plunged into that chaos of a book. Heavens!

what mud, what hospital stench, what futile repetition, what a mania for sickly psychology! That's the sort of book to which all that you say in your letter about this style of literature applies word for word." For all that, when an unusually unintelligent outburst of criticism assailed *Fathers and Sons* its author acknowledged that Dostoevsky, almost alone, had grasped his exact meaning in that epoch-making novel.

In spite of this, Turgenev's rival in *Demons*—an admitted answer to *Fathers and Sons*—saw fit to ridicule him in the person of Karmazinov a malevolent novelist who has out-lived his vogue. "They tell me," wrote Turgenev to Polon-sky, "that Dostoevsky has brought me upon the stage; much good may it do him! He paid me a visit at Baden-Baden five years ago, not in order to repay me the money that he had borrowed, but in order to insult me in every kind of way on the subject of *Smoke* which, according to him, ought to be burnt by the common hangman. I listened in absolute silence to this philippic. What did I learn later? I had expressed to him all sorts of criminal opinions which he had hastened to communicate to Bertenev—Bertenev, in fact, wrote to me about it. This would be a calumny pure and simple, if Dostoevsky were not out of his mind, as I have very little doubt that he is. Perhaps he dreamed all that. But Heavens! what miserable tittle tattle!" In the end, the merciful and forgiving Turgenev was to use the phrase, "*C'est du Dostoevsky*" as the most scornful of all comments and to label and libel the author of *The Brothers Karamazov* as a badly balanced mediocrity.

It is a profound misfortune that these two great Russian novelists, whom nature had meant to be complementary each to each, should have so profoundly misjudged one another. The artist who best of all interpreted the soul of Russia to the West, became the personal enemy of the veri-table confessor of that soul. For the incohate message of the Russian was primarily Dostoevsky's secret by right of suffering, of self-knowledge, of divination. He it was and neither Turgenev, nor Tolstoy who felt in his own heart the mysterious inner wound of the Slav. He it was who, in the Russian manner, uninfluenced by Western logic, believed without reasoning, divined without analysing, felt without knowing and comprehended, best of all, the great mass of the Russian people because, in actual personal experience, he had not been severed from their aspirations and their despair. Tolstoy knew well that there lay in the heart of Dostoevsky everything that he himself was striving to make articulate without the experience of his formidable rival. But when Russia acknowledged tumultuously her loss in the death of Feodor Mikhailovitch Dostoevsky, realizing with a sudden insight of grief that he was her own national symbol, Turgenev, who ought best of all to have understood, turned coldly and derisively away.

With Belinsky, on the other hand, Turgenev's relations were happy from first to last. The critic had fallen on evil days when Turgenev met him in 1843. He was in great poverty at this period, and was already in the grip of phthisis. Yet in spite of these afflictions he enjoyed those Russian talks with Turgenev with whose general views he sympathized far more than he did with Dostoevsky's. The Russian critic, like the future author of *Smoke*, believed in the necessity of Western civilization for his country, though he admired—almost as deeply as Dostoevsky himself— what seemed to so many to be the national soul of Russia. Oddly enough at this period, prior to the unfortunate misunderstanding with Dostoevsky, both Belinsky and Turgenev felt themselves bound to take the author of *Poor Folk* to task for the disorder of his life though without much result. For in the same letter that Dostoevsky alludes to these well-intentioned cautions he goes on to say with all the exaggeration of contrition: "I cannot live correctly; I am a complete debauchee." For the ill-fated critic it was becoming more and more difficult to live at all, and in 1846 his health broke down completely. He was compelled to leave the "Otechestvennya Zapiski" in which so many of Dostoevsky's earlier works appeared and went abroad the same year.

But there was someone who influenced Turgenev on his return to Russia far more profoundly. Pauline Garcia, Malibran's sister, came to sing in Petersburg for the first time in 1843. From the moment of their first meeting Turgenev became her slave; he praised her to everyone including, most unwisely, his own mother. To Belinsky he described the ecstasy of a moment when the singer had brushed a perfumed handkerchief across his forehead. The same year he met, on a shooting expedition, Monsieur Viardot who had undertaken the task of introducing to the French public the masterpieces of Russian literature. A little later the diva became Madame Viardot and it was under her direct influence that Ivan Turgenev began his career as a serious writer. She it was who brought him to the west. "I should never have written *The Annals of a Sportsman,* if I had stayed in Russia," Turgenev has frankly admitted. Though he felt nostalgia for Russia when abroad the novelist frequently experienced something paralysing in the atmosphere of Russia; this was to repeat itself during the flying visits of his later years. He has himself commented on the feeling of compulsion that drew him away from Russia, in spite of his love for his native land: "The existing state of things, the whole social fabric, and particularly the class to which I belong—the class of landlords, of serf-owners—held out no inducement which could have kept me in my own country. On the contrary, almost everything that I saw about me distressed me, filled me with indignation and scorn. I could not remain undecided for long. I had either to submit, to walk meekly in the common rut, the beaten path, or tear myself away with one wrench, casting off everything and everybody at the risk of losing many who were near and dear to my heart. I chose the latter course."

Few writers in the world have been more steeped in irony than Turgenev and yet the irony of life—so different from personal irony—played mockingly enough with him. With every instinct of his being he opposed the idea of owning a fellow human being and yet, in 1841, he who had sworn the oath of Hannibal in Berlin, purchased a serf girl. At the house of a rich uncle in Moscow he met a young cousin, Elizabeth Turgenev, a fair girl of about sixteen, who had a property of her own near Orel. Elizabeth administered the affairs of her village and her cousin began to visit her at least once a week. She had at this time a young *femme de chambre*, a serf girl whose name was Feodista, but who was called Fetistka. She was by no means beautiful, but she appealed to Turgenev just as those silent wistful serf girls in his sketches appealed to him. "Fetistka," writes Pavlovsky, "did not strike one at first glance; her beauty was not at all extraordinary. A brunette, thinnish, not ugly, but not pretty, nothing more, one might have pictured her readily thus; but on observing her more closely, one found in her drawn features, in her pretty face tanned by the sun, in her sad glances something which attracted and charmed." Turgenev observed Fetistka very closely and for the time being at least, he was charmed.

Elizabeth Turgenev was attached to her *femme de chambre* and had her dressed like a lady. Ivan, whose object in life was the abolition of the serfs, none the less desired to purchase this particular serf girl and made an offer for her which Elizabeth refused. In one of the sketches of *The Annals of a Sportsman*, the novelist reproduces, with one knows not what bitter sting of memory in his heart, this ignoble haggling over the ownership of a human being. In the story the rich mistress refuses to sell her slave and the would-be purchaser carries her off. In the end, however, the serf's hiding place is discovered and she gives herself up to her mistress, as though she were not a living woman, but merely a piece of stolen property endowed with the curse of being able to feel. In *Fathers and Sons*, too, Turgenev reverts with delicate sympathy to this same question of a serf girl owned and oppressed by the added bondage of love. In that book, it must be noted, it is not Bazarov, the heir of the future, but Pavel, the inheritor of the past, who brings home to the girl's master that a serf is a human being.

The son of "*le beau* Serge" inevitably regarded serf girls

as human beings. Like Sanin, and with the softness of Sanin still clinging to him, he searched not only for the meaning of life, but for its savour. This savour is said to have come to him only through the frou-frou of a mondaine's skirts, but there is an allusion in the poem *Parasha* to wild flowers that are fresh and sweet but wither too soon. "I have gathered two or three of them," he notes with the insousciance of youth.

But years later the memory of a serf girl was not insousciant. At one of those Magny dinners in Paris the Russian felt himself transplanted into the quietude of his native plains. Suddenly to his nostrils, suffocated by the miasma of the boulevards, there returned the old sweet sharp scents as he visualized across that sophisticated dinner table the gathering of one of those wild flowers that wither too soon. He had asked, it seems, a poor serf girl what she would like him to give her and she had answered "soap" so that her hands might be like those of other women whose fingers men such as Sanin kissed. That, too, had its rightful place among the arid dissections of old passions which are revived only by the brain.

But in 1841, self-accusation was stifled. After much bargaining with Elizabeth Fetistka's price was fixed at seven hundred roubles, though a serf girl at that time was valued at a maximum of fifty. Turgenev took his purchase to Spaskoë Selo and remained in retirement with her about a year. During this time he endeavoured to teach her to read, but not with much success. He seems to have wearied of her only too quickly and to have taken again to sport as a relief from love. In any case, there was born on the 8th May, 1842, an infant daughter and to her at least the novelist remained faithful to the last day of his life.

But poor Fetistka was lightly forgotten when Turgenev followed the singer in 1847. At Berlin, however, he deserted the Viardots and went to see Belinsky at Stettin. The critic was nearing the end; Turgenev accompanied him to Salsbrunn in Silesia. Here, while taking the waters, the dying man talked with all his old gusto to his friend, who after a few weeks abruptly disappeared. "The devil alone knows where he has gone," is Belinsky's comment, but at Petersburg they assigned him as a matter of course to the Viardots. Gossip had already been mockingly busy over this infatuation. "*La Clairon*," noted one observer with envious malice, "has always some Russian *pot-au-feu*, who is content with kissing her hand." Turgenev was in no sense of the term *pot-au-feu*, but apart altogether from his obsession he had a devout belief in the genius of the singer, fully endorsing the verdict of George Sand: "Pauline Garcia-Viardot, *le plus beau genie de femme de notre époque*." On her side, whatever their actual relations were or were not, this superb artist gave the Russian not only the music which to him was almost a physical need, but those other rare gifts for which he craved so uselessly in her absence—sympathy and comprehension.

There was yet another link between the diva and Turgenev; it was poor Fetistka's small daughter. The novelist took Madame Viardot into his confidence about this little being and she consented to supervise her bringing up and education. There are frequent references to the younger "Pauline" in Turgenev's letters, and curiously enough it was Fetistka's daughter who indirectly strained the relations between Turgenev and Tolstoy. For it was during a discussion about her education that the two writers quarrelled and more than once this incident, almost as trivial as that incident which poisoned Turgenev's relations with Dostoevsky, very nearly led to a duel.

It was at a house party at Spaskoë Selo; among Turgenev's guests were Tolstoy and the poet, Fet. The visitors were lunching hurriedly as they were on the eve of departure. One of them happened to ask Turgenev where his daughter was. "Always abroad," was the reply. "She was receiving an education exclusively French. That, however, did not suit my ideas, and I have recently given her an English governess, a worthy and excellent woman."

Tolstoy glanced at his host with a sarcastic smile. "And this governess," he interrupted scoffingly, "she will pay visits with your daughter to the poor, while they are out for walks. She will leave money with medicines."

Turgenev, naturally irritated by this gibe, answered "that in any case there was no harm in that, since the poor would receive a little relief and his daughter would be developing a sense of duty towards all who suffer."

"Then," observed his younger rival, "if it is not one thing it will be the other. If your daughter is not receiving a good education, the poor at least will have received something. She is your natural daughter is she not?"

"Yes, and what next?"

"What next! But you are making an experiment *in anima vili!*"

Turgenev grew white with anger and called out in his high-pitched voice: "Be silent, Tolstoy, or I will throw my fork at you."

At the moment, Tolstoy's eyes expressed merely delight at having exasperated his host and he returned then and there to his own property, while Turgenev and another friend of Fet's accompanied the poet to his estate where they spent a few days. The incident seemed to be closed, but on his return home Turgenev found two letters from the count, in the first of which he begged him to accept his sincere apologies, while in the second, he informed Turgenev that the insult to him, Tolstoy, could be washed out only by pistol shots and invited him to a duel without seconds at six o'clock in the morning. The next day Turgenev despatched his friend Borissov to Tolstoy to arrange a duel in accordance with ordinary usage, but after some parleyings the count declared that he would not fight.

Once more the matter seemed to have ended, but Turgenev felt that his friendly relations with his young rival were definitely broken by this unfortunate squabble over the education of the serf girl's daughter. "I have quarrelled point blank with Leo Tolstoy," he wrote to a friend. "We were within a hair's breadth of a duel. At this moment the hair's breadth has not been passed yet. The fault is in me, but all that was only the result of a long-standing hostility,

FEODOR DOSTOEVSKY

COUNT LEO TOLSTOY

of an antipathy between our two natures. I divined well enough that he hated me, and I could not understand why he kept coming to me all the same. I was compelled to hold myself at a certain distance from him. I tried to approach him, with the result that we were very nearly approaching each other with pistols. I have never liked him. . . ." Four months later, Turgenev learned both in Petersburg and in Paris that Tolstoy had circulated a defamatory letter about him in Moscow, and he determined to call him out. With this object he wrote him the following letter:

"Sir, I learned at the last moment before my departure from Petersburg, that you were speading all over Moscow a copy of the last letter that you had addressed to me, and that besides this, you were referring to me as a coward, asserting that I refused to meet you in a duel, etc. I was unable at that time to return to the government of Toula and continued my journey. But, as I regard your way of behaviour, *after all that I have done to make amends for the words that escaped me,* as dishonouring for me and dishonest, I must inform you that this time I shall not allow this matter to pass without issue, that is to say, that, on returning to Russia next spring, I shall demand satisfaction from you by arms. I must inform you at the same time, that I have written to this effect to my friends in Moscow, in order that they may contradict the malevolent scandal that you are circulating about me."

Count Tolstoy replied by a point blank contradiction of these accusations. He assured Turgenev that he had circulated no copy of the letter and with that the matter was fortunately allowed to rest.

The relations between these two novelists were difficult, but they never became impossible as the relations between Turgenev and Dostoevsky were to become. Nobody appreciated the work of Tolstoy more heartily than did Turgenev who did his very best to secure his rival a hearing in Paris. Turgenev was incapable of that literary jealousy which has warped so many famous lives; even on his death bed, he remembered the great service that Tolstoy had rendered to Russian literature and implored him to go back to it. Pushkin and Lermontov were both killed in duels; one cannot be too thankful that a merciful chance prevented the author of *Smoke* and the author of *Anna Karenina* from assassinating each other, on account of a squabble over the education of Ivan Turgenev's daughter.

But in this year, 1847, the little Pauline was only five years old; Count Tolstoy was still in his teens and the Sanin who was Ivan Turgenev had not lost the softness, which is so much stressed in *Spring Torrents*. He was at a stage of transition; a new era was commencing for him. His orientation towards the west was now definitely formulated though his work was to remain Russian to the core. Primarily and essentially an artist as he was, it must be remembered that he not only wrote the book of political emancipation, but he also depicted the nihilist who was to flower eventually in the cold logic of Lenin. It must be remembered, too, that Turgenev depicted in the self-made Russian a type that was to blossom in the kulak who has proved fodder for a political scythe which, for all its sharpness, is still so powerless against the cunningly inert mass of the Russian peasantry. That inertia Turgenev realized to the full; but he detected all sorts of curious new roots sprouting up in different directions just beneath the surface of the Russia that was mouldering before his eyes in the charmed garden of Spaskoë. Potentially, he had become already the novelist who might well claim the historic significance which he himself had claimed for Gogol.

CHAPTER VII

THE SERFS

IN 1846, "The Contemporary" had been founded in Petersburg, a review to which Turgenev contributed while abroad with indefatigable zeal. "Not a week has passed yet," he writes after being some time in the west, "without my sending a *MSS* to my editors." Among the results of this industry were, *The Annals of a Sportsman* and *The Diary of a Superfluous Man*, the two works which best reveal, respectively, the objective and the subjective side of the great writer.

He visited France for the first time in 1847, and his first impressions, like those of Dostoevsky, were the reverse of enthusiastic. For the younger novelist, Jacques Bonhomme was antagonistic to every Russian ideal, and in Paris he detected the essence of that satisfied bourgeois spirit which was peculiarly inimical to his own temperament. In his essay on the bourgeoisie the constant bias of Dostoevsky, which made him so remote from Turgenev in many ways, reveals itself with characteristic irritability: "It is ignoble and base to steal, that leads to the hulks; the bourgeois is ready to pardon a great deal, but he does not pardon robbery, even if you were to be dying of hunger, you and your children. But if you steal through virtue! All will be forgiven you. You wish then to make a fortune and amass property, that is to say to accomplish the duty of nature and humanity. That is why they have very clearly designated in the Code cases of robbery with a base intention, that is to say from pure necessity, and robbery from the highest virtue. This last is strongly supported, encouraged, and very solidly organized." Dostoevsky never really abandoned that attitude towards France as the interpreter of Western culture. Turgenev was to accept gratefully that culture, to welcome even the croupier, as its lowest symbol.

In reality, Turgenev was dissatisfied not so much with French life, as with the absence of Madame Viardot who wrote to him frequently from Dresden. "All the details that you give us," he wrote in December 1847, "of your life in Dresden are read and re-read a thousand times; they are decidedly a good people, *les Dresdennois*." He is now perfectly at home with the Viardots and the diva's mother has become "Maman." In the same month, he writes of his interest in Madame Viardot's native tongue and speaks of steeping himself in Caldron, "the greatest catholic dramatic poet that there has been as Shakespeare was the most human, the most anti-Christian."

Already his preferences in art have shaped themselves into permanence; he detests the emotional convulsiveness in opera, exactly as he was to detest it in the novels of Dostoevsky. Even at this stage the artistic influence of Garcia's daughter is striking; that influence was also to remain permanent. As to the exact nature of their relations, it is perhaps difficult to attribute to the diva an attitude similar to that enforced platonism which is now alleged to have been Madame Récamier's sole reward to the long homage of Chateaubriand. But there is nothing whatever in the published letters of Turgenev to Madame Viardot to suggest a long and winding love affair of sustained emotionalism. In the present days such an intimacy, if it existed, would appear with cynical frankness; but it must be remembered that in the last century other nationalities, besides the English paid discreet attention to the *qu'en dira t'on*, of posterity. As a mentor in art, at all events, no Egeria could have been more unerring than this artist whose influence has been so gratefully acknowledged by the whole world of music. Only, underneath all that, one divines that this Russian novelist felt in his heart towards Madame Viardot, as Musset felt towards her sister:

Oui, oui, tu le savais, et que, dans cette vie,
Rien n'est bon que d'aimer, n'est vrai que de souffrir.
Chaque soir dans tes chants tu te sentais pâlir.

Tu connaissais le monde, et la foule, et l'envie,
Et, dans ce corps brisé concentrant ton génie,
Tu regardais aussi la Malibran mourir.

Madame Viardot enriched the artistic life of Ivan Turgenev. "I remember," he writes to her, early in 1848, "a penetrating and just observation that you made one day on the little movements, at once agitated and restrained, that Rachel permits herself, while at the same time preserving a calm and imposing attitude; that was with her, perhaps only *savoir faire;* but, in general, it is calm *arising from a strong conviction, or a profound sentiment,* calm, which envelops, so to speak, on all sides, the despairing outbursts of passion, which communicates to them that purity of line, that ideal and real beauty, the true, the only beauty of art. And what proves the truth of this remark is that life itself—in rare moments, it is true, in moments when it rises above all that is accidental and common—raises itself to the same genre of beauty. The greatest sorrows, you have said in your letter, are the most calm; one might add, are the most beautiful. But one must know how to unite the two extremes, or otherwise, one will appear cold." Never has the truth of this profound criticism been more poignantly illustrated than by the work on which the novelist was busy at the time when he wrote this letter.

Yet at this period, the suavity of Turgenev's genius would often lose itself and he would become disconcerting to all around him. Years before, people had noticed his odd pranks in the Russian capital. In Paris, they were to become almost abnormal. It is recorded, for instance, that about this time he was frequently seized by curious fits of spleen. Once, during an attack of this kind, he tore a blind from a window and made out of it a high-pointed cap. Decked with this cap, the man who was then writing *The Annals of a Sportsman,* literally put himself in a corner with his nose to the wall and waited until the mood had passed. In 1849, he wrote from Courtavenel, Madame Viardot's country house in Brie: "I have a great deal of time here, and I make use of it by doing the most perfectly useless things. From time to time, this is necessary for me. Without this safety valve I should be in danger of becoming very stupid one day for good and all."

Still, there is very little trace of these abnormal moods in the correspondence which, though it is for the most part a blend of the sombre with the gay, is lit up invariably by Turgenev's love of art and by his even more profound love of nature. His artistic predictions were unerring; he foresaw the success of the composer Serov, and of the sculptor, Antokolsky. At the commencement of Tolstoy's literary career, he wrote to a friend: "I am delighted at the success of *Adolescence*. May God give Tolstoy a long life, and I have a firm hope that he will astonish you all : his is a talent of the first order." But the artist, Turgenev, even during this first visit to France, was by no means blind to the sweep of modern progress in the applications of science: "In my opinion, the greatest contemporary poets are the Americans who are going to pierce the Isthmus of Panama and talk of establishing telegraphic communication across the ocean."

Yet the supreme solace of Turgenev, the solace beyond the dreams of art and science and the love of women, lay in Nature herself. For this reason, while he rejected so many famous French writers, he capitulated at once to George Sand, in whom he recognized his own delicate responsiveness to Nature's moods. He caught from her the aroma of long lost perfumes, the sounds of night, the rustlings of poplars, the tracings of fantastically edged pictures in clouds, the unforced revelation of her moods untainted by the alloy of any pathetic fallacy. He himself, at Ville-d'Avray in 1848 as long before in the garden of Spaskoë, and in the Black Forest of his Berlin student days, could not "see without emotion a branch covered with foliage outline itself clearly against the blue sky."

Nature may have remained to him almost to the very last *la grande Indifférente*, but she held him with every spell of her changing moods and his sombre pessimism seems to float away from him when, on some dry restless morning, he catches through films of dust, the peace of a drowsy hillock, or the deep recess, saturated with shadows, of some low-lying copse. He absorbs the sounds, the perfumes of summer, the timid caresses of spring, the low calls of the woods, the startling splashes at night in the rivers, the buzzing of insects over stagnant water, the whole hushed landscape of the plain on which man moves in unconscious unison with every other manifestation of life. And because the moujik, more easily than a convoluted type, blends with the setting of such scenes, the artist in Turgenev, as distinct from the emancipator, had long been pre-occupied with the Russian peasants as part and parcel of the loved Russian landscape.

The great Russian novelists of the nineteenth century all alike realized the necessity of understanding the mass of the Russian people. Tolstoy imagined that in the moujik he had discovered a new and deeper Socrates; Dostoevsky believed that the Russians were the most unspoilt of peoples and that the moujik, as the simplest type of Russian, was the most unspoilt of all. Both he and Tolstoy detected in the common people of their country a great motive power of nationality in the sense of brotherhood.

"I have always been a true Russian," wrote Dostoevsky, in 1856, and in the same letter he goes on to speak of "our Sacred Mother" who is to become the saviour of Europe. "I assure you," he continues, "that I, for example, am so near to everything that is Russian, that the convicts themselves did not alarm me; they were Russians, my brothers in adversity, and I had more than once the good fortune of meeting with greatness of soul in the heart of even a brigand for the sole reason that I was able to understand him, being myself Russian."

For Turgenev, the Russian peasant was neither a new Socrates, nor the potential leader to a destiny of mystic nationalism. He was content to draw him lovingly and simply as he was, allowing his picture to speak for itself. If occasionally a vibration of anger quivers through his serenity it passes quickly and, veritably like Tacitus, he continues to speak in undertones. Still he, no less than either of his rivals, saw in this crushed Atlas of Imperial Russia, a being who preserved a strange dignity throughout the indignities of his life and an impassive fortitude in the face of death, a being, moreover, who starved by reality, was none the less so close to Nature as to share something of her brooding dreams. Turgenev was to see in this manifestation of life—seemingly the last and least of men—not a philosopher, but yet one who, for all that, possessed an incongruous kinship with him who drank the hemlock as though in sombre derision of the powerful folly of mankind.

Writing from Paris in the summer of 1849, Turgenev sketches the catastrophe in a family of Russian peasants whose harvest has been suddenly destroyed. The women wept, but the father of the family, his head and breast bare, uttered no word: "I approached them, I tried to console them, but at my first word, the peasant let himself fall slowly face downward on the earth, and with his two hands pulled his grey linen shirt over his head. It was the last gesture of the dying Socrates, the last mute protest of the man against the cruelty of man or the brutal indifference of Nature." And the novelist goes on to give the very key-note of his reasoned pessimism: "That is what she is: she is indifferent, there is soul only in ourselves and perhaps a little around us. . . . It is a feeble radiation that old night seeks eternally to devour." But he goes on to admit that this "*scélérate de Nature*" is, for all that, admirably beautiful. Such is the philosophy that underlies every one of these sketches of Russian life which were to light up, for the second time, the dark morass of Russia.

It is difficult to believe that *The Annals of a Sportsman* was actually written abroad, so permeated is it by the sounds and scents, the dim languor of Russian summers and the cool hush of Russian nights. It seems almost impossible that he could have conveyed to us in such minute detail from far away those scenes of izbas and country houses, those long tramps through woods and plains, those chance meetings at isolated post houses, those uproars in traktirs, the rush of troïkas, the dust and din of the horse fair, the straining of hounds—all that long rapturous medley of Russian outdoor life. He seems to be writing always with his eye on the object, always in the open air of Russia, but perhaps he was never so near his native land as when he paced the boulevards of Paris. Russian critics, however, never understood that imaginative nostalgia which went so far beyond the range of Zola's industrious notebooks. "Now," Turgenev wrote in the course of a letter with reference to this old quarrel, "let us pass to your little old woman that is to say to the public, or to the critics. Like every old woman, they cling obstinately to vulgar or pre-conceived opinions, on however slight a basis they may rest. For example, they always maintain that after my *Annals of a Sportsman*, all my works are bad, thanks to my absence from Russia, of which, if one is to believe them, I can have no knowledge whatsoever; but this reproach can only refer to what I have written after 1863. Up to that date, that is to say up to my forty-fifth year, I remained in Russia almost without stirring from it, except from 1848 to 1850, during which period I wrote precisely, *The Annals of a Sportsman*, while *Rudin*, *Liza* and *Father and Sons* were written in Russia." This old quarrel between the creative writer and his assailants might be passed over as faded and meaningless, but for the fact that, even to this day, Turgenev is so often judged not by what he accomplished as an artist, but what he failed to accomplish in the political maelstrom. This particular book, at all events, did accomplish a great political reform, but it is wholly free from the special pleading, self-consciousness and over-emphasis of the ordinary novel with a purpose. Fortunately, both for Russian freedom and for universal literature, Turgenev kept the oath of Hannibal, sworn in his youth and yet remained the artist he was by nature.

It was his own youth that gave him the secret of the thing, the open Sesame to the driest and most disillusioned hearts. It was his own youth that made him able to renew the historic spell of *Dead Souls*, to renew the illusion of passing for the very first time through the background of Imperial

Russia over the mapless wastes of dwarfed lives. He had only to close his eyes to recall as human beings Nicholas Jakovlev, Ivan Pretov and Egor Kondratiev, his mother's serfs, with whose lives she had played more carelessly than a child with already broken toys. He knew, in a deeper sense than Gogol, that these also were men and through him, Imperial Russia itself began sluggishly to understand.

The whole world has acknowledged the livingness of these admirable sketches which won the author so high a tribute from George Sand, but few people realized that for all their objectivity, and, seemingly, impersonal detachment they are as close to the actual autobiography of Turgenev as even *First Love* and *Spring Torrents*. Scattered all through the two volumes, there are allusions to the home life of Spaskoë which are an ample corroboration of Varya's chronicles. In *Raspberry Spring*, for instance, we have from a serf this glimpse of a landowner who kept an establishment, quite on Madame Turgenev's scale, even to the orchestra: "Embroidered coats, wigs, canes, perfumes *eau de cologne* of the best sort, snuff boxes, huge pictures: he would order them all from Paris itself! When he gave a banquet, God Almighty, Lord of my being! there were fireworks and carriages driving up! They even fired off the cannon. The orchestra alone consisted of forty men. He kept a German as conductor of the band, but the German gave himself dreadful airs; he wanted to eat at the same table as the masters; so his excellency gave orders to get rid of him! 'My musicians,' says he, 'can do their work even without a conductor.' Of course he was master. Then they would fall to dancing and dance till morning, especially at the *écossaise-matrador*."

In *My Neighbour Radivol*, we have an impression of lime trees, recalling the days when the boy Ivan would steal out into the garden to keep an appointment not with a bright-eyed maiden, luring him through the ghostly moonlight, but only with a lime tree. In *The Peasant Proprietor Ovsyanikov*, there is a biting reminiscence of the old ancestral régime. The peasant proprietor tells his interlocutor

what happened when his father complained of having his
land taken away from him: "Your grandfather at once
sent his huntsman Baush with a detachment of men. . . .
Well, they seized my father, and carried him to your estate.
I was a little boy at that time; I ran after him barefoot.
What happened? They brought him to your house and
flogged him right under your windows. And your grandfather stands on the balcony and looks on; and your grandmother sits at the window and looks on too. My father cried
out, 'Gracious lady, Marya Vasilyevna, intercede for me!
have mercy on me!' But her only answer was to keep getting
up to have a look at him. So they exacted a promise from
my father to give up the land and bade him be thankful
that they let him go alive. So it has remained with you. Go
and ask your peasants—what do they call the land indeed?
It's called 'The Cudgelled Land' because it was gained by
the cudgel. So you see from that, we poor folks can't bewail
the old order very much."

The cruel confusion in the life of a serf by turning him
first into one thing and then into another is reproduced, as
from personal memory, in *Lgov*. Here a serf is suddenly
transformed from a coachman into a fisherman and told to
shave his beard. Before this he had been a cook and then
a coffee bearer. Asked what his duties had then been he
answered: "I don't know, your honour. I stood at the side-
board and was called Anton instead of Kuzma. The mistress
ordered that I should be called so." Besides being a coffee
bearer, the bewildered serf was employed as an actor. Asked
what he did in the theatre, he became comparatively lucid:
"Don't you know? Why they take me and dress me up; and
I walk about dressed up, or stand, or sit down there as it
happens, and they say, 'See, this is what you must say,'
and I say it. Once I represented a blind man. . . . They
laid little peas under each eyelid. . . . Yes, indeed." One
detects in all this the unhesitating touch of Madame Turgenev herself; but the serf's odyssey of activities is by no
means exhausted. He had begun his career as a page, became a postilion, then a gardener, then a whipper-in. This

last was a dangerous occupation from more than one point of view: "Yes, I rode with the hounds and was very nearly killed; I fell off my horse and the horse was injured. Our old master was very severe; he ordered them to flog me and to send me to learn a trade to Moscow, to a shoemaker." The impassive sportsman asked him if he had ever been married, and his reply is the final comment on the ownership of human beings: "No, your honour, I have never been married. Tatyana Vassilyevna—God rest her soul!—did not allow anyone to marry. 'God forbid,' she said sometimes, 'here am I living single—what indulgence! What are they thinking of?'"

But it is perhaps in the counting-house that the whole system of Spaskoë flashes most clearly from memory into life. The sportsman asked the clerk if his mistress keeps many serfs in the house, and is told that there are not a great many. Pressed for an exact number, he says that it probably runs to about a hundred and fifty. His own great accomplishment is good plain handwriting, and he shows a document which might have been signed by Madame Turgenev. It is worth quoting in full, because it seems to be stamped not by the "Seal" of the chief office of the Manor of Ananyevo, but rather by the Seal of the old Russia:

"ORDER

From the Chief Office of the Manor of Ananyevo to the Agent, Mihial Vikulov.

No 209.

Whereas some person unknown entered the garden at Ananyevo last night in an intoxicated condition, and with unseemly songs waked the French governness Madame Eugène and disturbed her; and whether the watchmen saw anything, and who were on watch in the garden and permitted such disorderliness; as regards all the above-written matters, your orders are to investigate in detail and report immediately to the office.

Head Clerk. Nikolai Hvostov."

In exactly this spirit, Madame Turgenev issued her famous decree: "I give orders that to-morrow morning, the disobedient servant, Nicholas Yakovlev, Ivan Petrov, and Egor Kondratyev, shall sweep the court in front of my windows." In exactly this spirit, Sobolev had been reduced from major-domo to sweeper of the yard. In exactly the same spirit, Polyakov had been banished to a distant property. In exactly this spirit, the deaf mute had been robbed of Mumu. Even the glass of water which had led to poor Sobolev's degradation finds its way into this sketch. The clerk, for his part, though he admits that a merchant pays no wages, thinks that life is less impossible with a merchant: "But with a gentleman, it's a woeful business. Nothing as he likes it—this is not right, and that he can't fancy. You hand him a glass of water, or something to eat: 'Ugh, that water stinks positively stinks!' You take it out, stay a minute outside the door and bring it back: 'Come now, that's good; this doesn't stink now.' And as for the ladies, I tell you, the ladies are something beyond everything! . . . and the young ladies above all. . . ."

A little later, a bewildered peasant rushes into the counting-house with the news that he has just been turned into a stoker. His comrades jeer at him delightedly, but he warns them that their own day of reckoning may not be far off: "It's the mistress's orders, but just you wait a bit. . . . They'll turn you into swineherds yet!" There follows an ugly quarrel between a married man who is persecuting a serf girl and an unmarried man who loves her. "I mean marriage," he exclaims, "I am acting straightforwardly." "How am I to blame in that? Andreitch, Pavel Andreitch," answers the married man, "the mistress won't permit you to marry; it's her seignorial will!" In the end it is neither of the rivals, but the poor serf girl herself who is banished by order of the châtelaine.

But the most poignant of all these sketches from life is perhaps the vignette in which is to be found almost the only direct, concrete plea for the Russian slave. It is put into the mouth of Lukarya who had been a servant in the sportsman's old home when he was a boy. She had been then a "tall, plump, pink-and-white, singing, laughing, dancing creature," but now her face has become, through illness, "strained and dreadful." He can scarcely recognize her when she asks faintly, "do you remember who used to lead the dance at your mother's, at Spaskoë? Do you remember, I used to be leader of the choir too?" They chat over old times, and then he asks her what he can do for her; she tells him that she is content and in want of nothing. "But there, Master," she adds, "you might speak a word to your Mama—the peasants here are poor—if she could take the least bit off their rent! They've not land enough and no advantages. . . . They would pray to God for you . . . but I want nothing; I'm quite contented with all."

Quietly, indirectly, in everyday scraps of talk, the good old times are illumined in the true perspective of accusation. Turgenev makes no comment; but there is often the stress of silence after a statement of fact. It is the silence of condemnation and it is more impressive than pages of Tolstoy's moralizings over the moujik as the instructor of humanity. For Turgenev, the moujik is not at all a moral instructor, but he is a man whom his fellow men have turned into a thing.

A little dressmaker in Moscow implores her owner to allow her to purchase her freedom, but he refuses to give a direct answer as though her poor little life were too trivial a matter for serious discussion. A peasant is sent off to be a soldier for spilling chocolate on the new dress of one of his master's mistresses. Orders are given that a serf girl's hair is to be cut off, that she is to be dressed in sack cloth and sent into the country because, when marriage had been denied to her, she had dared to love by stealth. The little details accumulate, always without annotations, until one begins to grasp the real background of Holy Russia. They are not things, they have never been things, these men and women essentially sensitive to the call of liberty and love, that is to say of life. And moments do come to them when they are free, at least in dreams. Suddenly in a tavern, at a singing competition for a bet, a voice with genius in it utters the very secret of the plains which is the sombre secret of the race. Instantly, the tavern loungers are roused from their inertia of endurance and become men with the winding memories of men. A peasant, "hunted down like a hare" by what he has accepted as his fate responds, at the very first touch of human kindness, with a fidelity that is almost worship.

Turgenev very seldom expresses in terms of set praise his penetrating sympathy; for him the Russian peasant is neither a newly-discovered philosopher, nor potentially the innovator who will one day galvanize Europe. He seeks neither to learn from him nor to instruct him; but he wins his confidence and listens to him, as half-grudgingly and as though bewildered by something twisted in his destiny, he chatters out the simple mutilation of his life. One definite tribute, however, the novelist does pay to the moujik, in his recognition of the quiet courage with which at all times he faces death—a courage which cannot be put down merely to "indifference or stolidity." A moujik is informed by his doctor that it is a matter of life and death for him to remain under medical supervision: "The peasant simply shook his head, struck the horse with the reins and drove out of the yard. The road was muddy and full of holes; the miller drove cautiously without hurry, guiding his horse skilfully and nodding to the acquaintances he met. Three days later he was dead." Death is the Russian slave's ceremony of freedom; he dies as he has lived without making any fuss, or being conscious of any heroism. "It is my hour," is his traditional comment; a comment by no means without significance on the lips of slaves. For they who have robbed him of life are powerless to retain his servitude. This *is* his hour and he has dignified it by that impassive courage, which neither seeks nor needs the praise of words.

Yet, every now and then, in the course of this accusing book, one detects a faint recognition by the peasant of the tyranny which consumes him as something not necessarily in the nature of things. At such times the new spirit seems to intrude upon the old, but for the most part is it not the resentment and revolt of the peasant, but his endurance and, above all, his silence that find expression. In these dwindling days of serfdom in which "the old is dead, but the young is not born," a master punishes his servant unjustly, but the sense of wrong dies out with the sensation of actual physical pain. Well, life is like that, even life on a far more complex scale, and has always been like that. It is only the Old Russia, muses Turgenev, who in these very sketches was evoking the charter of the New.

Still, in Old and New Russia alike, Nature at least is unendingly the same and in this book, as in so many other of Turgenev's, hers is almost the only alleviation for crushed lives. Day after day the lazy golden hours repeat themselves; and again and again with that art which throws genius into the slow monotony of the seasons—so close to the essential monotony of human life beneath the froth and fret of human passions—Turgenev translates for us the Russian summer days. He leads us into the shade of birch woods, into the coolness of low river banks, into the gold-filmed haze of flat stretches and in our ears, as in his, there sound the songs of birds and all the humming, buzzing underlife of insects, the cheerful accompaniment of man's day which at night becomes uncertain and mysterious. In *Byezhin Prairie*, especially, he runs almost the full gamut of homely summer sounds that night has made inexplicable. One can see the group of boys round their supper on the open steppe listening—now interested, now perturbed by the mystery that prowls closer and closer to them through the darkness—to that mysterious menace of nature which, for Turgenev, is always hovering over human destiny. The boys chatter on old Russian superstitions, on the *russalka* and haunted places when a dog barks suddenly and a horse is heard galloping. A little later one of the boys leaps from the horse and the others ask him what it was that had caused the dog's alarm. "I suppose the dog scented something," he answered carelessly. "I thought it was a wolf."

Here, Turgenev makes one of his rare comments: "I could not help admiring Pavel. He was very fine at the moment. His ugly face, animated by his swift ride glowed

88

with hardihood and determination. Without even a switch in his hand he had without the slightest hesitation rushed out into the night alone to face a wolf. . . . 'What a splendid fellow!' I thought, looking at him." Certainly one dislikes the thought of Pavel being swamped in that swarm of urchins who in Spaskoë waited at the beck and call of Madame Turgenev.

But, though the dawn of the new Russia was not yet, a sense of change was dimly perceptible among the peasants. Among their owners it was already obvious. "The smallest landowners," says Ovsyanikov, the peasant proprietor, "have all either become officials, or at any rate do not stop here; as for the larger owners, there's no making them out. I have had experience of them—the larger landowners—in cases of settling boundaries. And I must tell you; it does my heart good to see them, they are courteous and affable. Only this is what astonishes me, they have studied all the sciences, they speak so fluently that your heart is melted, but they don't understand the actual business in hand; they don't even perceive what's their own interest; some bailiff, a bond-servant, drives them just where he pleases, as though they were in a yoke."

The pictures of the landowners indeed, while lacking the shafts of sudden savagery in *Dead Souls*, are in artistically dark colours. There are, however, exceptions and among them is the portrait of *The Hamlet of the Shtchigri District*, a sketch which has some ironical references to those samovar nights which elsewhere are always alluded to with sympathy and even with a sense of loss. This Hamlet of the steppe rails fiercely against the students' "circle" which played such an important part on Turgenev's university programme, both in Moscow and Berlin: "The circle is a hideous substitute for society, women, life; the circle . . . oh, wait a bit, I'll tell you what a circle is! A circle is a slothful, dull living side by side in common, to which is attached a serious significance and a show of rational activity; the circle replaces conversation by debate, trains you in fruitless discussion, draws you away from solitary useful labour, develops in you the itch for authorship—deprives you in fact of all freshness and virgin vigour of soul." The man's whole nature has become embittered by a sense of impotence in coping with Russian life, but when he begins to talk of his dead wife, all his blind rage falls away from him, leaving behind it only a bewildered and morose regret.

He had married a young girl in the country, and even now that she is dead he cannot be certain as to whether he ever loved her or not. He cannot be certain that he ever really came close to her. It was as though she had died without that impenetrable veil between them having been raised for a single instant. There was a "secret wound" in her life. Neither of them could divine its origin; but both knew that it was always there. In her lifetime there had been no explanation of that permeating melancholy which came upon her like a mist from the plains. She did not pine because she was love-sick for an old memory. The light did not fade day by day from her eyes because she had brooded too long over *les neiges d'antan*. The man who mourns for her hints that the cause of this life wound may have been simply, "living too long in the country." Yes, it may have been the sadness of Russia herself that withered her, the sadness of too long patience, the sadness of being unable to seize happiness when one has been too long inured to endurance. She had pined away like a bird without complaints, without conscious regret, and in the very moment of death, her eyes retained exactly that "dumb look" which had been hers in life.

It is this dumb look that is symbolic of the old Russian life, uniting this wife of a Russian landowner to the voiceless multitude of serfs in a common silence of unconscious loss. Nowhere more than in *The Hamlet of Shtchigri District* does one experience the oppression of Russian life which Turgenev experienced so often on his visits to his own country. Masha, a gipsy girl, who is loved by the hero of another story, tries to express the overwhelming sameness of the plains against which her whole body revolts. She cannot allow the lid of Russian life to close in upon her for ever. She tells her lover that "weariness, the divider" has come upon her and she must go. At any cost she must wander on and on over the steppe, seeking to escape from the coma of Russia, seeking to escape not only from her lover, but from herself. As for Tchertop-Hanov, the eccentric lover whom she deserted, he at least is not devoid of the fierce generosity of the old Russian noble at his best. And when at last the Commissioner of Police forces his way into the room of the dying man, it is the veritable voice of the old Russia that rebukes the intrusion: "Panteley Eremyitch of the ancient hereditary nobility is dying; who can hinder him? He owes no man anything, asks nothing from anyone. Leave him, people! Go!"

Certainly, in some aspects both of life among the nobles and life among the serfs the old order preserved a certain glamour against the rawness of the new. In *The Tryst*, Turgenev sketches a young serf girl of the old Russia coming to meet a peasant of the new Russia which she cannot understand. He is a manikin of attitudes and affectations, but she is grateful to him for deigning to look at her. But Victor is tired of the little dead romance and is returning to Petersburg with his master. One sees the very soul of the valet grinning through the rich clothes of his master at this poor serf girl who is content with her lot. Progress and refinement are for him, Victor, but not for such as her. So they part, the man to return to the capital, the girl to become absorbed once more in the dumb life of the people.

"I should have been glad indeed, to take lessons of her —of Russian life, I mean—but she's dumb, the poor dear," exclaims the Hamlet of the Shtchigri district in his puzzled despair. It was the genius of Turgenev's *Annals of a Sportsman* that was to make this dumbness vibrant to the world. Turgenev, indeed, continued where Gogol had left off. Turgenev went from izba to izba, to carry the messages of those who could not utter them, to express the hopes of the hopeless, to claim pity for those who asked for none. Gogol shows what Russian life was; Turgenev shows what the Russians are beneath the harsh surface of that life. In his *Annals of a Sportsman*, he has recorded the common daily routine of the serf's life but, repeatedly, he has pierced through all the externals of degradation to the very heart of that inner dream of which he himself is only sub-conscious.

First and last, Turgenev is pre-occupied with reality; he knew, none better, that the deep dark undercurrents of reality belong more naturally to the hut, than to the palace and that the moujik's izba is by no means a negligible seismometer for the cruel life-pressure of the whole world movement. Without apology, without effort, he gossips his way into the hearts of men and though you seem to be listening merely to time-worn stories, told by the rough products of the Russian plains who are not dressed up for the occasion, these people are teaching you, without in the least intending it, the subtle secret of compassion. And though, on the surface, Turgenev's genius has placed you almost on hail-fellow-well-met terms with the lowliest of human beings it has also brought you into very close touch with the elemental forces that are the real masters of human destiny.

One recalls Turgenev's explanation of what "method" meant to him when Zola and Flaubert were discussing style in literature. "I go to Oka," he exclaimed, on that occasion. "I find his house—that is to say, not a house, a hut. I see a man in a blue jacket, patched, torn, with his back turned to me, digging cabbages. I go up to him and say, 'Are you such a one?' He turns, and I swear to you that in all my life I never saw such piercing eyes. Besides them, a face no bigger than a man's fist, a goat's beard, not a tooth. He was a very old man." Well, that was the method; Turgenev had no need to leave the boulevards of Paris to recapture the aroma of his poor Russia because he was part of her himself. Such scenes as these were of the very warp and woof of his life and his art regarded as one. *The Annals of a Sportsman* is a work of personal memory in which the lives of others have been written down, to no small extent, from their own lips. In another work, during this same visit to France, the great artist was to reveal that *vie interieure* of the Slav, which he found just as dumb in its oppression as were the external lives of the Russian people.

CHAPTER VIII

THE RUSSIAN CROW

I T can be seen that Turgenev was never closer to his own country than he was at this particular period abroad. Yet he had penetrated the real atmosphere of French country life in Courtavenel, Madame Viardots château. Here he forgot his monetary difficulties and continued with sustained energy his work for the Russian review. He was almost unconscious of being *déraciné*, when suddenly in a French field he caught sight of a common grey crow. "The sight of this compatriot appeals to me," he wrote to Madame Viardot in the summer of 1849, "I raised my hat to him and asked him news of my country, in truth, I was almost touched. Come, I say to myself, let us make a pretty little piece of verse out of that. Something simple, graceful; in short, let us produce, Béranger, what!" The result was the following address to this Russian ambassador:

> "Corbeau, corbeau,
> Tu n'es pas beau
> Mais tu viens de mon pays
> Eh bien! retourne-z-y."

Yet, in spite of this careless dismissal, he was haunted again and again in the fields of *la douce* France by the reminder of the Russian crow, who, he knows well will claim him in the end. "Russia will wait," he writes a little later, "this immense and sombre figure, motionless and veiled like the Sphinx of Oedipus. She will swallow me up in a little while. I seem to see her massive inert look fasten upon me, with a mournful attention that becomes those eyes of stone. Be at ease, Sphinx, I shall return to thee, and thou wilt be able to devour me at thy knees! Leave me in peace for a little time longer I will return to thy steppes."

93

In reality, the Russian crow haunts him like the raven of Edgar Allan Poe. While he is gossiping urbanely to Madame Viardot about the art of foreigners, about the perfection of her own art and the ineptitudes of others—Coletti, for example, "sings like a paterfamilias"—while he is telling her about his walks and his dogs and his dreams, while he is discussing the language of his idol and the drama of Shakespeare, while, in brief, he is himself in the process of becoming an epitome of this alien culture, one feels that the Russian crow is flapping its wings close to him all the time.

But in this foreign interlude he is happy at least on the surface and in this very letter he continues, in a vein of unruffled serenity: "It is a beautiful day to-day. Gounod has been walking all day in Blondureau wood in search of an idea, but inspiration, capricious as a woman, has not come and he has arrived at nothing. At least, that is what he tells me himself. He will have his revenge to-morrow. At this moment he is lying on the bear's skin 'in travail.' He has a determination and a tenacity about work which compel my admiration. To-day's barrenness makes him very unhappy; his sighs would almost blow one away, and he is incapable of rousing himself from his preoccupation. In his depression he falls foul of the libretto. I have tried to cheer him up and think I've succeeded. It's very dangerous to let oneself go like that; one ends by folding one's hands and saying 'Bother the whole thing.' I've listened to his complaints with a slight smile, for I know that all these little clouds will disappear at the first breath of inspiration, and I am much flattered at being made the confidant of the small woes of creative genius."

Some two years before the date of this letter, during the rising of the Parisians in 1848, Turgenev had written to Madame Viardot a minute and detailed account of what he himself had witnessed on the famous Monday in May. He had studied the mass consciousness of Paris wholly in the western manner and his verdict was: "They had the air of waiting till the end of the storm." He goes on to ask as his future friend, Gustave Flaubert would have asked, "What then is history? Providence, chance, irony or fatality?" The Russian novelist had, as already indicated, eliminated Providence from his vision of the scheme of things; variation in series and cycles he could not eliminate any more than he could control; irony and fatality persist through all his work.

It has been said of the Slavs that they, the barbarians, "have lizzards' eyes." Undoubtedly, Turgenev's eyes were lizzard-like towards external life, whether on the boulevards of Paris, or in the quiet haunts of Courtavenel during this interlude. And yet not only did he produce during these two years that objective, minutely observant series of sketches known as *The Annals of a Sportsman*, but he was also busy on one of the most curious studies in the long literature of introspection.

The Diary of a Superfluous Man, the book that appealed so much to Guizot, may be called the confession of a human soul to itself. Such confession is conspicuous in the works of all three of the great Russian realists of the last century. But in nothing are they more sharply differentiated from each other than in their manner of revealing the inner recesses of the human heart. In *My Confession*, Count Tolstoy, glancing back at the panorama of his life, writes unhesitatingly of himself as of someone else whom he has studied only to condemn: "I honestly desired to make myself a good and virtuous man, but I was young, I had passions, and I stood alone, altogether alone, in my search of virtue. Every time I tried to express the longings of my heart for a truly virtuous life, I was met with contempt and derisive laughter; but directly I gave way to the lowest of my passions I was praised and encouraged. I found ambition, love of power, love of gain, leachery, pride, anger, vengeance, held in high esteem. I gave way to these passions, and becoming like unto my elders, I felt that the place which I filled in the world satisfied those around me."

Unlike the author of *Anna Karenina*, Dostoevsky is secretive about his personal life. Even in regard to his exile in Siberia, he remained curiously reserved. "It will be noticed," he says in *The Diary of a Writer*, "that up till now I have scarcely ever spoken of the years that I spent in prison. The recollections of *Buried Alive* which I published some fifteen years ago are apparently the work of an imaginary person. I gave them as though they had been written by a Russian noble who had assassinated his wife . . . I may add in this connection that a great many worthy people imagine to-day that I was sent to Siberia for the murder of my wife." One finds, then, in the works of Dostoevsky no real parallel to the repeated confessions of Count Tolstoy. But one does find in one book, *The Underground Spirit*, a record of enquiry into the workings of the human soul, that cuts far deeper than does the accumulated self-accusation of Tolstoy. Intellectual curiosity led Dostoevsky to search for the ape in man far below the level of ordinary contrition. And when Ordinov speaks against himself one realizes at once, not the experience of a moral reformer, bent on reforming himself, but rather the septic wound of one who has vivisected the human soul and absorbed no little of its poison. What has Count Tolstoy, or any one of his projections from Irtenyev to Nekludov, uttered to compare with the self-loathing of Dostoevsky's subterranean hero? "At times, I suddenly plunged into a sombre subterranean despicable debauchery, or semi-debauchery. My squalid passions were keen, glowing with morbid irritability. The outbursts were hysterical, accompanied by tears and convulsions of remorse. Bitterness boiled in me. I felt an unwholesome thirst for violent moral contrasts and so I demeaned myself to animality. I indulged in it by night, secretly, fearfully, foully, with a shame that never left me, even at the most degrading moments. I carried in my soul the love of secretiveness; I was terribly afraid that I should be seen, met, recognized." Such a lacerating exhibitionism is foreign to Tolstoy and anti-pathetic to Turgenev.

The artist of *Smoke* presents a scene in which a man, or a woman reveals the core of character through what one may call normal admission of fact. It is the truth, but Tolstoy would begin at the point where Turgenev had left off; the artistic picture would be transformed into a tabulated human document. But when the last rag of deception had apparently been stripped from the human soul, Dostoevsky would begin where Tolstoy had left off. The verbally truthful confession extorted from himself by the moralist would now become the broken, distorted cry of one who, essentially secretive, is listening only to the promptings of atavism behind the façade of words. When everything has been torn from the witness box there are odd whispers from Dostoevsky. When the truth has been proved up to the hilt, Dostoevsky knows well that there is something behind all that. The delicate scrutiny of Turgenev, the blunt registration of Tolstoy, are mere first rough readings of the truth to the man who translated the subterranean soul of Ordinov.

For all that, *The Diary of a Superfluous Man* is in its delicate fashion a parallel to the underground spirit in exactly the sense that Turgenev's poignant pictures of the peasants is a parallel to Dostoevsky's equally poignant pictures of the proletariat. Coming from the reserved Turgenev, this book is as remarkable as its parallel from the pen of the secretive Dostoevsky. In either case, it is absurd to read a personal confession into a work of art, but it is very interesting to note the habit of introspection, as revealed by authors so temperamentally hostile to each other. In both books, it must be added, there are personal reflections which undoubtedly do not belong to fiction.

At most periods of his life, Turgenev was pre-occupied by the idea of death, and the habit of mind betrayed by this diarist, was only too familiar to him even in his youth. Besides, there are in this book, as certainly as in any one of the admittedly autobiographical novels, memories of the early days in the garden of Spaskoë.

Dostoevsky is not Ordinov, but when the subterranean hero discusses certain topics he is speaking for Dostoevsky and for no one else, as, for example, in the following fragment: "Everybody knows this truth: it is by that especially that we are distinguished from foreign countries. We are very little ethereal, we are not pure spirits. Our own romanticism is wholly opposed to that of Europe; and their's and ours cannot be reduced to the same terms. (I say romanticism; excuse me. It is a little word which has humbly performed its duties, it is old and everybody understands it). Our romanticism understands everything, *sees everything and often sees with a clarity incomparably more living than that of the most positive intelligence*. . . ."

In the same way, though Ivan Turgenev is not the Superfluous Man, it is he who recalls personally the garden scenes, the cool swish of the long fresh grass, the sun-dried sweetness of those stolen Novgorod apples. It is Turgenev who is tasting again those memories of first love which seem to bring Zenaïda herself back into the garden. It is Turgenev who sees himself once more breathless and tongue-tied before a young serf girl whom he has brushed against by accident among the raspberry bushes.

It is all twenty years ago; but the savour is so physical in its intensity that he seems to be waiting, not for death, but for the incarnation of loveliness and youth that is haunting him as from yesterday. It is to the garden, the pond, the crooked silent paths, the rustling birch trees, the waiting lime trees that he reverts when reviewing the happiness that has swept past him like a wave, which has no share in his life, and yet consumes him like any other juggernaut of man's dreams. From the beginning, he has been "the fifth wheel" in the relations of life, moving among men and women like oil on water. He is superfluous among his fellows exactly as Dostoevsky's subterranean hero is superfluous. But, again like Ordinov, just because he is detached from the whole life of ordinary humanity, he is peculiarly fitted for the despairing scrutiny into the workings of lacerated hearts. He is, in short, in Flaubert's phrase, "a born onlooker" and, because there was so much of that attitude towards life in Turgenev himself, this record of introspection has a peculiar significance.

For the rest, his little love story is as it were, the malady of Vladimir grown old; only while Vladimir is scanning for the first time the different landmarks of passion, the Superfluous Man annotates each one of them with self-torturing minuteness. And, whereas Ordinov remains stifled in the dissecting room of Dostoevsky, Turgenev's hero—stricken though he is—moves always in the open air, while he watches the young girl he loves being dazzled by a brilliant rival. So far, however, as an artist dealing with surface values can at all indicate the inner depths Turgenev's hero is certainly laid bare. Every by-way of thought, every nuance of self-torment, every pause of exasperation is indicated. One sees the man with his eyes wide open mocking himself in his fool's paradise.

Liza, too, though her eyes are not wide open, is equally emmeshed in her own fool's paradise, captivated by her Prince, exactly as the Superfluous Man is captivated by her. The poor heart-broken fellow clumsily insults his rival and the incident is followed by a duel à la barrière. He wounds the Prince very slightly and prepares to advance to the barrier. But his adversary, too contemptuous even to torment him, fires in the air, exclaiming: "The duel is at an end." The Superfluous Man has become superfluous even as a victim.

Instead of being an object of indifference to Liza, he is now the monster who has sought to kill her Prince Charming. Her family regard him in the same light and he is cut off from her. But as she drives past him with her parents and the man who has bewitched her, the Superfluous Man, instantly realizes that the psychological moment in the game of passion has already been reached. Liza has already surrendered and though the horses gallop too quickly past for him to observe the Prince's face, he fancied that "he, too, was deeply touched."

A little later, he sees her again at church and again he studies her as though she were a veritable book of passion, whose pages he must read though they torture him. On returning to his own quarters he whispers to himself, "She is lost." She could deceive others who watched her hour by hour, but not for a moment could she deceive the man who was being consumed by her own malady. And now, mixed with his pain and his sense of loss, he finds a certain acrid pleasure in the thought that at last there is something which she must share to the uttermost with him.

Liza's dream passes only too swiftly. Her Prince Charming returns to the capital, leaving the girl to the busy tongues of her acquaintances. The tide turns in favour of the Superfluous Man, who is admitted once more into Liza's family circle. Long, long ago—a few weeks ago—he had watched the child advancing tremblingly to girlhood. A little later, he had watched the girl expanding like a flower to the radiation of love. In each of these transformations there had been a natural ripening as of the dawn of spring and the passing of spring into the summer. But now there was something new in the tell-tale record of this, too well-loved face. Something had shrivelled her youth before its time. Something had hardened her, robbing her of all the sap and savour of girlhood's expectancy and yet denying her the ampler calm of experience.

Liza feels neither regret nor shame for this still dear secret. She has been a spendthrift of her girlhood and her beauty and her honour, but she sheds no tears for these. More than ever, she is contemptuous to this faithful man a mere foil to the dear one who has ridden lightly away. Not for a moment does she see in him the good love as opposed to the bad. The ironical and suspicious Turgenev has peered into the human heart too honestly for any such recipe of human conduct. On the contrary, never is Liza more utterly the slave of the man who has betrayed and deserted her, than when his rival offers her once more the protection of his unending love. "You can say anything you like," she murmurs, "but let me tell you that I love that man, and always shall love him, and do not consider that he has done me any injury—quite the contrary. . . ." It is the last transformation of all; another is allowed to supplant the Superfluous Man in shielding Liza from the consequences of her unregretted passion. Even in this, the final sacrifice, he remains the "fifth wheel" of the wagon of normal life. Everything has been denied to him, even the right of self-denial.

The hurt of this book is almost oppressively intimate as though Turgenev shared with Flaubert that *peur de la vie* which the author of *Madame Bovary* confessed to George Sand who, on her side, knew little or nothing of it. In all Turgenev's novels one recognizes the essential cruelty of life, the stupid external cruelty as of a scythe-chariot lashed by a madman through a crowd of cripples. But in *The Diary of a Superfluous Man* one seems to catch something of the inner hurt of Turgenev himself, the hurt of one who feels himself incorporated in this brutality, not only its victim' but its confederate. It is a register of the *vie interieure* of the Russian, just as *The Annals of a Sportsman* is the register of his external life. One is complementary to the other and it is exceedingly curious that the two books should have been written within this brief period, during which their author was apparently saturated by French influences.

In the depths of Courtavenel he could not hide from that Russian crow, flapping its wings in morose protest against this exile. It was the same in Paris, where he had not commenced that essentially Parisian existence which he was afterwards to enjoy, so far as he could enjoy anything. But, soon after his arrival in 1847 he was presented to George Sand in Madame Viardot's house. Here he also made the acquaintance of Prosper Mérimée, who was already known for his translations from the Russian. About the same time Turgenev renewed his acquaintance with Charles Edmond, whom he had met in Berlin, and who, years afterwards, was to introduce the Russian to the élite of the French literary world. But at this period Turgenev was poor and obscure; it was not until many years later that, through Gustave Flaubert, his intimacy with George Sand began. Now he was merely a young Russian exile living rather precariously and utterly unable to take any part in *la vie parisienne*. It was perhaps for the best. The quiet retreat of Madame Viardot's country house was peculiarly suitable, not only for recapturing the atmosphere of the Russian plains, but also for stimulating that *vie interieure* which finds such imaginatively sensitive expression in *The Diary of a Superfluous Man*.

Already the novelist's attitude towards life, both in the individual and in the abstract, had become what it was to remain with little modification to the very end. In a letter to Madame Viardot from Courtavenel he defines this attitude which was to permeate so many sombre master-pieces. In this letter he refers to the common belief that the stars inspire the sentiment of religion while protesting that this is not the effect produced on anyone who regards them impartially: "Thousands of worlds cast in profusion in the most remote depths of space are nothing but the infinite expansion of life, of this life which embraces all, penetrates everywhere, germinates without aim and without necessity a whole world of plant and insect life in a single drop of water." All this, he urges, is the product of a movement, at once instinctive and irresistible and not a work of reflection. As to what it is, this life, he admits that of this he knows nothing except that at the moment it is everything in its full flower and force, that it makes his blood flow in his veins without his knowing why just as it makes the star rise like "*boutons sur la peau*" without its costing it any more effort, or without its deriving, for that matter, any greater merit: "This entity, indifferent, imperious, voracious, sel-fish, overwhelming, it is life, nature, it is God; call it what you will, but do not adore it; let us understand one another, when it is beautiful, when it is good (which it is not always), adore it for its beauty, for its goodness, but do not adore it either for its grandeur or its glory! . . . For there is nothing either great or small for it; there is no more glory in creation than there is glory in a stone that falls in water that flows, in a stomach that digests; all that is unable to do anything else than follow the Law of its existence which is Life." Then, with an "Ouf" at such outpourings on speculative mechanism, Turgenev passes on to lighter themes. But it was this conception of nature—against which there were to be such definite protests in later times—on which his pessimism was formulated. It is not one of his least distinctions that it never made him an alien from his fellow man.

It is all there in that one letter, the mournful philosophy of *Smoke*. Unlike Tolstoy, who dreaded it, and Dostoevsky, who rejected it, Turgenev accepted stoically the cold indifference of that resultant of aimless forces which had flung him, among inumerable other insignificant units, into this little hour of conscious life. It was not so much philosophy as the resigned acceptance of fact, which shaped the mental evolution of this writer and though his moods changed, his tastes changed, his distractions changed, his political sympathies changed; from this starting-point of coldly reasoned pessimism he was at no time to escape. Yet at this period he was almost happy and when the news of his mother's illness forced him to return to Russia, he wrote in June 1850, to Monsieur Viardot to express his regret at being torn away from this loved corner of France: "There is no spot on earth that I love so much as Courtavenel. I can never tell you how touched I have been by all the proofs of friendship that I have received during the last few days; truly I don't know how I have deserved them; but what I do know is that I shall keep their memory in my heart as long as I live."

Three months later, in a letter from Turgenev, he informed Madame Viardot of his plans for his daughter's welfare: "As for the little Pauline, you know already that I have decided to follow your injunctions and I am only thinking of the means of doing it quickly and properly. I will write to you from Moscow and Petersburg telling you day by day everything that I am doing for her. It is a duty that I am fulfilling and I fulfill it with happiness from the moment that you take a personal interest in it." Thus, clearly enough, the fate of the serf girl's daughter swung in the balance of the diva's sympathy. That sympathy was sustained and because of this, Turgenev's sense of responsibility as a father never weakened through the years. Incidentally, there is another interesting little girl, alluded to in this same letter. She was the natural daughter of Turgenev's uncle and a serf girl. Her name was Anne, and in his story *Acia*, he was later to give a study of a child of mixed origin which was undoubtedly based on the childhood of his little cousin, *de la main gauche*. Anne, it seems, was once punished by Madame Turgenev for having remained nearly an hour with Ivan. The châtelaine did not know that it was her son who had taken the child away, but Anne was instructed not to tell why she had been punished. Turgenev entered his mother's room and noticed the child in a corner, silent and sad. Madame Turgenev explained to him that Anne had been disobedient. When Ivan mildly reproached the child, she turned her head away without uttering a word. Early the next morning, however, Anne came into the writer's room where the following explanation took place: "You believed yesterday what Mama said about me?"

"Yes."

"Well, you were wrong. This is why I was punished. . . . I had promised not to tell you, and I would not have told you if you had not believed Mama."

"Did you cry when you were punished?"

"Oh, no . . . but I cried when you came up to me in Mama's room."

"Ah, that is why you turned away your head?"

"You noticed it and you didn't see that I was crying?"

"No, I must confess I didn't."

Anne then sighed heavily at this lack of comprehension, kissed her friend and went away. "I assure you," comments Turgenev, "that she is a very curious little creature and I study her with interest. She is not yet five years old."

That is the last reminiscence, in the correspondence at least, of the autocracy of Spaskoë. Madame Turgenev died within the year and the novelist was left a man of independent means. His tutelage was over and with it his youth which had closed so much more mercifully than the youth of many of his contemporaries. Things had been happening in Russia while he had been basking in the quietude of Courtavenel. Dostoevsky had been sent to Siberia; Belinsky

SHOOTING IN THE STEPPES

AVENUE AT SPASKOË

had escaped the same fate only by death. The Sphinx of Oedipus, in short, had been dealing in her own way with those who presumed to bring fire to the Russian snows. Yet, Turgenev, the apparent deserter, was in his own fashion a Slav Prometheus. Down there, far away from the Russian steppes he had been keeping faith with the voiceless ones to whose liberation all that was best in him, that is to say his art, was dedicated. Scarcely conscious of it himself he had continued in France the historic work of Gogol. It is difficult to exaggerate the significance of this work which, after so long a lapse of years, can now be viewed in its true perspective.

Historically, the position of the Russian peasant was a continuation of a servitude that, politically, Russia had shaken off. Russia had emerged from the Tartar yoke into her former position as a free state. But the Russian peasants, who had not always been serfs and who had never lost the idea of owning land, found themselves—while the state became free—transformed into veritable slaves of the landowners. Their situation was all the harder, because they realized dumbly that their enslavement, like the former enslavement of Russia herself, was not from time immemorial. The people, like the State—only more despairingly—had clung to the idea of liberty as to some vague clouded memory of long ago. And this memory—a veritable race-memory—lent a new sting of degradation to the serfdom of Spaskoë, that genuine microcosm of the old Russian landowners.

For centuries Russia had been significant in the affairs of Europe; but the great mass of the Russian people had remained an unknown quantity until Gogol's voice broke the unendurable silence, thus heralding the fulfilment of Madame de Staël's prophecy that some day there would be Russians who would speak to the Russian people. Now the heirs of Gogol, each in his own way, focussed men's attention, not on Imperial Russia, but on the frozen multitude of Russians. Turgenev's work is of incalculable importance because he formulated his message of compassion as a universal artist, speaking not only to his compatriots, but to the west.

He was now thirty-two years old. At first glance his had been a careless insousciant youth compared with the ordeal of penury, hardship and injustice that had already mutilated the early manhood of Dostoevsky. Yet, from the standpoint of his art, Turgenev's boyhood, adolescence and youth had been singularly fruitful. By a fortunate chance this apparently unimportant young man had realized sensitively, in the background of his own home, the background of the Russian people. Because he was what he was, to him nothing was lost, nothing was dim; nothing was vulgarized or dulled, but the routine of tyranny. Every experience became vivified in those romances of reality which retained the charm of life because they were engendered by life itself. Childhood in Spaskoë, his school days in Moscow, the samovar nights at Moscow University, the Petersburg days with their memories of Pushkin and Gogol—all were to ripen naturally into the fruit of art. Nor to his dying day was he to forget that voyage on the *Nicholas I*, the first fresh delight of his sense of freedom in Berlin, the friendship of Bakunin and Porkorsky, the little adventures with Porphyre, the travels to Italy and Switzerland, the marred romance of Frankfurt. No emotional experience had left him cold and untouched. On his return to Russia in 1841, he remembered and was always to remember not the mere facts of an episode, but the heartbeats that had brought it into life. Even the tedious days when he had played with the notion of becoming a bureaucrat had not been wasted. The serf girl who had borne him Pauline, had also ministered to his art. The friendship of Belinsky and his incalculable infatuation for Madame Viardot remained his most precious possessions all through his life. Attracted to the West, he had returned to it six years later, but between him and complete absorption in an alien culture there had stood always the persistent memory of his race. The foreign nightingale, even in the person of Madame Viardot, had never lured him from the Russian crow.

Never was he more Russian at heart than when pacing the boulevards of Paris or brooding in the peaceful fields of Courtavenel. And what he was when he crystallized his sombre philosophy in a letter to Malibran's sister, that he was to remain to no small extent until the same incomparable artist watched at his bedside the last convulsions of life. But had he died now, in 1850, at the same time as his mother, he would still have taken his place in the literature of the world. For he had already written the book of compassion and liberation; he had already translated to the last nuance of hesitating despair that *vie interieure* which is the most jealously guarded secret of the Slav.

But there was in him a yet deeper potentiality and his mother's death made its realization possible. It meant for him artistic independence and it meant for literature those seemingly cosmopolitan, but in reality essentially Russian studies of the Russian people that were in their own way, as purely national as the most extravagant dreams of the Slavophils who derided him. And he, pre-eminently a realist who drew only from life, was none the less to evolve more than once a veritably new type of Russian, just as it was he, pre-eminently the detached onlooker of the present, who was to divine the future outlook of the serf whom he had helped to free.

Certainly it was neither the moralist in Tolstoy, nor the seer in Dostoevsky who was permitted to project upon a single overwhelming canvas the background of the Russian people. It was the artist in Turgenev who was to accomplish this : and even his vision of the future was perhaps surer than that of either of his rivals. Tolstoy detected in the moujik a wisdom which could only be approached by a ruthless stripping off of every trapping of European progress. Dostoevsky, accepting mystically—like Gogol before him—the mystic goal of Russian advancement, accepted as part and parcel of it the autocracy of the Tsar and the dominion of the Orthodox Church. The national forces through which Russia had emerged from slavery seemed to him the only ones beneath whose aegis the Russian people should emerge into freedom.

But, for Turgenev neither the simplification of life on the Tolstoy plain, nor the perception of a mysterious goal in the future were of real significance. His was neither the dream of moujik simplification nor that larger national dream of a renewed Byzantium. His was rather the simple conviction that the Russian people, marred as they were by their past, were still capable of sharing, in their own individual manner, the common fruits of European freedom, the common aspirations of European culture and progress. Already in his youth he had summed up, from this standpoint the past of his country; in his maturity he was, from exactly the same standpoint, to divine the future of the great mass of Russians in their relations with the dreams of such revolutionaries as Bakunin.

CHAPTER IX

LIZA

MADAME Turgenev's attitude towards her sons, according to her adopted daughter, had considerably softened in the last days of her life. The novelist, however, formed a different opinion. "I am ashamed to say it," he wrote, "but in her very last moments she thought only of ruining us, my brother and me. The last letter that she wrote to her intendant contained a precise and formal order to sell everything at a miserable price, to set fire to everything so that nothing might be. . . . But it is better to forget."

For weeks Turgenev was absorbed in accounts, but his final conclusion was that financial ruin had been averted: "I shall never have less than twenty-five thousand francs a year and with that one is rich." Already he had begun to plan a return to France; but among other pre-occupations there was the settlement with his adopted sister. Varya was eventually bought off by the two brothers for a sum of sixty thousand francs payable in three years, together with six per cent interest for that period. In addition to this, Varya received the whole of Madame Turgenev's wardrobe, etc., etc.: "she gave us a receipt and now we are quit of her! Ouf! That has been a heavy charge." And in this same letter from Moscow, in which he finally disposes of Madame Turgenev's biographer, Ivan goes on to speak of a one-act comedy of his that met with considerable success in the old capital. Though his health is beginning to trouble him more and more he is always eager to write to Madame Viardot, "*un volume, et pour Gounod*," he adds after alluding to the rehearsals of *Sapho*, the work which had so troubled the composer at Courtavenel in the spring of 1850. Turgenev and Gounod were always friends. "Gounod," wrote Madame Charles Gounod to E. Halperin-Kaminsky, "had a profound admiration for the illustrious poet. He often chanced to meet him at the houses of mutual friends, but I think that their intimate relations ended there, for among Gounod's numerous letters which I have just recently been sorting, I have not found a single signature of Tour-guénieff." This is a pity for in this very letter to Madame Viardot, promising "*un volume*" for herself, Turgenev declares that he will not leave Moscow without writing at length to the composer of *Sapho*. "What is the little Pauline doing?" he continues. "Is she good? Is she learning French and the piano?"

The novelist, in spite of his health, is tranquil enough as the months glide by until he is startled by the death of Gogol in Moscow. The publication of *The Annals of a Sportsman* in book form this same year had made Turgenev not only famous all over Russia, but also an object of sus-picion to the authorities who were hostile to his great pre-cursor. "There is not a single Russian at this moment," Turgenev wrote on first hearing the news, "whose heart is not bleeding." In a letter to the press he had the hardihood to call Gogol "a great man." The censors of Petersburg objected to the letter which Turgenev contrived to publish in Moscow; in consequence of this he was at once arrested. In a letter dated May 13th 1852, he explains the whole matter to his friends in France: "I will begin by telling you that if I didn't leave St Petersburg a month ago, it was quite against my will. I am under arrest, by the Emperor's order, in a house belonging to an officer of police, for having printed in a Moscow newspaper an article of a few lines on Gogol. This was only a pretext, the article being in itself entirely unimportant. I have been looked askance upon for some time, and they have seized on the first opportunity which turned up. I do not complain of the Emperor: the matter has been wilfully misrepresented to him so that he couldn't well have done otherwise. The fact is the authori-ties wish to put an end to all that was being said about Gogol's death, and they were not sorry at the same time to put a stopper on my literary activity."

But his treatment was very different from that meted out to poor Dostoevsky some three years before. Turgenev admits that he is well treated, has a good room, is provided with books and is even permitted to write. During the first few days he was allowed to see visitors, but this privilege was cancelled because so many flocked to see the author of *The Annals of a Sportsman* even in prison. Sometimes there were humorous incidents. His gaoler not only condescended to drink a bottle of champagne with him, but went so far as to click glasses in a Russian prison "to Robespierre!" This was certainly a contrast to Dostoevsky's preliminary imprisonment in that miserable cell lit by one small lamp, a cell so wet that even the Commandant on his morning rounds exclaimed, "This is really not proper!"

Turgenev's health seemed to improve under this mild arrest but he found himself aged in appearance. "I could send you a lock of white hair, without exaggeration," he tells his French friends, "yet I don't lose heart." Like Dostoevsky in the fortress he continued to work faithfully and it was while he was in prison that he wrote *Mumu*, the story which so touched Carlyle who knew nothing of life at Spaskoë.

The imprisonment lasted only for one month, after which Turgenev was despatched, "by Administrative Order," to Spaskoë which he was forbidden to leave. Apart from the sensation of being still a prisoner, life at Spaskoë was tolerable enough and the novelist's one complaint was the lack of good music. "No one here," he exclaims in the autumn of 1852, "has the musical hunger which torments me." The torment must have considerably deepened when Madame Viardot came to Petersburg the following year, while he remained a prisoner at Spaskoë. For all that, except on the eve of the anniversary of Gogol's death, Turgenev's letters to Madame Viardot at this period are cheerful in tone. He sympathizes with the diva in her long series of triumphs in Paris, London, Petersburg and Moscow and tells her of his own shooting exploits, never forgetting the charm of his garden: "My garden is splendid at the present moment, verdure is radiant, there is a youth, a freshness, a vigour about it of which I can convey no idea; I have an avenue of great birch trees in front of my windows, their leaves are still lightly creased; they still preserve the impress of the sheath, of the bud which enclosed them only a few days ago; that gives them the holiday air of a brand new dress in which the creases of the stuff are visible. The whole of my garden is full of nightingales, of orioles, of thrushes: it is a perfect benison! If I could imagine to myself that you would walk in it one day! It is not impossible, but it is scarcely probable . . ." In another letter of about the same time the novelist goes into his personal accounts with the great singer: "There is a hundred and fifty roubles due to Monsieur Viardot for a gun and four hundred for the *pension* of the little Pauline up to the March of the following year." As different writers have assigned the liaison, to which little Pauline owed her birth, to the period commencing with Turgenev's return to Russia in 1841, it may be as well to quote this precise fragment from a letter dated May 24th 1853: "I had given you this day as little Pauline's birthday, but according to a document that I received lately, she was born on the 8th May 1842. She is a fortnight older than I thought. All the same, I don't think that it will be necessary to change the date. Give me news of her."

Towards the end of 1854, the novelist was permitted to go to Petersburg where his reputation was now established as the first writer in Russia and the veritable successor of Gogol. The Crimean war seemed remote to Turgenev who was consoled for the fall of Sebastopol by an unexpected work of art; it came from the pen of the young Count Tolstoy. "Have you read his *Sebastopol!*" he wrote to Serge Aksakov in 1855. "As for me, I read it and cried 'Hurrah' and drank the author's health." Soon afterwards he met the future author of *Anna Karenina*, but from the very beginning, as has been shown already, their personalities clashed. The foolish and dangerous squabble over the little Pauline's education was by no means the first altercation as this picture from the pen of P. A. Sergyenko shows pointedly enough: "I looked at Lyeff Nikolaevitch and I seemed to see spread out before me those stormy scenes in Nekrasoff's lodgings, which took place in the Fifties, when young impetuous Count L. Tolstoy, presenting a living embodiment of Tchatsky (the hero of Griboyedoff's famous comedy, *The Misfortune of Wit*), played in St Petersburg literary circles the part of Gadfly, and in the harshest form expressed his protest against everything which seemed to him conventional and false! 'You cannot imagine what scenes these were,' relates D. B. Grigorovitch. 'Oh, Heavens!' Turgeneff would squeak and squeak, clutch his throat with his hand, and, with the eyes of a dying gazelle would whisper, I can endure no more. I have bronchitis.'

"'Bronchitis,' Tolstoy would growl out immediately, 'bronchitis is an imaginary malady—bronchitis is mental.'"

Thus they wrangled while Nekrasov, the editor of *The Contemporary*, naturally did his best to conciliate the two most important contributors, but seemingly with little success. "Tolstoy," continues Sergeyenko, "is lying in the middle of the room which serves as corridor, on a morocco-coloured divan, and sulking, while Turgeneff parting the skirts of his short pea-jacket, with hands thrust into his pockets continues to stride back and forth through all three rooms. With the object of averting a catastrophe D. Grigorovitch approaches Tolstoy. 'My dear Tolstoy, do not be vexed. You do not know how he values and loves you.' 'I will not permit him to do anything to harm me,' says Tolstoy, with swelling nostrils. 'Here is he marching to and fro past me and wagging his democratic haunches.'"

In the meantime, the formidable rival of these two great writers was buried alive in Siberia, and perhaps it was well for literature that he was. Fate had snatched Leo Tolstoy from the Fourth Bastion at Sebastopol, so that he might become one of the few world novelists. Fate was equally merciful in her very irony when she taught Dostoevsky, through the outrages of Siberia, the lowest depths of human nature without robbing him of access to its noblest heights. The Crimean war was to mean freedom for him also, and it was not in vain that he urged Baron Wrangel to plead his cause with Todleben, "the veritable hero of Sebastopol." Dostoevsky had been a private soldier in the Seventh Battalion of the Line of Siberia, in 1854, a non-commissioned officer in 1855. In 1856 he regained the rank of officer and received the Imperial pardon for a crime that he had never committed. In this same year, the mildly punished, but equally guiltless, Turgenev received permission to leave Russia.

Turgenev crossed the frontier in the summer of 1856. He was to return repeatedly to his native country but never to settle down permanently. This year he went at once to Courtavenel and thence to Paris. The following year he took a trip with Tolstoy to Dijon and afterwards to Geneva. In spite of his own bad health and Tolstoy's difficult temperament, there was no incident between the two travelling companions. At this period, indeed, Turgenev had the highest opinion of the younger novelist . . . *"Mais pour Tolstoy: il est sérieusement, et pour tout de bon un talent hors ligne,"* he confides to Madame Viardot, writing from Spaskoë in 1858. In the same letter he refers with the deepest regret to the death of Ary Scheffer, a very old friend of the Viardots.

Dissatisfied with his own country, Turgenev was discontented with France, the country to which he was always returning. In Paris he would be seized by nostalgia; it seemed to him that it was only for the sake of the Viardots and the little Pauline that he could bring himself to hide from the Russian Sphinx. He was revolted by the materialism of the French and at this time their greatest authors were repugnant to him from Victor Hugo and Lamartine, to George Sand and Alexandre Dumas. In this state of mind, he produced a book that would seem to place him definitely and permanently among the Slavophils.

The Paris of *Liza,* is essentially the Paris of Lavretzki's wife: " All of them brought their friends and *la belle Madame de Lavretzki* was soon known from Chaussée d'Antin to Rue de Lille. In those days—it was in 1856—there had not yet arisen the tribe of journalists and reporters who now swarm on all sides like ants in an ant-hill; but even then there was seen in Varvara Pavlovna's salon a certain Monsieur Jules, a gentleman of unprepossessing exterior, with a scandalous reputation, insolent and mean, like all duellists and men who have been beaten."

Such was the spirit of the West for the essentially western Turgenev during the writing of this beautiful novel, the dates in which have been perhaps purposely confused. It has been said that *Liza* is, in a sense, a younger book than what one may call its companion volume, *Rudin*. But in another sense it is a product of conscious reaction. In any case, Lavretzki cannot be accepted as connoting for Turgenev what Levin, for example, connotes for Tolstoy.

Turgenev's hero is essentially the home-loving Russian of the Fifties, just as Rudin had been the Russian wanderer and *déraciné* of the Forties. The hero of *Liza* is not at all a man of genius, or even of genuine talent, but he possesses precisely what was always lacking in Rudin. One need not labour the point that Lavretzki's avowed intention of "cultivating the land" has a deeper political significance than the words suggest. One need not stress his significance as a reformer; but one must accept him as a Russian who derives his strength from the very entrails of his own country. He is the antithesis of Panshin, the chattering "Westerner", whose mind is fed by the mere refuse and garbage of the Paris boulevards. Turgenev was in the frame of mind to present life from this standpoint, admittedly a *volte-face*. Like his hero, he was able to approach Russia, conscious not only of the brilliant civilization of the West, but of its shallowness for the Russian who had not assimilated its depths. In *Liza*, as in *Rudin*, he was not making up a story, but re-reading the pages of memory.

Like himself as a child, Lavretzki was submitted to a system of training under foreign influences. These innovations ranged from a Scotch kilt and cap to Swiss gymnastics. He was severed from national Russian influences as Turgenev had been severed from them in Spasköe. Ignorance of reality was fostered in each case. The young Lavretzki was prevented from knowing women and when at last love came to him it was for a woman who had lisped lies from her infancy. They married; she betrayed him; that was in the nature of things, a life-story like any other. But, when he discovered her treachery something dumb and deep, something of the very warp and woof of the stagnant background of the steppes oozed up to the surface, making this Lavretzki something different from the wronged husband of fiction. He wishes to kill her and her paramour with words on his lips, which are not at all the rhetoric of melodrama: "You were wrong to play your trick on me; my grandfather used to hang the peasants up by their ribs, and my great-grandfather was himself a peasant." But the atavistic savagery died down. He separated from his wife to continue life alone, while she became more than ever a *lionne*, exploited from time to time by Monsieur Jules of Paris. She had arrived at notoriety when Lavretzki returned to Russia "to cultivate the land." He had come back perhaps to teach, but he remained to learn. For here in a remote corner of Russia, he happened upon what is best and strongest in the whole birth-right of the Russian race.

Panshin, the clever talkative young bureaucrat who represents the West in this Russian provincial town, even Panshin responds vaguely to the silent impenetrable charm of Liza. Lavretzki is perturbed at the thought of this quiet Russian girl being dazzled by the shallow wordmonger. "Well, but Liza," he asks, "is she indifferent to him?" It is Marfa Timofeevna, the old great-aunt, a simple Russian who yet anticipates one of the deepest secrets of Debussy: "She seems to like him, but there, God knows! The heart of another, you know, is a dark forest and a girl's more than any." One does not argue about that even in favour of cultivating the soil; the political thesis is sloughed from the novel, but the heart of Liza remains. She has become the secret of Russia to Lavretzki and, when he returns to his old country place, so permeated is he by the sense of something peaceful which has suddenly risen in his heart that at last he is reconciled to his lot: "And again he fell to listening to the silence, expecting nothing—and at the same time constantly expecting something: the silence enfolded him on all sides, the sun moved calmly in the peaceful blue sky and the clouds sailed calmly across it; they seemed to know why and whither they were sailing. At this same time in other places on the earth there is the seething, the bustle, the clash of life; life here slipped by noiseless, as water over marshy grass; and even till evening Lavretzki could not tear himself from the contemplation of this life as it passed and glided by; sorrow for the past was melting in his soul like snow in spring, and, strange to say, never had the feeling of home been so deep and strong within him."

Such was Lavretzki's frame of mind when a paragraph in a Parisian newspaper, a florid paragraph from the pen of Monsieur Jules, informed him that his wife was dead. He is free to speak to Liza to whom already something of his secret has communicated itself without words. Now he can speak openly and honourably. His love secret seems to him fresh and pure as the wind across the steppe at night, at once tremulous and unhesitating, open and yet with a thousand hidden vibrations, at once shy and steadfast like the light in Liza's eyes. Hugging this radiant secret in his heart, he returns to his house to be startled by the too familiar scent of patchouli. His wife is not dead, but has come back to beg for forgiveness; she has brought her little daughter Ada with her to plead for them both. He must forgive and forget. As for her, she will live only to atone. Penitence adds a new grace to patchouli all through the easily spoken appeal. It is not only the cheeks, but the soul of the woman that is roughly rouged; Lavretzki reads the inner mask as easily as the outer. But others do not read his wife so easily. Liza's mother in particular is quickly charmed by her. Panshin, whom Liza has rejected, is quickly consoled by this incomparable and inconsolable demi-veuve who has brought with her into the atmosphere of the steppe, the patchouli-drenched miasma of the boulevards.

It is this woman who is to brush aside the man's delicate,

almost wordless love for Liza, the elder sister of Natalya from whom fate demands a yet harsher sacrifice. Liza is national without knowing that one can be anything else: "the Russian turn of mind gladened her." She is a Christian in the same sense and just as inevitably. "One must be a Christian," she forced herself to say to Lavretzki once, without claiming originality, "not so as to know the Divine . . . and the . . . earthly, but because every man has to die." But when she speaks of herself and for herself she says: "I have no words of my own." Yet her instincts are un-erring; she judges unhesitatingly between the reserved Lavretzki and Panshin who talks so glibly about the Russia that she loves too well to search for words of praise. She listens in silence to Panshin's western jibes at the hidden wound of her country: "Russia has fallen behind Europe; we must drive her on. It is maintained that we are young—that's nonsense. Moreover, we have no inventiveness: Homakov himself admits that we have not even invented mouse-traps. Consequently, whether we will or no, we must borrow from others. We are sick, Lermontov says—I agree with him. But we are sick from having only half become Europeans; we must take a hair of the dog that bit us." The girl listens in silence, but Lavretzki is stung at last into answering this cheap-jack of the West, in the name of that Old Russia who, like Liza herself, means so infinitely much, but yet has no words of her own.

It is as though Turgenev had deliberately placed Lavret-zki and Liza on the side of the Old Russia and Panshin and Madame Lavretzki on the side of the New. Even as a child Liza had responded not to Melle Moreau, her frivolous French governess, but to Agafia her old Russian nurse. Turgenev stresses Liza's early training and it was due to Annenkov, by whose advice he once suppressed an entire novel, that he inserted the minute, detailed description of Liza's education. "Thanks to him," he observed to Pav-lovsky, "I have been able to correct a serious error in *Liza*. In the manuscript of that novel not a single word was said of the education received by the heroine; and in order to understand her character, it is absolutely necessary to know the history of this education. Annenkov detected this, he insisted that I should make up my mind to write in a chapter and it was only after having done so that I realized that without it, the type of *Liza* would be pale and incomprehensible." As the book stands, it reveals not only the flower, but the deep hidden roots of that Russian girlhood so little complicated, almost naïve, which Turgenev was to reveal to the whole world as something fresh and strange.

Madame Lavretzki herself is no mere foil to Liza, but is in her own way equally strongly defined. She is not the conventional erring comedienne, but a highly individualized character bored by the necessity of being seriously hypocritical for very long at a stretch. She is a touch-stone to character. What is shallow in Liza's mother responds instantly to Lavretzki's wife. She herself in spite of her age has a natural inclination for bright lights, laughter and perhaps even for the scent of patchouli. At all events, after a little preliminary stiffness and one or two half questions prompted by curiosity, she agrees to stage a comedy of reconciliation between husband and wife. She argues the point at great length with the husband and then dramatically produces the wife, hidden traditionally behind a screen: "Take your wife back from my hands," she exclaims, enjoying every second of the romantic situation. But a cold compromise follows and, baulked of sentimentality Liza's mother is frankly disappointed. She had hoped that the wife would fall on her knees before the husband and that both would weep, as she herself was weeping luxuriously. "How was it you didn't understand me?" she expostulated after Lavretzki had gone. "I kept saying 'down.'"

Whether the comedy in her mother's drawing-room was or was not artistic, the daughter's love story was spoilt for ever. Liza entered a convent and Lavretzki saw her only once again. After years of wandering he returned to Liza's old home, only to find the laughter of a new generation ringing out the ghosts of the old. The children are grown up and the old people, including Lemm, the German music

master, who was one of Liza's best friends, are all dead.
The young people are polite; they even invite Lavretzki
to join them, but he is busy with other things. "Please
play your games," he tells them, "don't pay attention to
me. I shall be happier by myself, when I am sure I am not
in your way. And there's no need for you to entertain me;
we old fellows have an occupation which you know nothing of yet and which no amusement can replace—our
memories."

Then, in that remote corner of Russia, Lavretzki catches
one fleeting despairing glimpse of Liza as she crosses from
choir to choir. Not so much as a whisper passes between
them. She did not so much as glance at the man who remembered, "only the eyelashes on the side towards him
quivered a little, only she bent her emaciated face lower,
and the fingers of her clasped hands, entwined with her
rosary, were pressed still closer to one another. What
were they both thinking, what were they feeling? Who can
know? Who can say? There are such moments in life, there
are such feelings. . . . One can but point to them—and pass
them by."

To the last, Lavretzki preserved his memories; to the
last, he was permeated by the perfume of Liza's soul. And
something of this perfume was to haunt Turgenev himself
to the end. Rudin's dryness of disillusion, Rudin's recognition of imposture and of self-imposture doubtless persisted throughout his life. But with it, permeating it and
redeeming it, there survives always the antidote of that
mute and pervading regret which has made Liza at once
so naïve and so exquisite. The novelist was to experience,
to the fatigue point of satiety, every promise and every
falsehood of passion, but he was also to preserve his insight
into the depths of innocence; this perhaps was his most
precious inheritance and it never lost its freshness. The
irony of his nature, in conflict with his innate compassion,
produces often the effect of a disconcerting duality. But,
in the probing of youth's troubled heart he is always
single-minded and utterly disarmed. Here at least, one

never divines that hesitating mockery with which he so
often chills those who would intrude too closely upon his
dream. Here at least, one does not become conscious of that
merciful, but final, pessimism which hems in, as with an
impenetrable nebula, so many of his creations.

In the heart of Turgenev there survived through the
years two essentially Russian figures, each sombre, one by
reason of an inner coldness and the other by reason of the
external irony of life. These figures are Rudin and Liza;
it is by no accident that it is the woman who expresses that
serene confidence in the goodness and kindness of humanity
to which, in spite of all his pessimism, Turgenev clung as to
an axiom of life. Never was he wholly a prey to the fatigue
of him who sees too clearly to love and to pity. Cynicism
was wholly alien from him and he, who had analysed so
remorselessly the rhetoric on Rudin's tormented lips, bowed
always humbly before the candour of Liza's eyes.

The novel was received on all sides with acclamation.
Everybody felt the charm of Liza's renunciation and even
if Lavretzki was scarcely a representative Slavophil, Slavophils welcomed the portrait of Panshin as the representative
of their opponents. But in this same year, 1859, Turgenev
published a very different novel from quite another standpoint and this was to meet with a quite different reception
in Russia.

He was at work on this book in the summer of 1858 and
he refers to it in a letter to Madame Viardot from Spaskoë:
"Here is what I have been doing during the last nine days.
I have worked a great deal at a novel which I have begun
and which I hope to finish by the beginning of the winter."
The book was to appear under the title of *On the Eve*,
and after alluding to an unsuccessful shooting expedition,
to his difficulties with tenants and relations and to arrangements with committees he returns to the subject again in
the same letter: "I have just spoken to you of a novel
which I am busy writing. How happy I should be if I
could lay the plot of it before you, describe its characters,
and the object which I've set before myself. How carefully

I should treasure your remarks! This time I have thought over my subject for a long time and shall avoid, I hope, those rash and abrupt deductions which so rightly jarred upon you. I feel in the vein for work and this notwithstanding that I have left the enthusiasm of youth far behind me. I write with a calmness which astonishes me. Let us hope that the work will not suffer therefrom. Coldness generally implies mediocrity." It is well to stress this particular letter in proof of the fact that Turgenev was directly under Russian influences while writing this novel which was so ironically assailed by Russian critics. In reality—one cannot repeat it too often—Turgenev never lost touch with the national life of his country; his heart was never more in Russia, than when he traversed the boulevards of Paris.

CHAPTER X

ON THE EVE

TURGENEV did not consider himself absolved of his oath of Hannibal through the publication of *The Annals of a Sportsman*. He was still faithful, in his own fashion, to the great central idea of liberation. It has been said of *On the Eve* that the only character in it capable of action, as opposed to general conversation, is not a Russian, but a foreigner. For all that, it is a novel of action in the Turgenevian manner in which and through which dynamics can always be found by those who seek. Certainly in no other novel of Turgenev, not even in *Virgin Soil*, is one so penetrated by the atmosphere of expectation, the tension of waiting for a blow to be struck at last. It is admittedly significant that it is a Bulgarian who is prepared to strike it. With Insarov, indeed, we are a long way from Rudin and those other will-less heroes who, inflaming themselves and their followers by words, remain powerless to translate into action a solitary fragment of rhetoric. Insarov is not at all one of these self-condemned, forceless and yet driven people; he is rather a man of action in the uncomplicated Anglo-Saxon sense.

In most of Turgenev's novels we are presented to people who are waiting for something to happen without quite knowing what it is. In *On the Eve* we meet at last the man for whom they wait and he knows for what they are waiting. Confused by no inner problems, swamped by no side-issues, Insarov is prepared to strike when the moment arrives. But around him there circles the old familiar group of talkers and speculators in general ideas, the hesitating folk who paralyse each other with noble generalities. They at least are Russians, though one character among them, Schubin the sculptor, is French on his mother's side. But this accident of birth merely accentuates in Schubin. making it clear and articulate by right of his Western glibness of utterance, the immeasurable gulf between the inspiration of a moment and the slow, dogged preparation for the accomplishment of one purpose. Even in his art, Schubin is a stricken being. With his quick clever hands he fashions busts and statues, only to destroy them. He mocks at his own dearest hopes; he parodies his own ideals. It is as though the novelist had symbolized in this one character the whole series of those apostles of Russian liberty for whom words were their first and their last sacrifice.

As usual redemption lies in the soul of the heroine. Elena is a yet deeper reading of *la femme russe*, than either Natalya or Liza. She has words of her own, though her inheritance of felling is the same as theirs. She is capable of initiative while retaining the same impulse for self-sacrifice. And though she has unconsciously hardened herself for the storm and stress of human conflict she has remained, again like Natalya and Liza, very close to the heart of nature. For here, as in all Turgenev's books, that *scélérate de Nature* is so merciful in her beauty that one almost forgets her indifference to human hopes and aims. When Odysseus happened upon Nausicaa in the hour of his need, he compared her with a young palm tree and, through all the centuries, no writer of any country has ever improved on his exquisite adroitness. Bersenyev, the typical Turgenevan figure in this novel, detects in the faint summer rustling of leaves the frou-frou of a woman's skirts. And as the drowsy scents and sounds crowd in upon his senses they evoke the image of a Russian girl, fresh and virginal as though budding into life with the universal awakening of the spring. Like Schubin the artist, he loves Elena, though he knows well, as Schubin also knows, that they and such as they are without the inner force to win her. She belongs to Bersenyev only in his dreams, but none the less she permeates his life with the pantheism of beauty which he cannot formulate in words.

No other heroine of Turgenev comes quite so close to one as Elena who speaks where Liza had no words of her own.

Her self-sacrifice, too, is active whereas Liza could only bow passively before the impassive irony of reality. In her girlhood, Elena had shared the formless longings of Natalya and Liza; but as she emerged into womanhood, she recognized resolutely and unerringly the man who, alone for her, could translate the meaning of the Sphinx's smile. No chatterer could deceive her as Natalya was deceived. Less static than Liza, she accepted what it was impossible for Liza to accept. Yet in that Russian capacity for pity Elena was simple and direct like those other two. In childhood this pity had fastened upon animals. Starved dogs, homeless cats, every maimed and helpless thing found a friend in Elena. She performed the duty immediately to hand, but she was always waiting, like a young conscript, for the trumpet call to larger action. Turgenev's heroines are always waiting, but Elena and perhaps Elena alone had in her eyes the inspiration of forlorn hopes and lost causes and on her lips the radiant whisper, "At last! at last!"

The meeting between her and Insarov for the first time is cold enough in its simplicity; he is not the inconnu, nor she the donna fatale of romance. There is nothing of melodrama about this silent man who, in spite of his physical strength, is so non-heroic in his personal appearance. But instinctively she divines that he is not as the others, that he is absorbed in something definite and central, something beyond the zone of generalities on freedom. She divines that what others wish vaguely this man wills intently. In the very depths of her being, she realizes something grand and terrible in this man's self-dedication to a national cause. He and he alone is prepared to strike; with him at last, it is really "on the eve."

A trivial incident crystallized this instinctive girlish confidence. Anna Vassilyevna had arranged a picnic and the young Bulgarian drove with them to see some ruins. The weather was delightful and they were all enjoying themselves when they were suddenly disturbed by a party of Germans—the familiar intrusion of Turgenev's novels. The inevitable drunken German officer accosted the

Russian ladies. Schubin mocked him with malignant wit, only to be brushed aside like an obtrusive mosquito. Quietly Insarov came forward and informed the German officer that if he advanced a single step he would be thrown into the lake. In spite of the closeness of the water the officer advanced; the next instant he was splashing and fuming in front of them. Schubin's wit had meant nothing to the German; but he understood Insarov's quiet lesson and when he was eventually dragged out, he merely threatened "the Russian scoundrels" and promised to make the regulation complaints.

But not only the German had understood the little incident; Elena had understood it. The verbal shafts of Schubin and his like would always be like the stings of mosquitoes at the very best. But here a very simple idea had been translated into immediate action and the girl realized sharply the abyss between action and words. The critics might jibe, as jibe indeed they did, at the insignificance of the incident. To the young girl it was the symbol of the magnetic unknown—the blow that so many were preparing for in words, the blow of so many samovar talks, the blow that seemed to be swathed, muffled, paralysed by the rage of talk that had so long both anticipated and obscured it.

Her first subconscious, involuntary choice now became definite. Here at last was the man. Secretly in her diary she confessed the strange new happiness that had brought a meaning to her life. The diary in English fiction has been only too often a fatiguing device for avoiding the impact of reality. But this delicate and sensitive confession of Elena has nothing in common with *Mes Larmes* of Thackeray's derision. Here we have not only the analysis of an individual temperament, but, as it were, the ultimate secret of those wordless ones from Natalya who failed to redeem Rudin to Liza whom fate denied to Lavretzki. In her diary Elena told things to herself, shaping into words all those formless hopes and fears which had begun to haunt her with a more acid insistence than the long vague pity of her early youth. All unknowingly, too, in this little hidden journal she explored the secret depths of the Russian woman's soul which perhaps has changed so little though all the formulæ of conduct have changed so much.

It is this articulateness of a deep nature that makes the heroine of *On the Eve* more significant than the heroines of *Rudin* and *Liza*. Elena was not merely a young girl betraying to herself the troubling secret of her youth; she was a Russian woman stammering out that imperishable love whose very exaltation has its origin, as Turgenev so well knew, in self-immolation. Elena is *la femme russe* incarnate, a veritable Slav Antigone who chooses the noble and the dangerous as instinctively as others choose the practical and the safe.

Yet even in this intimate personal confession abstractions inevitably intrude. What was the meaning of Elena's youth? Why had she been given a soul? What was the hidden intention of it all? Was there anyone who could answer these questions? One after the other they passed before her, the men who offered her their love, but who possessed in themselves nothing to sustain it. Here again, one becomes conscious of an altogether larger, more national meaning than one might expect from the mere diary of a Russian girl. In Elena's circle of admirers there were precisely those types by which the purpose of Russia had been so long frittered away. Instinctively the girl shunned Schubin; instinctively she distrusted art as something remote from the immediate need of the ever narrowing circle of life as she now divined it. People like Schubin explain and illumine, but she was weary of the explanations and illuminations of words. Poor Schubin had his own reality, his own sincerity; volatile and capricious as he was, he had preserved not only the artist's power for self-torment but the artist's divination of another's sorrow. But now that they were on the eve, Schubin and such as he must surely stand aside. Then there was Bersenyev, the "go-between of science" whom romance had entangled in equally difficult coils, a man of wide and brotherly sympathy, quixotic even against his own dearest interests, so Russian that, like the hero of Dostoevsky's *Injury and Insult*, he was capable of helping another to win the woman of his heart. None the less, he was helpless in the atmosphere of action so he also must yield place to the long expected one who alone can translate the common will in deeds.

Someone has entered Elena's life who will march forward even if he has to march alone. "I am a Bulgarian," he exclaims, "and I have no need of a Russian's love." But, literally as well as figuratively, love is the alchemist whose gold is life and whom none may reject. So, in spite of his self-dedication to the cause of liberty that other even older cause which has its origin in the very source of life, springs up swift and unbidden in the Bulgarian's heart. Unwillingly he loves this Russian girl and he is worthy of her in every sense. It is as though Natalya had met a Rudin who was strong and as though Liza had found a Lavretzki who was free.

Immersed in the national cause, the Bulgarian suppresses his personal secret, but Elena tears it from his eyes. She knows that her lot must be with this man whose only aspiration is to advance against desperate odds to death. She knows that the old safety and quietude of her life must be abandoned. But not for a second does she hesitate. Like flame leaping to meet flame, her own love, blending with self-sacrifice, irradiates this wordless courage which she recognizes as the one answer to all the questions of her youth. But even in *On the Eve* something of the old hesitancy persists. The ancient oppressions, the wrongs of centuries fester in Insarov's blood. With his whole soul he welcomes the war for Bulgarian freedom. But foreigner though he is, Insarov is too surely a creation of Turgenev to be wholly free from the malady of reflection, even when reflection can avail nothing.

He is conscious of that paralysing note of warning, "We are not ready"; even now there is something of the Russian "nichevo" in his heart. None the less, he prepares for instant action and in this moment Elena comes to him, bringing with her the weakening atmosphere of passion. But not for a moment does the Russian persuade this soldier to exchange a bayonet for her arms. Her love is no lure to soil his honour. She is overwhelmingly on the side of action. Let him start for the front at once and she will accompany him. His cause has become hers; her life has become part of his. Her marriage settlement shall be a Turkish bullet and her dowry the afterthrust of a Turkish bayonet. She is well content. Only they must go together, always together, upon this hard honeymoon.

Alone once more in his poor dark room, Insarov wonders if he has been listening only in a dream. For surely in the whole world of women there are none such as she, who had seemed tenderly, but sternly, to sacrifice her love even in its first golden moment. Are there women who are to be won not by the promises of luxury and ease, but by the certainties of danger and hardship? Are there women who will share gladly the anonymous burden unillumined by glory, serving without hope of personal reward the losing cause of liberty? But it had been no dream; the Russian girl had really come to him offering unconditionally her beauty and her youth, her courage and her compassion. And still there lingered, fresh and perturbing as the dear memory of her promise, the scent of migonnette. With that scent a thousand haunting memories throng into his heart, beautiful and stainless even as this courageous and selfless passion which has ennobled suddenly the dusty hardships of his life.

Again and again in his novels Turgenev recaptures the tang of physical sensation associated with a particular flower. From the printed page the woman herself seems to escape with the flower's scent. The faint forgotten swish of skirts, a half sigh in the darkness, a suggestion of muffled laughter, light steps as of ghosts tip-toeing down haunted corridors—these things come back to us like the remembered perfume, which has won back as from the dead the remembered women. It is in the art of Turgenev to recall to each his own most precious memories. At his magic touch the old rapture is restored, the old burden renewed. Old graces come back with a deepened glamour and for the moment, the very ashes of a dead transport glow with a phantom warmth. But nowhere else, even in the novels of Turgenev, does a flower recall a living personality more vibrantly than this spray of mignonette through which Insarov evokes, in his dark miserable room, the radiance of Elena.

It is no wonder that the Bulgarian tells her that Russians have hearts of pure gold! Turgenev, the cosmopolitan, maintains that his compatriots were "the strangest, the most astonishing people on the face of the earth" and if he has made one of his very few men of action a foreigner, he has given us in Elena one of the simplest and noblest creations in the whole world of literature. Insarov had need of such a woman for at the eleventh hour he was struck down by illness. While he was struggling back to bruised life she came to him again; he felt her breath upon his cheeks. It was too much for him and he implored her to leave him. But Elena's pity had no hesitations and in that moment she gave herself to this man in the same sense of uncalculated sacrifice that he had given himself to the cause of his country's freedom. They were secretly married and poor Bersenyev did everything in his power to help them, forming as it were for the time being a Russian *ménage à trois*, as opposed to that of Western fiction. Essentially Russian, too, was the forgiveness of Elena's father who had been so bitterly opposed to this marriage, but whose heart was softened under the near menace that overshadowed these young lives.

But, after all, Insarov was not to die by Turkish bullets. He was already a stricken man as they lingered over their sombre honeymoon in Venice, waiting for the coming of a certain Renditch who was to accompany the Bulgarian to the front. . . . Even in *Liza* the beautiful moments are those of unspoilt happiness. Poor old Lemm, the German exile, has one such moment on the night when inspiration comes to him at last and he exclaims exultingly to the astounded Lavretzki, "I wrote that for I am a great musician." It is another such moment when love steals from Liza in the garden absolutely as perfume steals from a rose at night.

Such moments are ultimately happy so that no after loss or disillusion can ever rob them of their pervading fragrance. But in *On the Eve*, even the beautiful moments are darkened by the certainty of calamity.

One such moment came to this bride and bridegroom as they listened together to "La Taviata." A quite unknown singer, unattractive and with a feeble voice, suddenly "found herself" in the part of Violetta as from the very depths of her being she pleaded against the waste of youth. Elena, listening to that despairing "Lascia mi diviro— morir si giovane," knew well that the singer was pleading for her own youth, for this stricken Bulgarian, for Elena herself, for all the wasted youth of the world. Elena felt cold in the beautiful moment as she caught the echo of "morir si giovane" with the dying man at her side. But at least he must be permitted to die for the cause so sacred to him. Everything was in progress; the Dalmation fishermen had made bullets of their very dredging weights. Insarov used to murmur the name "Renditch" even in his sleep. They were on the very eve of action, but when Renditch crossed from the Slavonic side of the Adriatic it was only to find Insarov, the Bulgarian, already dead.

For Elena there is now nothing in the world. She leaves with her husband's corpse for Zara so that he may be buried in Slavonic earth. From that moment mystery veils her. Of the others we have at least hints, but of Elena we know only that while life remained to her she would be faithful to the dead. Somewhere on that Dalmatian coast there may have lingered a sombre woman whose very presence penetrated, like a faint subtle perfume, lives that swept heedlessly past her own. In this atmosphere, so impregnated by the blended genius of Latin and Slav, the noblest of Turgenev's heroines may have continued silently and unobtrusively the tradition of Russian womanhood as it appeared to Turgenev. But "morir si giovani" that, after all, is the real portent of *On the Eve*. This Russian girl who had it in her to inspire an army was permitted only to cherish a memory. She, who might have roused with her life blood an oppressed race was left only to defend the misunderstood meaning of a lost cause.

Here once more appears the old, old antithesis between character and intellectuality. The clever thoughtful people in the background are water-logged by reflection. They comprehend everything, but they realize nothing. Characters familiar to English fiction are almost their exact opposites and when deprived of the safety-valve of action become listless and inert. The art of living in a variegated and interesting world means less than nothing to them. The very cult of courage, fostered at the expense of intelligence, narrows their horizon and tends to make them tedious in their very heroism. But this, it may fairly be urged, is the fault of the English novelist and not of the ideal of English character. At all events, in spite of certain muddled reactions against this national tendency, there is little danger of Anglo-Saxons falling into the abyss in which Turgenev's will-less intellectuals invariably find themselves. But in the last century there was undoubtedly no little danger of an Anglo-Saxon type being fostered so utterly devoid of all intellectual curiosity that it was threatened with isolation in the onrush of European culture. In the meantime, now as then, effectual character is superior doubtless to ineffectual intelligence. It is perhaps better to give even a stupid order and enforce it than a clever one which no one will obey. It is undoubtedly better to perform even stupid actions than to dream impossibilities that have no reference to human life. From Turgenev to Chekhov this maxim has been driven home and in a welter of blood the long series of talkers have at last been cruelly silenced. The intellectuals have perished in Russia their natural home, but even in Bolshevik fiction their ghosts rustle ominously enough. You may whitewash the leopard, but he does not change his spots. You may change the formulæ of conduct, but you cannot change the national reactions to the formulæ. As Dostoevsky prophesied long ago the Russian in atheism itself will become religiously fanatic. The old dreams are dead doubtless, but the national tendency to dreaming, as distinct from laborious achievement, can be noted just as clearly to-day as when *On the Eve* was penned. Still, the typical Russian in this book is neither Schubin nor Bersenyev, hopeless and helpless as they are with all their gifts; it is Uvar Ivanovitch Stahov whose inertia is monstrous. Schubin with his surface of Western glibness hails him as a "primeval force"; the words are mere sounds to Stahov. The artist may chatter out something of the suffering which is festering beneath his glibness. Bersenyev may pour over his books and endure silently as he watches happiness floating past him for ever. Insarov may go quietly to his death asking only to serve with his body the *ignis fatuus* of liberty. But Uvar Ivanovitch is remote from them all. He alone can wait as the Asiatic waits. Hearts and lives may be broken around him; hopes may fail, love may waste itself on corpses, but he, the "primeval force," continues to stare into nothingness. But sometimes into this darkened mind stray gleams flash only to die away leaving the blackness more intense. One such gleam came to him when Schubin, unconsciously echoing that question of Madame de Staël, asked him if there would ever be men among the Russians. "There will be," he answered. But when, on the very last page of *On the Eve* the question is repeated, this Russian of all the Russians merely flourishes his fingers and stares gloomily into the remote distance.

Turgenev was preoccupied with the subject of this novel long before the book was actually written. An acquaintance of his, on the eve of departure for the Crimean war, had confided to him his own personal love story. He had met a young girl at Moscow and fallen in love with her. His love was reciprocated, but she had afterwards made the acquaintance of a Bulgarian and had followed him to his own country where in a little while he died. "At that time," says Turgenev, "various impressions were swarming in my head. I wished to settle down to write *Rudin*, but the thesis I was trying to develop in *On the Eve*, sometimes rose up before me. The type of the chief heroine, Elena, then a new type in Russian life, was defined quite clearly in my imagination. I had no hero, the man to whom Elena, with her vague, but powerful leaning towards liberty, could give herself."

As among Russians there was no corresponding type worthy of the heroine Turgenev selected the Bulgarian of his acquaintance's spoilt romance, promising him that he would not allow the story to pass into oblivion. The actual story had been roughly jotted down in a notebook by the soldier who became a victim of typhus in the Crimea. But Turgenev did not set to work on it then and there: "I was busy with something else. After *Rudin* I began *Liza*. . . . In the winter of 1858-1859 at last, finding myself in the same village and the same milieu as during my relations with Kratieff, I felt that the slumbering impressions were beginning to germinate. I found the notebook again and re-read it." Inspiration seized him and taking up his pen he gave the world the story of Elena and Insarov. The book was published in 1859 and, as already indicated, created a bad impression on Russian critics. The following year, Turgenev discovered in a veritable Russian those qualities of energy, initiative and tenacity for which Elena had been waiting so wistfully until the coming of her Bulgarian.

CHAPTER XI

TWO GENERATIONS

In a letter to Madame Viardot from Spaskoë, dated April 1859, while he was still in the throes of composition Turgenev shows himself curious on the subject of the diva's new rôle, that of Lady Macbeth. "If we act *Macbeth* at Courtavenel," he adds, "I want to be the ghost of Banquo, for he does not speak."

The Russian novelist is now obsessed by a quite new type who is not a foreigner. Asked whether he had taken the nihilist of *Fathers and Sons* from actual life, Turgenev replied: "That particular type had already absorbed me for a long time when, in 1860, while travelling in Germany I met in a railway carriage a young Russian doctor. He was consumptive, tall, with black hair and a bronzed complexion. I made him talk and was astonished at his keen and original opinions. Two hours afterwards we separated, and my novel was done. I gave two years to writing it, but that was no work for me; it was merely a matter of putting down on paper a work already complete. You have perhaps observed that my Bazaroff is a blond. It is the surest proof that he was sympathetic to me. In my works all my sympathetic heroes are blonds. From my own observation I have come to the conclusion that blonds are always more sympathetic than dark people. For example, Belinsky, Hertzen and the others. . . ."

So concentrated was Turgenev on this new type, that while he was writing *Fathers and Sons* he kept a Bazarov journal: "If I read a new book, if I met an interesting man, or even if an event of importance, political or social, took place, I would enter it always in this journal from the point of view of Bazarov. The result was a very voluminous and curious manuscript. I lost it unfortunately. Someone or other borrowed it from me to read, and did not return it to me."

The idea of the book first came to him when he was taking sea baths at Ventnor in the Isle of Wight and the chance meeting with that young doctor in Germany made the mental sketch a living and actual portrait. "In that remarkable man," he wrote of Bazarov years after the book was published, "was incarnated to my ideas the just rising element, which, still chaotic, afterwards received the title of Nihilism. The impression produced by this individual was very strong. At first, I could not clearly define him to myself. But I strained my eyes and ears, watching everything surrounding me, anxious to trust simply in my own sensations. What confounded me was that I had met not a single idea or hint of what seemed appearing to me on all sides. And the doubt involuntarily suggested itself. . . ."

Before approaching his Prometheus manqué, the strongest creation which ever emerged from Turgenev one must remember that stagnant background which still overshadowed, in spite of the approaching emancipation of the serfs in 1863, the fermentation of the new Russia. One must remember the ingrained inertia of such figures as that of Uvar Ivanovich. One must remember that though Madame de Staël's question had undoubtedly been answered by creative writers of Russia, men of action were still swamped in the morass from which, even theoretically, there seemed to be no escape. Rudin could only talk about this or that panacea of the West; Lavretzky could only make the best of endurance while refusing to bow down before charlatans; Bersenyev could only make his little sacrifice of personal happiness; the Bulgarian Insarov's vision was clouded by the long stare of Uvar Ivanovich. Voices indeed had sounded—Turgenev's the most magical of them all—but men were still lacking. For though there had been heroic rebels there had been none to interpret, in action, the challenge of freedom coherently, scientifically, from the head, in short, rather than from the heart. In *On the Eve*, Turgenev had found the necessary Russian woman; in *Fathers and Sons* he was to find the necessary Russian man. Bazarov would be a formidable creation in the

Western Europe of the twentieth century; in the Russia of the early 'sixties he was like no one else.

At once he ruffled the quiet country house into which he burst suddenly with his little disciple Arkady. But there was nothing melodramatic about his face: "It was long and lean, with a broad forehead, a nose flat at the base and sharper at the end, large greenish eyes, and drooping whiskers of a sandy colour; it was lighted up by a tranquil smile and showed self-confidence and intelligence." His manner was rought, but manly, and there was nothing whatever about his external appearance to provoke apprehension, except the sense of power which emanated from him without his being conscious of it himself. The two elderly country gentlemen, Arkady's easy-going father and his fastidiously correct uncle, were at once vaguely uneasy about this newcomer. Arkady described him proudly as a Nihilist, "a man who does not bow down before any authority, who does not take any principle on faith, whatever reverence that principle may be enshrined in." Bazarov, for his part, does not bother about the niceties of definition. When confronted with the views of the older generation as personified by Nikolai Petrovich, his host, and Arkady's uncle, Pavel Petrovich, he dismisses them contemptuously to the limbo of dead conventions. "Aristocracy, Liberalism, progress, principle," he exclaims, "if you think of it, what a lot of foreign . . . and useless words! To a Russian they are good for nothing."

The Nihilist, briefly, denies everything and is particularly harsh towards the savour of old salves. He makes no god of the Russian people but, when Pavel refuses to acknowledge a man who thinks like this as a Russian, he answers haughtily: "My grandfather ploughs the land. Ask any one of your peasants which of us—you or me—he'd more readily acknowledge as a fellow-countryman. You don't even know how to talk to them." Pavel reminds him that while he, Bazarov, talks to the peasant he is despising him all the time. The Nihilist admits indifferently that this may be true and then in a single speech, broken by occasional ignored interruptions, he gives, once and for all, the point of view for which he stands. And in giving it he sums up all the hopelessness and helplessness, all the sense of impotence, the chattering of failure, the futile idealism of the typical Russian of Turgenev's novels. It is as though in a single speech he was silencing Rudin, galvanizing Lavretzky and annihilating Schubin:

"I'll tell you what we do. Not long ago we used to say that our officials took bribes, that we had no roads, no commerce, no real justice. . . . Then we suspected that talk, perpetual talk, and nothing but talk, about our social diseases, was not worth while, that it all led to nothing, but superficiality and pedantry; we saw that our leading men, so-called advanced people and reformers, are no good; that we busy ourselves over foolery, talk rubbish about art, unconscious creativeness, parliamentarianism, trial by jury and the deuce knows what all; while all the while, it's a question of getting bread to eat, while we are stifling under the grossest superstition, while all our enterprises come to grief, simply because there aren't honest men enough to carry them on while the very emancipation our Government's busy upon will hardly come up to any good, because peasants are glad to rob even themselves to get drunk at the gin-shop. We decided not to undertake anything."

But it is little Arkady and not Bazarov, who permits himself to observe: "We shall destroy, because we are a force." Then indeed, in his turn, Paval Petrovich sums up what after all may be accepted as Turgenev's involuntary attitude towards the civilization of the West in relation to his own country: "Force! There's force in the savage Kalmuck, in the Mongolian; but what is it to us? What is precious to us is civilization; yes, yes, sir, it's fruits are precious to us. And don't tell me those fruits are worthless; the poorest dauber, *un barbouilleur*, the man who plays dance music for five farthings an evening, is of more use than you, because they are the representatives of civilization, and not of brute Mongolian force! You fancy yourselves advanced people and all the while you are only fit for the

Kalmuck's hovel! Force! And recollect you forcible gentlemen, that you're only four men and a half, and the others
are millions who won't let you trample their sacred
traditions under foot, who will crush you and walk over
you!" This is unmistakably in line with Turgenev's avowal
of gratitude to the occident, gratitude even to the croupier
as its lowest symbol. Nihilism, lisped through the innocent
lips of Bazarov's disciple, was to be repeated textually more
than half a century later. But the man Lenin was able as
well as willing to destroy; the position of Bazarov was
wholly different.

Still, in the jog trot atmosphere of this country house it
was easy enough for him to cope with the representatives of
the older generation. Verbally, he could sweep aside every
arbitrary trammel of the past. He feels that he is strong
enough to accomplish the great upheaval and to drag his
own generation at his heels. Bazarov seems to have no vul-
nerable point. He despises the old love story that has broken
Pavel's life just as a bolshevik of to-day would despise it as
so much bourgeois sentiment. Arkady pleads that his uncle
is a product of his education, but his mentor thrusts aside
that shibboleth of the centuries: "Education? Every man
must educate himself just as I've done, for instance. . . .
And as for the age, why should I depend on it? It's rather
it that depends on me. No, my dear fellow, that's all
shallowness, want of backbone! And what stuff it all is
about these mysterious relations between a man and
woman? We physiologists know what these relations are.
You study the anatomy of the eye, where does the enig-
matical glance you talk about come in there? That's all
romantic, nonsensical, æsthetic rot. We had much better
go and look at the beetle." That is indutably the language
of the Moscow of to-day and Bazarov speaks it as to the
manner born. Figures like Rudin and Lavretzky annotate
a particular decade; Bazarov stands out as a demiourgos,
a veritable moulder of centuries to be. He is actively what
Uvar Ivanovich is passively—a primeval force. And like a
primeval force, obeying only the law of his own being, he

prepares to sweep aside the obstacles not only in his own life, but in the national life of his country. Yet even he is to meet with his match in spite of all his knowledge of physiology.

Bazarov, the active plebeian, encounters an indolent aristocratic widow and interests her as something new in the sleepy comfortable routine of life. Madame Odintsov likes to listen to him, enjoying the sensation of her own power over a man of whom she is always half afraid. He must teach her chemistry and while he is teaching it she will learn something much more interesting—a new type of Russian. From time to time, he snarls at her, but beneath the snarl there lurks always something else that gratifies her sense of power which has already so undermined his. At last brutally, abruptly, the Nihilist bursts out with the confession of all this savage, pent-up feeling that had hidden itself behind the mask of scientific instruction: "Madame Odintsov held both her hands out before her; but Bazarov was leaning with his forehead pressed against the window pane. He breathed hard, his whole body was visibly trembling. But it was not the tremor of youthful timidity, not the sweet alarm of the first declaration that possessed him; it was passion struggling in him, strong and painful—passion not unlike hatred and perhaps akin to it. . . ." Madame Odintsov felt sorry for Bazarov, but she was definitely afraid of him. Musing over the scene afterwards she recalled, "his almost animal face as he had drawn her savagely to him." She had been playing with something very dangerous, but her "peace of mind was not shaken." He must go away; it would be better for him to go away, better for both of them. And so she returns to the comfort of orderly emotions and to the stimulus of French novels, while Bazarov returns to science only to be dragged into a duel with Pavel for the sake of a serf girl who is the mistress of Nikolai Petrovich.

In this scene, so different from the duel in *Spring Torrents*, and yet given with corresponding irony, the representatives of these alien schools and alien generations stand out in the clear perspective of final antagonism. Faithful to his code, listlessly correct, Pavel confronts this strange being whose very existence is an insult to every instinct and every tradition of the old Russian noble. Bazarov, to whom fear is an unknown emotion, is almost perturbed by his opponent's icy tranquillity. This man who is so blind to the torment of the Russian underworld, who is so heedless of the dawning strength of a democracy which he, Bazarov, means to harness, this man who is haunted merely by a fool's passion of long ago that has nothing in common with the life force which will sweep him and such as he aside, this figurehead of a frozen school as opposed to the life-giving Prometheus of the new, has but one solitary intention—to shoot and to shoot to kill. Bazarov is puzzled by this glacial intensity, this fierce concentration upon so petty an object. "He is aiming straight at my nose," he thought, "and doesn't he blink down it carefully, the ruffian! Not an agreeable sensation though. I am going to look at his watch-chain."

Bazarov wounds Pavel slightly and the duel closes with even less romanticism than that which had surrounded poor Sanin in the early days at Frankfurt. The real opponent of Bazarov is not the wounded Russian noble, but the perfumed indolent woman who is not unwilling to see him when, like a singed moth, he returns to her from time to time. At last he sends for her and on his death-bed he whispers to her, of all people in the world, what had been his golden hope and is now an irrevocable loss. The wolf cry rings human at last, but even now the wolf is not broken: "Noble-hearted! Oh, how near, and how young and fresh and pure . . . in this loathsome room! . . . Well, good-bye! live long that's the best of all, and make the most of it while there's time. You see what a hideous spectacle; the worm half-crushed, but writhing still. And you see, I thought too: I'd break down so many things, I wouldn't die, why should I! there were problems to solve, and I was a giant! And now all the problem for the giant is how to die decently, though that makes no difference to anyone either. . . . Never mind; I'm not going to turn tail."

The sluggish ignorance of the old Russia had beaten the innovator. Bazarov had cut his finger while dissecting a corpse and the district doctor was without caustic. The would-be Prometheus, whose brooding rage had so perturbed his peasant parents, was now babbling as though the coma of old Russia had entered his veins. He had wished to conquer the background of Russia, but it was this very background that was to consume and absorb him. His last faint dream was passing; he was to become part and parcel of that Russian earth into which he had sought to inject a new spirit and a new hope. He had stood not merely for a new generation, but for a new race of Russians, yet he was to die stupidly because a district doctor had no caustic.

The Russians had never known Bazarov; only the old people—drawn so livingly by the great artist who had fashioned this poisoned eagle of the steppes—mourned for their son as Priam and Hecuba mourned for Hector. Bazarov had been beaten not by external enemies, but by the inertia against which his restless anger beat itself out in vain. His voice had never been heard. His energy had been strangled at its very source. In the whole world only two people felt the scald of his loss. There are but few words in such sorrow, but while they two at least drew breath that poor grave would not be wholly deserted: "Often from the little village not far off, two quite feeble old people come to visit it—a husband and wife. Supporting one another, they move to it with heavy steps; they go up to the railing, fall down and remain on their knees, and long and bitterly they weep and yearn and intently they gaze at the dumb stone under which their son is lying; they exchange some brief word, wipe away the dust from the stone, set straight a branch of a fir tree and pray again, and cannot tear themselves from this place, where they seem to be nearer to their son, to their son, to their memories of him. . . . Can it be that their prayers, their tears are fruitless? Can it be that love, sacred, devoted love is not all-powerful? Oh, no! however passionate, sinning and rebellious the heart hidden in the tomb, the flowers growing over it peep serenely at us with their innocent eyes; they tell us not of eternal peace alone, of that great peace of indifferent nature; they tell us too of eternal reconciliation and of life without end." So, with completely disarmed irony Turgenev closes the parabola of Bazarov.

The Annals of a Sportsman had made Turgenev the most popular author in Russia; the ineffectuality of Rudin had been forgiven him and the charm of Liza had more than atoned for the mildness of Lavretzky in "cultivating the soil." *On the Eve,* in spite of its hero's foreign extraction, had seemed definitely to establish Turgenev's position in the camp of the young Liberals. But *Fathers and Sons,* appearing in 1862, enraged both the old-fashioned Russians and *les Jeunes.* Each generation saw itself caricatured. The author was furious at this lack of comprehension. "At this moment," he wrote shortly after the book was published "there are only two people who have grasped my meaning, they are Dostoevsky and Botkin." As for the general effect produced by *Fathers and Sons* here it is in the words of Turgenev himself:

"I will not enlarge upon the effect produced by this novel. I will only say that everywhere the word 'Nihilist' was caught up by a thousand tongues and that on the day of the conflagration of the Apraksinsky shops, when I arrived in St Petersburg, the first exclamation with which I was greeted was 'Just see what your Nihilists are doing!' . . . I experienced a coldness approaching to indignation from people near and sympathetic to me. I received congratulations, almost caresses from people of the opposite camp, from enemies. This confused me, wounded me; but my conscience did not reproach me. I knew very well I had carried out honestly the type I had sketched, carried it out not only without prejudice, but positively with sympathy. . . . While some attacked me for outraging the Younger Generation, and promised me with a laugh of contempt to burn my photograph, others on the contrary, with indignation, reproached me for my servile cringing to the younger generation. . . . 'You were grovelling at the feet of Bazarov. You pretend to find fault with him, and you are licking the dust at his feet,' says one correspondent. Another critic represented Monsieur Katkoff and me as two conspirators, 'plotting in the solitude of our chamber our traps and slanders against the forces of young Russia' an effective picture! . . . My critics called my work a pamphlet and referred to my wounded and irritated vanity. . . . But a shadow lay on my name. I don't deceive myself. I know that shadow will remain."

The reactionaries read Bazarov exactly as Pavel had read him. Again and again Turgenev returned to the defence of a hero whose temperament was in reality the very antithesis of his own. "The death of Bazarov," he wrote in a letter, "which the Comtesse de Sallis called heroic and criticizes for that reason, should in my opinion give the last touch to his tragic figure; your young people, they see in it only an accident. I end on this remark. If the reader does not love Bazarov with his roughness, all his harshness, his pitiless dryness, his asperity—if he does not love him, I say the fault is in me. I have not attained my aim. To flatter like a spaniel I have not wished although by that means I might have been able to win over all the young people to my side, but I had no wish to purchase a popularity by concessions of that kind. It is better to lose the campaign (and I believe that I have lost it), than gain it by such a subterfuge. I dreamed of a figure, sombre, untamed, great, only half emerged from barbarism, brave, wayward, honest, none the less condemned to perish since it is always on the threshold of the future."

In another letter he writes of this hero who stands head and shoulders above the familiar Turgenevian onlooker: "The sentiment of beauty, an excellent sentiment of patriotism in the true sense of that word, that is all that is wanted at the present moment. And Bazarov on the other hand is a type, a precursor, a great harmonious figure, with a certain prestige, not without a certain halo." Finally, the consummate artist did not disdain to explain explicitly his own method of artistic presentation, which seemed to him to have caused this perverse mis-reading of his aims: "The whole ground of the misunderstanding lay in the fact that the type of Bazarov had not time to pass through the usual phases. At the very moment of his appearance, the author attacked him. It was a new method as well as a new type, I introduced—that of Realizing instead of Idealizing. . . . The reader is easily thrown into perplexity when the author does not show clear sympathy or antipathy to his own child. The reader readily gets angry. . . . After all books exist to entertain."

The distrustful Turgenev was not dogmatic even in regard to *la grande Indifferente;* he was little likely, then, to accept trustfully the dogmatic destructiveness of Bazarov. Behind his explanation of that strange hero, there is something instinctive and temperamental. For all his admiration of Bazarov, Turgenev is too instinctively alien from him, too fastidious not to protect even a woman whom he dislikes from the savage caresses of this primitive who had emerged from the background of Russia. He dislikes Madame Odintsov, admittedly, but he will not give her to Bazarov even though he permits her to hesitate about giving herself. Again, involuntarily he shares Pavel's physical repugnance to the idea of Bazarov caressing even a serf girl who chanced to be *de la même famille,* as the well loved woman who had forsaken him. "I can't bear any insolent upstart to touch . . ." he whispered, and Turgenev, although he saw around and beyond Pavel deep into the wolf heart of Bazarov, understood and perhaps in spite of himself shared that prejudice.

But the creator of Bazarov valued the depth and energy of this new Russian; above all, he felt the poignancy of his death. For that was more pathetic than the *morir si giovani* —to die of the disease of which one is endeavouring to cure others. As time passed the young people in the novel became almost ashamed to speak of the dead Bazarov whom they had failed to understand in life: "'To the memory of Bazarov,' Katya whispered in her husband's ear, as she clinked glasses with him. Arkady pressed her hand warmly in response, but he did not venture to propose this toast aloud."

Dostoevsky at least had understood the book. Years afterwards he published a reply to it. It was said of the heroes of
Demons that they were the heroes of Turgenev in old age.
Yet, in that extraordinary novel, Dostoevsky not only
turned his back on everything for which Bazarov stood, but
deliberately caluminated the author on *Fathers and Sons*.
Karmazinov, the admitted caricature of Turgenev, is a
fatuous novelist who has returned from abroad only to
amuse these demons of the New Russia by platitudes on
the Russian God. "I believe in no God," he assures them
eagerly, "I have been calumniated in the eyes of the Russian youth." Opposed to this pale denier of the old faith,
the hero Stavrogiun can after all only half deny. "One can
discuss infinitely on everything," he admits, "but from me
there has issued only a negation without grandeur and without force." Modern criticism is claiming that Stavrogiun is
one more portrait of Bakunin, but in this extraordinary
figure we are certainly a very long way from poor Rudin.
In any case *Demons* is a denial of this very negation and a
formidable protest against the nihilism of Bazarov whose
successors have become veritable monsters under Dostoevsky's touch. A duality, not merely of generations, runs
through this terrible novel in which are opposed two gods,
two faiths, two demons and two loves.

Bazarov, the nihilist, is certainly a normal figure perfectly
comprehensible to the West, compared with these dis-
possessed ones of Dostoevsky who belong essentially to the
East. Bazarov, in spite of his theory of destruction, is con-
structive, a man of the future who will be no longer a nihilist
when he has cleared away the clogging obstructions of the
past. But the creations of Dostoevsky are actual demons,
suffocated and convulsed, whose resting place is fittingly
assigned, not to the hearts of one generation or the other,
but rather to the bodies of swine. Yet there is another
message in *Demons*; it comes from the Apocalypse and it
also is of the very essence of Dostoevsky's faith. It speaks of
him who is neither hot nor cold, but only tepid; of him who
believes that he is rich and has need of nothing, unable to

comprehend that in reality he is wretched and unhappy, poor and blind and naked. Merciful to every type of sinner from Marmeladov to Raskolnikov, Dostoevsky opposed with all his heart that paleness of temperament which in the West is so often confounded with goodness. Even in this answer to *Fathers and Sons*, in which he condemns the excesses of his demons, he makes it quite plain that if he regards the nihilist as a monster he also refuses to exalt the tepid person who, without faith, believes himself to be without sin.

Externally, the plot of *Demons* resembles that of *Virgin Soil* rather than that of *Fathers and Sons* in so far as it describes an attempt at a conspiracy in a Russian provincial town and the utter detachment of the great mass of the people from the conspirators. Strictly speaking, it has little bearing on Turgenev's earlier book and, stupendous as Stavroguin is in spite of so many efforts to dwarf him by a pedestal, Bazarov retains easily his own original significance. To this significance the Russians responded at once, in spite of the storm of professional criticism. The word "nihilist," popularized by Turgenev, passed into everyday language and the young Russians began to imitate respectfully the man who had been hailed as a caricature of themselves. Reproached for having "played the game of the reactionaries," Turgenev made, if not an apology, at least an apologia: "I wrote without afterthought, astonished as much as anybody else at what came from my pen and forgetting in my literary preoccupation that to speak of *les Jeunes* was to make a political work. . . . I ought to have sacrificed literary to civic duty and to have discarded not an error, but perhaps, in view of the times, an injustice . . . Bazarov had quite as much right to idealization as my other heroes."

So much for the pacification of *les Jeunes* by Turgenev, so different from the pacification by Karmazinov. In reality the figure of Bazarov, "sombre, untamed, great, only half emerged from barbarism, brave, wayward and honest," had no need of being idealized. He is the hero among Turgenevian heroes and Turgenev, who had done so much for the past with his *Annals of a Sportsman*, had accomplished little less for the present with his so undeservedly notorious *Fathers and Sons*.

At this period he was coming once more under the influence of Germany. When reproached for his one-time love of the French, he exclaimed: "I gallomane! You will see if I am." It has been thought that he depreciated France in order to mollify his compatriots, but just at this time he was not only absorbed in Mommsen, but was also under the sway of Italy. For the rest, his pacification of *les Jeunes* was a half ironical gesture, as he was soon afterwards to prove very clearly to the world at large. His cosmopolitanism, now as always, was only on the surface, but it was exceedingly valuable to him because, through it, he arrived at the detachment necessary for seeing Russian life in relation to Western progress. He and he alone among Russian writers was able to throw upon a canvas, types that were immediately recognized as standing for a particular period, and even for a particular decade. Dostoevsky who hated him was gratified by that critique on *Demons* which hailed his characters as those of Turgenev in their old age. In reality, Dostoevsky in spite of his genius, and perhaps even because of it, failed to produce such convincingly representative figures as Turgenev produced seemingly without effort. National as he was and steeped in the mysteries of that Russian soul upon which derision was so soon to fasten, Dostoevsky none the less worked only in that "fantastic" atmosphere in which ordinary humanity cannot breathe. From Raskolnikov to the "Idiot" his characters are Russian to the core, but they are not representative Russians as are the less highly charged, but more artistic creations of Turgenev.

Nor did Tolstoy punctuate, as it were, nearly half a century of Russian development as did the author of *Smoke*. Irtenev, Olenin, Nezhdinhov, Pierre, Levin, Nekhludov, do not mark the spiritual and political development of Russia, but rather the moral and spiritual advancement of Count

Leo Tolstoy. It was the artist Turgenev and neither the seer, Dostoevsky nor the reformer, Count Tolstoy, who really mirrored the Russians as they were not only to the outside world, but even to themselves. Their very exasperation with him was in its own way an acknowledgement that he was doing, on a comparatively minute scale, what Balzac did on an immense one. Turgenev in his quite different way wrote that inner complementary history, in its relation to the general ideas of Europe, that for his work also justifies the title " *Comédie Humaine.*" And it was just because he was so unerring in his analysis of Rudin and Lavretzky in regard to the past and of Bazarov in anticipation of the future that his compatriots resented so passionately his seeming desertion of the cause of liberty.

The English novelists of the nineteenth century offer no parallel to Russian fiction as a register of national life in relation to the Zeitgeist of Europe. They are, for the most part, proudly detached from general ideas. In reading *Vanity Fair*, for example, one might easily forget that such a world storm as the French Revolution had ever taken place. Balzac gives us the fresh deal of the cards, the fresh way of thinking, the ravenous competitiveness for life on the part of those to whom it had hitherto been always denied. Balzac aimed at and succeeded in creating a whole society, but it was essentially a society of the future, whereas Scott in England, with something at least of the same amplitude of conception, reverted to the past and recreated the very feudalism from which Europe was doubtfully but, on the whole, thankfully escaping. Other English novelists of the same century while refusing to blind themselves by the glamour of the past none the less fostered the fading feudalism of the old wealth, only to pass on to salute the tranquil exploitation of the new. There is a whole world not merely of individual, but of European experience between Thackeray's " Jones at his Club," haunted by an invitation from a duchess and the *jeune premier* of *Père Goriot* fighting his way into the surviving society of old France. The genius of Dickens carried his creations all over the world, but he was not a world novelist. Little less than Thackeray, he worked essentially in an insular medium and great as he was no one could say of his work what Dr A. Brückner has said, with such imaginative insight, of Dostoevsky's: "Not in 'Faust', but rather in 'Crime and Punishment' does 'the whole woe of mankind take hold of us.'"

It was not for Turgenev to communicate "the whole woe of mankind", but it was for him to reveal, in a manner comprehensible to the West, the wound of Russian life, which in his opinion was being treated by one generation after another of quack doctors. He had been attacked again and again and very soon he was to strike back, this time almost without dissimulation. In the meantime, he grew weary of Italian associations with the past and of the rough homeliness of German taste. "*Ce scélérat de Paris, je l'aime pourtant,*" he exclaimed, but before settling down finally in the French capital, he was to find for himself an almost equally advantageous "nest in Europe."

CHAPTER XII

THE RUSSIAN TREE

IT was in 1863 that Turgenev presented himself for the first time at one of the famous Magny dinners. Here he met the élite of the Parisian literary world—Sainte-Beuve, Gautier, the Goncourt brothers, Taine, Renan and Flaubert whom he had known slightly since 1858. There is a note in the *Journal des Goncourts*, which describes the occasion: "Charles Edmond brought Tourguenieff, that foreign writer with such a graceful talent, author of the *Mémoires d'un Seigneur Russe*, and of the *Hamlet Russe*. He is a great big charming fellow, a gentle giant with bleached hair and looks like the kindly genius of a mountain, or a forest. He is handsome magnificently, immensely handsome, with the blue of heaven in his eyes, and that charming Russian sing-song voice, in which there is just something both of the child and of the negro. Being put at his ease by the ovation that was given to him, he talked in a curious and interesting way about Russian literature which he declares to be well launched upon the side of realism from the novel to the play."

Guizot had for some time wished to know the author of *The Diary of a Superfluous Man* and Lamartine has described his delight at his first meeting with the great Russian novelist. Later on, through Flaubert, Turgenev met the representatives of the naturalistic school and joined "the Company of Five," Zola, Daudet, Ed. de Goncourt and Flaubert being the other four. They dined every month together, sometimes at Flaubert's and sometimes at the de Goncourts, calling their repasts "the dinners of the hissed authors." Flaubert, Alphonse Daudet has told us, was a member of this dining society through the failure of his *Candidat*, Zola through the reception of *Bouton de Rose*, Goncourt on account of *Henriette Maréchal*, while Daudet himself claimed admission through his *Arlésienne*. "As for Tourguenieff," he adds, "he pledged his word that he had been hissed in Russia and as it was a long way off, we did not go there to find out." Such was the prelude to the purely Parisian period of Turgenev's life; then at Baden he discovered an excellent *point d'appui* from which to study his compatriots abroad.

Turgenev was delighted with Baden and in the spring of 1863 he wrote to Flaubert: "I am leaving Paris in a week's time in order to settle at Baden. Won't you come there? There are trees there such as I have never seen anywhere, right on top of the mountains. The whole place is full of vigour and youth, and, at the same time, of poetry and grace, and it does a great deal of good to one's eyes and to one's soul. When one is seated at the foot of one of these giants one feels, as if one took in a little of its sap, that it is very good and helpful for one. Seriously, do come to Baden, if only for a few days. You will carry away from it some famous colours for your palette." Undoubtedly, Turgenev found at Baden admirable colours for his own palette, and one cannot help contrasting his delicate and sophisticated experiences with those of poor Dostoevsky in the same place a few years later. "Finding myself quite near Baden," wrote the author of *Crime and Punishment*, in a letter to Maikov, dated August 1867, "I had the idea of visiting it." The result of this visit was a gain of four thousand francs with which his second wife, Anna Grigorievna, implored him to be satisfied. "But there was a chance," continues Dostoevsky in the same letter, "so easy and so possible, to remedy everything. And the examples? Besides one's own personal winnings, one sees every day others winning 20,000, 30,000 francs (one does not see those who lose). Are there saints in the world? Money is more necessary to me than to them. I staked more and I lost. I began to lose my last resources, enraging myself to fever point. I lost. I pawned my clothes, Anna Grigorievna has pawned everything that she has, her last trinket. (What an angel!) How she consoled me, how she wearied in that accursed Baden! in our two little rooms above the forge, where we had to take refuge! At last, no more, everything was lost. (Oh! how those Germans are vile! They are all without exception userers, scoundrels and rascals! The proprietor, knowing that we had nowhere to go until we received money, raised his prices.) At last, we had to save ourselves and leave Baden."

Turgenev endured neither such temptations, nor such miseries as he settled down in a small one-storied house with a garden. It was a suitable resting-place, this Baden whose "Russian tree" was to form the pivot of his next, this time almost frank and direct onslaught on *les Jeunes*. Here he could watch, with that luminous, but equivocal gaze in which the vision of the dreamer blended with the inquisition of the analyst, those emancipated ones who asserted themselves to be the vanguard of Russia. They were openly deriding him now as one wholly out of touch with their aspirations and their intellectual life, but, shortly after the new year, he determined to visit Russia. In this year, 1864, Madame Viardot was retiring from the theatre. Turgenev writes to her from Berlin: "I seem to be like a man in a dream: I cannot get used to the idea that I am already so far from Baden and people and objects pass in front of me without seeming to touch me." The next letter is headed: "*Bade, hélas Non! Saint-Pétersbourg!*"

The Viardots settled down in Baden and Turgenev was soon back beside the Russian Tree. While he watched and waited his external life flowed on with the limpidity and the tranquillity of his prose. He was once more almost happy. He was content with that sameness of one day with another, which, wanderer though he had been, and exile though he continued to be, seemed to him, as to Flaubert, a good thing in itself and for itself. He would enjoy music with Madame Viardot and he would shoot with her husand. Gossip had long been malignant on this friendship of three, which it asserted to be the traditional *ménage à trois*. But to gossip Turgenev was lazily indifferent. The life suited him, giving him exactly that phase of a quite exotic domesticity which appealed to a temperament at once deeply sophisticated and disconcertingly naïve. Besides, both the cosmopolitan types and the true Russian types were there always to hand.

By the Russian Tree he could watch all manner of men and women idly busy in pursuit of excitement or rest— foreigners airing their superiority or dissimulating their provinciality, Russians furtively imitating the oddities of the foreigners they condemned, Russians preaching the gospel of freedom while their pockets bulged with the roubles of the moujik. And in this fashionable European resort the *frou-frou* of some *mondaine's* skirts might, at any moment, revive in the novelist that thrill of expectation which is Turgenev's one solitary concession to the glamour of illusion. No better background could have been found for his peculiar powers, first as a cosmopolitan student of the younger Russia that mocked him and secondly, as a prober into those secrets of the human heart into whose windings so very few in the whole world of literature have been able to penetrate with even a tithe of his artistry, so naïve and so ironic, so hesitating and so ruthless.

But his health continued to trouble him and from time to time that Russian crow would begin to remind him of Spaskoë. Then he would return, not merely to receive his revenues, but to recapture the old freshness of his impressions of Russian life at home. No one interprets more sensitively than he that sense of return, the impression of long, empty corridors, of creaking neglected furniture with curtains rustling in empty, but pervaded rooms. Here at Spaskoë he would taste again those near memories of childhood which he could bring into art still quivering with their own life. Here he would inspect his property and resume those Russian friendships from which the more conventional life of the West was never to sever him.

Nor had he lost his old delight in mystification. On these visits he would magnify the glories of his estate and induce his friends to visit him through enticing descriptions of his house, his park and, above all, of a mysteriously beautiful neighbour. They would start, then, from Moscow only to discover that the country house and the park were nothing so very wonderful and that the neighbour was the very safest of human snares. But the novelist's hospitality and high spirits, the shooting, the swimming in the pond, the *champignons à la crème*, would more than make amends for their host's hospitable imposture. Private theatricals would be organized in which the perruque of Turgenev's Oedipus was the most significant stage-property. It was at one of these theatrical representations, incidentally, that the novelist ironically repeated that cry, once attributed to him in real earnest: "Save me! I am the only son of a rich widow."

But besides these amusements, there were serious pre-occupations with the peasants. Immediately after his mother's death, Turgenev had enfranchized his house serfs and endowed them with both land and houses. To the serfs on the land he had given the choice between *bartchina*, the corvée system, and *obrok*, tenure in money. In addition to this, he began to build a hospital for the peasants and, after the abolition of serfdom and the liquidation of accounts between the land-owners and the peasants, he endowed his servants gratuitously and even returned to the moujiks the fifth of the indemnity that they owed him for arable land. In addition to all these concessions, or rather actual gifts, he made them a present of wood and other per-quisites the right to which he renewed on his annual returns to Spaskoë.

Nothing could be more easy-going than the relations between Turgenev and his dependents. Once, while he was driving, the carriage pulled up abruptly in the middle of the road and the coachman began a game of cards with the footman. Turgenev waited quietly until the game was over. But best of all, perhaps, this characteristic little prophecy describes the novelist as he appeared to the Russian peas-ants, whom he had sought to emancipate. "One day," he remarked to his friend Polonsky, "we shall be seated behind the house drinking tea. Suddenly there will arrive by the garden a crowd of peasants. They will take off their hats and bow profoundly. 'Well brothers,' I shall say to them, 'what is it that you want?' 'Excuse us, master,' they will reply, 'don't get angry. You are a good master, and we love you well. . . . But all the same we must hang you, and him as well' (pointing you out, Polonsky). 'What's that? Hang us! . . . 'Oh, yes! There is a ukase that orders it. . . . We have brought a rope. Say your prayers. . . . We can easily wait a little while.'"

In reality life at Spaskoë was pleasantly sluggish, but at Petersburg, Turgenev found himself worried by the police the moment he left the train. He was also dragged into disputes with his fellow authors, bothered by Goncharov who had a grievance against him for plagiarism and harassed by Nekrasov for editorial reasons. With Tolstoy he was now on visiting terms, but Turgenev had no sympathy with the Count's theory of giving all that one has to the poor. On one of his visits to Yasnaya Polyana, this theory was discussed with his host over a game of chess. "What! everything that one has?" asked Turgenev, "then you will give everything, everything that is in this room, even the table on which we are playing?" To this Tolstoy answered grimly: "Even the table on which we are playing."

The so-called "conversion" of Tolstoy meant little or nothing to Turgenev, but no one welcomed more heartily than he the publication of *War and Peace*. He detected at once that what the public hailed with enthusiasm—namely the historical and psychological digressions—were precisely the weak points, while what was really of the first order was the long series of military and descriptive pictures.

Petersburg society greeted Turgenev coldly and he gained but little inspiration from his visits to the Russian capital. It was only at Spaskoë that he was able to renew the indefinable charm of Russia which at this period he and perhaps he alone, among contemporary writers, could interpret. This charm came to him in spite of all externals but he could not be blind to the poverty, squalor and rags that still remained typical of the great mass of the Russian people. On the whole, he was probably happier working and shoot-

A TYPICAL ISBA

TURGENEV IN OLD AGE

ing and listening to music in Baden where his friend and translator, Pitsch, would pay him a visit every autumn. They would have Russian talks together as this impression of an autumn evening with Turgenev in Baden, shows: "How well he knew how to express what he had thought and felt! Far off in the forest the cry of the screech owl saluted us, and in the garden the familiar murmur of the fountain; the leaves of the walnut trees rustled faintly in the silence of the night. From time to time ripe fruit detached itself from the pear trees and fell with their too heavy branches. Pegasus would detect some footstep and would growl. Over the fields stretched a whitish mist; the dawn would often find us on his doorstep; he still talking without ceasing and I all ears." Here in Baden, the novelist was as close to happiness as it was in his nature to be. And yet it was precisely now that he was summing up his whole life-experience in the most sombre of all his works.

Writing from Moscow in the spring of 1867, Turgenev informs Madame Viardot that Katkov has made him promise to deliver the last proofs of *Smoke* within the week. A few days later he informs her of a long conversation with Katkov who, it seems, begged him to modify the portrait of Irene for fear of recognition. Turgenev refused point blank. "Enough of Moscow with this sort of thing!" he exclaims in conclusion, "I swear to you that I feel here as if I were in prison." The altercation with his publisher ended in a compromise: "I have sacrificed one scene of insignificant importance and I have saved the rest," he assures Madame Viardot triumphantly.

His health continued to torment him and about this time he expresses pleasure at being able to walk without a stick in spite of the intense cold of Petersburg. "Botkine and I," he continues in the same letter, "spent yesterday evening at Madame Abaza's, she has organized some choirs of young ladies and they are not going too badly. We found Rubinstein and his wife there. He played like a lion, shaking his mane a little too much . . . speaking from the standpoint of music." Such entertainments were brief respite from the worries with his publisher over *Smoke*, with his uncle over the management of his estate and, above all from the pre-occupations with his health. But now, as always, he kept his mind open to every passing phase of Russian opinion and noted that at this time it had become peculiarly anti-French, the advance guard of Russian progress saluting the Prussian as the representative of movement and the future, and the Frenchman as the representative of routine and the past. How little Turgenev cared for the opinion of the advance guard of Russian progress was to be proved that very year, 1867, by the publication of *Smoke*.

In *First Love* and *Spring Torrents*, he has given us the inner story of his youth. In *Rudin* and *Liza*, he expressed his attitude towards the sowing of the seed of liberty, towards "cultivating the soil," while certainly in *On the Eve*, he seemed to detect if not the fulfilment of harvest, at least the means by which it might yet be reaped. In *Fathers and Sons*, however, in spite of Bazarov's genius of energy one divines only too clearly that the harvest is still remote. In all these books the Russian peasant appears in essentials exactly as he appears in the *Annals of a Sportsman*, In no one of them had Turgenev really committed himself to the opinion that the moujik was ripe for revolution in the Western sense. In one and all of them Turgenev's analysis of actuality can be clearly read, but in *The Diary of a Superfluous Man*, the intro-spective side of the author has been visibly laid bare; it is the necessary complementary book through which the art of Turgenev, so very close to that personal record which was burnt in the garden of Bougival, discloses itself in spite of all that reticence which the deceptive irony of Turgenev made inseparable from his work. He himself once advised a friend to write down this or that emotional experience even in the moment when it festered. Remembering this, one understands how in seemingly purely objective works there intervenes so often the subtle hint of personal memory.

In one book there is something of all the works of Tur-genev—his youth, his introspection, his real political atti-tude, his cosmopolitan outlook, his mature conviction as to the possibilities of fulfilling that oath of Hannibal sworn so light-heartedly in the student days. All these are to be found in *Smoke* and with them, stamping the book with a certain finality, that deep irradicable pessimism which with its author was never to be divorced from the simplicity of kindness. It is as it were, an unconscious résumé of the boyish worship of Zenaïda, of Sanin's remorse, of Rudin's verbose aspirations, of Lavretzki's disillusion of maturity, of the Superfluous Man's recognition of himself as a "fifth wheel," of Insarov's relentless passing in the hour of hope, of Bazarov's mocking doom, and of that realization of nature's eternal aloofness which had never ceased to chill him since the day, when as a boy he had observed for himself, in the garden of Spaskoë, her inalienable indifference to cruelty as to kindness.

Unlike *On the Eve*, and *Fathers and Sons*, this book has but little political significance beyond the laceration of imposture. Unlike Rudin, its hero has never been swayed by his own or others' rhetoric; unlike Lavretzki, he deserts at the call of passion, the immediate duty that lies to hand. He is as unlike the Superfluous Man as he is unlike the boy who loved Zenaïda in the garden of Spaskoë, or the youth who foresook Gemma at Frankfurt. But none the less, every one of these figures passes through the smoke rings of this enchanting work of disenchantment in which Turgenev, in the very deepest sense, utters his ultimate warning of disillusion. The very essence, too, of what romance meant to him whose pulse so often quickened at the *frou-frou* of a *mondaine's* skirt, strikes at us here, as from a remorselessly remembered past. Yet even in this book it is the young girl of Russia to whom his genius was finally dedicated no less than to the serfs for whose freedom he achieved his historic success, who appears at the last, as redeemer and consoler. Personal and analytic, at once subjective to the verge of introspection and objective with that intent habit of "realizing," this novel may be accepted as the philosophic conclusion of one who at no time posed as a philosopher.

Neither before nor after did Turgenev probe more uncompromisingly into the hiding-places of his own heart; neither before nor after did those eyes of his, sad· rather than triumphant in their irony, examine more minutely as through a new and powerful lens the patriots of young Russia. Not for nothing, here in Baden, had he observed these emancipated exiles whose chatter was to galvanize tired old Europe after it had penetrated the resisting arteries of young Russia. Politically the resultant was merely that of satire, but artistically the portraits are bitten in with the calm meditative malice of Turgenev, as a relief from that other malice of a too poignantly remembered passion.

In other novels of Turgenev we are plunged abruptly into the atmosphere of Russia, but here we are under the Russian Tree of Baden where the gossip of liberty and progress serve as an interlude to the gossip of gambling and chiffons. Litvinov is on his way back to Russia and is waiting at Baden for the arrival of a lady and her niece. He is engaged to the niece, and very soon all three will return home and then, it seems to him, just as it had seemed to Sanin at Frankfurt, all will be well. But whereas Sanin had been almost like a blank page awaiting the impress of experience, Litvinov had long ago been stamped by an old memory. It revives for him here in Baden through the only too familiar scent of a bunch of heliotrope, left by an unknown lady at his hotel. Instantly the romance of his early youth sweeps over him; he remembers how as a poor student he had given Irina a bunch heliotrope when she drove out of his life to a ball in the Hall of Nobility long ago. And he remembers how he had walked up and down outside the windows of that Hall and listened to the music of Strauss that, so mockingly and gaily, intensified his sense of loneliness and desertion.

The scent brings it all back to him in a turmoil of physical intensity of memory; he is scarcely surprised when the next day he finds that it really is Irina who has so subtly reminded him of her own broken promises of years ago. She is the wife of a Russian general now and a *mondaine* of no little importance, but none the less she has remembered

Litvinov and she wants him to forgive her for that desertion for which she cannot forgive herself. They must begin again together exactly where they had left off: the returned bunch of heliotrope must bridge over the interlude of years. What has happened to him in the meantime? "Why has he not told her the chief thing?" Litvinov blushes as he realizes how intuitively he has concealed the existence of his fiancée from this alluring worldly woman who had so light-heartedly broken his youth. From that moment Irina begins to wind herself round his life again, feeding herself on his passion and seeming sometimes to reflect it in her eyes. Truly, she is the Irina whom he had loved in the little white frock and the short cloak when the battered old coach had dragged her away from him, clumsily snapping the golden impulse of youth to youth. Only now he need be no longer outside the windows, listening to the music that is meant for others! Now he must be rewarded for all that; it is less than nothing to her that the rights of love and honour and fidelity are part of the price of passion. With her withering magnetism she closes in upon Litvinov just as that other woman had closed in upon Sanin.

And, like Sanin, he follows her brooding only on the physical spell which has made already so many suppliants for this soft captivity. As in a waking dream he is carried into her circle of pompous reactionaries which, even under this hypnotic influence, he studies closely and minutely just as the hero of *First Love* had studied Zenaïda's circle.

When, from time to time, he tears himself away from Irina it is only to enter an equally repellent atmosphere among the boastful idlers who called themselves the liberators of Russia. Bambeev, the child-like enthusiast, presents him to one mediocrity after another, exalting each as the man of the moment. But Litvinov discerns in none of them anything beyond the splashing of worn-out words and it is only the faint penetrating scent of heliotrope that seems real to him in this atmosphere of smoke.

It is in vain that Potugin, who has endured so long and so uselessly the same spell, warns this fresh victim of Irina.

It is in vain that the aunt of his betrothed implores him not to destroy his own happiness and that of Tatyana who loves him: "Leave this hateful Baden-Baden, let us go away together, only throw off this enchantment, and, above all, have pity—have pity. . . ." Tatyana understands; without a single reproach she gives him a letter to post, a letter marking the change in their two lives and accepting it as final: "Litvinov dropped the letter into the post box, and it seemed to him as though with that tiny scrap of paper he was dropping all his past, all his life into the tomb." He has given up everything for Irina, but now, just as years before the girl had hedged in the gamble of love, the woman hedges in the gamble of passion. She cannot give up everything, the world, her position in society, prestige, even for the sake of her lover. Besides, it is unnecessary. All that is necessary is that he should live near her and see her every day. They must continue to love each other certainly, but discreetly. The man will have none of this subterfuge of French romance. For him it must be one thing or the other and when she refuses to go with him, he prepares to go alone.

But at the very last, just as he is taking his place in the railway carriage, someone whispers his name. Turning round, he sees Irina wearing her maid's shawl and with her hair dishevelled. With her eyes she pleads to him, promising him anything and everything if only he will stay and dangle in the background as the secret lover of her heart. Litvinov utters no word, but points to the seat beside him. For a moment she hesitates, the whistle sounds and he is carried out of her life as long ago she had been carried out of his.

Then it is that the last illusion falls from him like the last withered leaf from a stricken tree. Every phase of experience personal and national, every battle cry of Russia's liberators, every platitude of the young generals in Irina's drawing-room, every boast of the noisy political enthusiasts—it all comes back to him to pass from him in so many smoke rings. The fresh first love of youth, the matured love of manhood, the dishonour in passion itself, all returned insistently, only to coil away in films of smoke.

The train sped on, passed Rastadt and Carlsruhe; Bruchsal was left far behind and then at Heidelberg shrill realities forced themselves pitilessly upon his morose reverie. All Bambeev's little gods had migrated from Baden to Heidelberg and now came rushing along the station platform to insult this laggard who had refused to believe in the cause of Russia as represented by themselves. Litvinov answered nothing, for this, too, was part of the universal smoke of life. And as he was whirled away from them there was only one word in his heart and brain and soul—smoke.

Soon afterwards he came across Bambeev, who under a French name, was employed as a menial in an obscure corner of Russia. The poor fellow admitted that one idol after the other had fallen from its pedestal, but at least it was still possible to believe in Russia: "Yes, yes, hard times have come! but still I say Russia . . . ah! our Russia, our Russia! Only look at those two geese: why, in the whole of Europe, there is nothing like them."

Litvinov passes on and gradually the coma of exhaustion is lifted from his soul; for at least there is left to him that merciful renewal which man is permitted to share with other manifestations of life. Slowly, but with the certainty of spring, love acts as an antidote to the poison of old passion. Tatyana, to whom he had been so merciless in his broken faith, heals him with that pity which perhaps, after all, is older and deeper and stronger than passion. In the whole world of smoke, she alone to him is beautiful and rare and real. But for the others with their mouthings and their boasts, their remedies and their revolts, nothing is left but their own rings of forgotten smoke.

Even Irina who had weighed carefully enough the scales of her destiny in the balance, even she cannot retain the little practical certainty to which she had sacrificed the lover of her youth and the man who had renewed in her the passion of womanhood. In an exclusive drawing-room in Petersburg the conversation happens to return on Irina of whom the

hostess observes: "I feel so sorry for her . . . she has a satir-
ical intellect . . . *elle n'a pas la foi.*" For Irina, too, nothing
had lasted, nothing had persisted. Her guess at happiness
and freedom had been as idle as all the other guesses.
Worldliness itself was after all only smoke.

Turgenev was to live to comparative old age, but, so far
as his interwoven art and autobiography are concerned,
this is his last word, as perhaps indeed, it was also his first.
Constantly he rebelled against the overpowering con-
clusions which are forced upon one so ruthlessly in this
book. But his conviction was formed long ago in the garden
of Spaskoë that there is no all-embracing pity in the stark
scheme of things on this planet. The very monotony of
motif in the novels, the monotony of Nature herself, arises
from this sometimes veiled, but always underlying, conviction. He knew, or felt that he knew, the blank meaninglessness of the suppliant's fears or hopes or laments. Nature
remained indifferent, inaccessible, and careless of death,
so long as there remains a spendthrift abundance of life.
The individual to her was negligible; the mother's cry over
her dead child and the nightingale's song were alike lost
in the tractless vaults of space.

But, as though in unconscious consolation for this immense remoteness, poor men and women were themselves
capable of pity; kindness was in them; it was from the
warmth of their own hearts that they had fashioned the
merciful eidolon of Nature. Above all, the compassion of
women for the wayward self-torment of men, made tolerable upon this earth the play of these coldly incomprehensible forces. Instinctively, they veiled the void as though
insensibly realizing that each fretful unit was but a part of
the great whole against which the rancour of words rang
ever meaningless. It is not strange that, holding this belief,
Turgenev expressed his inner convictions, not through the
words of men, but through the lives of his Russian women.
They at least, these steadfast and enduring heroines,
snatch something of beauty and permanence, as from their
own souls, through the smoke rings of human aspirations.

For them Turgenev retained a reverence deeper than verbal praise.

If one examines the work of Turgenev as a whole, one sees only too clearly that the *motif* of *Smoke* underlies every single one of his novels. Repeatedly, in *The Annals of a Sportsman* one catches, like a sudden shadow over a sunlit landscape, that pessimism which never loses its incongruous kinship with kindness. In those records of youth into which, though they were written so many years afterwards, his art has infused the very flush and expectancy of adolescence in its golden moment, it is the same. The exquisite Zenaïda is spoilt in life even before she is ruthlessly cut off in her youth by death. Sanin, who has been offered the very best in life, as though manipulated by mocking unseen forces, accepts the worst, knowing it to be so. In *The Diary of a Superfluous Man*, the human heart beats only to add to the general waste of nature. Rudin's instinct towards nobility fades into an incoherent atrophy of the will. Liza is cut off from Lavretzki in the very dawn of her virginal promise of love. Elena claims her Bulgarian on the eve, not of victory, but of death. Bazarov who strove to refashion the whole chaos of the Russian background perishes uselessly in that same chaos.

But in each case the redemption of human kindness is equally significant, as though poor human beings were striving consciously to modify the cruel indifference around them. The dying servant girl pleads with her former mistress's son, not for herself but for the peasants. Pity and not censoriousness is the last word before Zenaïda's coffin. Sanin's heart does not wither even though he has broken his faith with Gemma. The Superfluous Man, even he—"the fifth wheel"—has wrung a certain coherence out of his incoherent life, through the single-mindedness of his devotion. Rudin, who had chattered through life, dies fearlessly with no word at all on his lips. Liza, cut off as she was from the man of her choice, none the less permeates his life with something that is not all regret. Elena's self-sacrifice lives on to emulate the hearts of all brave men though Insarov lay cold in Zara. And Bazarov, whose health was drunk in silence, he who had hurled himself against the incohate mass which had smothered him, Bazarov in his death as well as in his life, had served the cause of humanity as though through nihilism itself came love.

While *Smoke* was going through the press, Turgenev made arrangements with his publisher for a complete edition of his works up-to-date. "I have sold my new edition," he says, in a letter to Madame Viardot, not without exultation, for the Spaskoë property had been badly mismanaged. "My new intendant," he continues, "finds literally chaos in the place; there are debts of which I had no idea. I must continue to strike while the iron is hot, that is to say work, write, while I am in the vein. I have promised for the new edition an immense preface of a hundred pages in which I shall narrate my literary and social recollections of the last twenty-five years, for in the spring of next year it will be just a quarter of a century since I first saw print, though it is true that the verses with which I made my début in 1843 were very mediocre!" He disliked the labour of arranging personal reminiscences as this fragment from a letter to Flaubert early in 1869 proves: "Apart from some fragmentary stuff in the shape of some literary memoirs, which I promised my publisher, I have never worked at this sort of thing and it isn't amusing. Oh, for two hours of Sainte-Beuve! I wonder if it amuses him much." Turgenev and Flaubert were now close friends as this extract from a letter written to him in 1868 shows conclusively: "Since the first time I saw you (in a kind of hostelry on the other side of the Seine) I have been conscious of a great drawing towards you. There are few men, especially few Frenchmen, with whom I feel so quietly at my ease, and so alive at the same time. I feel as if I could talk to you for whole weeks together; moreover, we are moles burrowing in the same direction. All this means that I shall be very glad to see you. I start for Russia in a fortnight's time, but I shall not stay there long . . ." The little Pauline was now grown up and married, and Turgenev informs his friend that he will probably be a grandfather when he comes to Paris in the following July.

For the last five years Turgenev had been a guest at the Magny Dinners and from his first appearance in 1863 he and Flaubert had understood each other. Alphonse Daudet has left us an admirable impression of this friendship between the author of *Smoke* and the author of *Madame Bovary*, under the benevolent auspices of the author of *Elle et Lui*: "It was George Sand who married them; the boastful rebellious quixotic Flaubert, with a voice like a Guards' trumpeter, with his penetrating ironical outlook and the gait of a conquering Norman, was undoubtedly the masculine half of this marriage of souls; but who in that other colossal being, with his flaxen brows, his great unmodelled face, would have discovered the woman, that woman of over-accentuated refinement whom Tourguenieff has painted in his books, that nervous, languid, passionate Russian, torpid as an Oriental, tragic as a blind force in revolt? So true is it that in the tumult of the great human factory, souls often get into the wrong covering—masculine souls into feminine bodies, feminine souls into cyclopean frames."

Flaubert undoubtedly reciprocated Turgenev's attachment to him. "But for you and Turgenev," he wrote to George Sand in 1870, "I don't know a single soul with whom I can talk freely about the things I have most at heart—and you both live so far away!" On one occasion he read aloud to Turgenev a hundred and fifteen pages of *Les Tentations de Saint Antoine*, followed by nearly half of the *Dernières Chansons*. "What an audience," he exclaims delightedly to the châtelaine of Nohant, "and what a critic! He dazzled me with the depth and accuracy of his judgment. If only all the people who meddle with literary criticism could have heard him, what a lesson it would have been! Nothing escapes him. At the end of a poem of a hundred lines he remembers a single weak adjective. On the subject of *Saint Antoine* he gave me two or three exquisite pieces of advice as to detail."

Turgenev had had a house of some pretensions built for him near the Viardots in Baden. It was finished in 1868, but the June of that year found its proprietor back in Spaskoë. He has news now for Madame Viardot of Dr Porphyre, the ex-serf who had accompanied him to Berlin in 1838. Porphyre's success in his profession seems to have been not very brilliant for this letter speaks of his having come to farm a small property that the novelist possessed in the Government of Orel. The misery of his native land came home to Turgenev with peculiar force during this visit. "The flood of people," he writes to Madame Viardot, "who consider me a milch cow! They are for the most part poor devils, starvelings, former servants, etc. . . . To refuse is almost impossible . . . but there is a limit to everything. . . . It is a regular *cour des miracles!* Whence come all these cripples, these blind people, these one-armed people, these decrepit beings whom hunger makes so peevish? What a profound misery there is all round. Holy Russia is far from being flourishing Russia; for the rest a saint has no wish to be flourishing." In another letter during this visit, he observes: "Spaskoë is the solitary village that I have seen up to now in which the thatched roofs are not gaping and God knows what a difference there is between Spaskoë and the humblest village of the Black Forest."

Only in his garden does he recapture the old charm of Russia: "Memories of childhood have forced themselves upon me, as they never fail to do. I have seen myself quite a little boy here, much younger than Paul (Madame Viardot's son) running along the alleys, lying down between the border plots to steal strawberries. Here is the tree where I killed my first crow; here is the place where I found that enormous mushroom, where I witnessed the fight between an adder and a toad, a struggle which made me for the first time doubtful of a good Providence. Then recollections of myself as a young student, as a full grown man, came back to me."

The next month he returned to Baden and wrote to Flaubert: "I have been here for four days, but unfortunately I have not come back from Russia alone. I have brought with me a fine attack of gout which first seized me at Mâcon, and again on my arrival at Baden. Here I am on the sofa with all the inevitable miseries—oil of Indian chestnuts, etc., etc. However, it is less violent than last year, and I am not without hope of getting to my baths towards the middle of next month and according to the programme I shall look you up at your lair." In the winter, Turgenev is in Paris and the beginning of 1869 finds him in Carlsruhe where he is longing for France: "I have often thought of Croisset, and said to myself that it was a good nest for the hatching of singing birds." Incidentally, the Russian novelist in a post-script to a previous letter had given this interesting, but unheeded suggestion: "Find another title—*l'Education Sentimentale* is bad."

The opening of 1870 found Turgenev at Weimar, of which he complains to Flaubert: "I have been here ten days and my one thought has been how to keep warm. The houses here are badly built and the stoves are useless. You'll see a tiny thing of mine in the March number of the *Revue des Deux Mondes*. It's a mere trifle. I am working at something more 'important', at least I am getting ready to work. I shall go to Paris before returning to Russia—it will be towards the end of April. We shall see a lot of each other. If you see Madame Sand, give her a thousand kind messages from me."

The reception of *Smoke* had added the last drop to Turgenev's well-filled cup of disillusion. His compatriots complained now of not even receiving from him what they expected. He had given them this time as a heroine, a *mondaine* instead of that young Russian girl, who so often had propitiated them for the lukewarmness of his heroes. Then, the novelist's old friends were disappearing one after the other and in this year Hertzen died. Turgenev felt that old age had stolen upon him before his time, but his pessimism remained singularly untinged by any wail of personal bitterness. He was naturally absorbed in the Franco-Prussian war, and, like Dostoevsky, he predicted the victory of French arms. He believed, indeed, that very soon the French uniform would show itself about the Russian Tree in Baden. "Everybody is going away," he writes to his brother on July 27th, 1870: "as for me, I remain, what can they do to me?" He was rather astonished at the subsequent course of events and though he had already handed on to Madame Viardot, as if he subscribed to it himself, the ready-made opinion that the Prussians represented the future and the French the past, he was quick to realize that the victors of Sedan were no better than any other conquerors. He protested vehemently against the annexation of Alsace. "Nationality," he insisted, "has nothing to say to it here. The Alsatians are French in heart and soul."

He would willingly have remained on German soil, but the Viardots left for England. Turgenev sold his villa at once in order to be with them. "If they had gone to Australia," he observed to a friend, "I would have followed them there."

CHAPTER XIII

THE PARIS PERIOD

IN spite of his desire to be with the Viardots, Turgenev spent the winter and the beginning of spring in his own country. It is from Petersburg that he condoles with Madame Viardot on the misfortune of France: "Here, everybody is full of sympathy for France, but that is only one bitterness the more." Dostoevsky's sympathies were equally pro-French. "You assert," he wrote to Maikov in December 1870, "that the spirit of the whole nation is now rising in France against brute force! But I have never doubted it from the beginning. . . ."

In Petersburg, Turgenev was actually fêted. He was invited to the annual dinner in commemoration of the emancipation of the serfs. Apart from the members of the Committee, who had taken part in the ground work of this historic reform, Turgenev was the only guest, an honour which did something to atone for the obloquy of years. The members of the Committee went so far as to drink the health of the author of *The Annals of a Sportsman*. Too profoundly moved to make any set speech, Turgenev merely stammered a few unintelligible words of thanks.

Some two months later, Turgenev was stopping at 16, Beaumont Street, Marylebone, from which address he writes to Flaubert on the subject of a startling rumour: "Happily, my dear friend, the news is absolutely untrue. Madame V. whom I see every day is no more dead than she is fifty-four years old. If the news had been true, I don't think I could have answered you. As it is, I can tell you that your letter has deeply touched me. It is very good to feel that one has a real friend and I am grateful to you for having proved it to me." In the same letter he gives this comment on English life: "I am in England, not for the pleasure of being there, but because of my friends who have come here to try and make a little money. Nevertheless, there is some good in the English people; but they all of them, even the cleverest, lead such a hard life. One has to get accustomed to it, as one has to their climate, and besides where else is there to go?"

The following August, Turgenev was in Scotland shooting *le Grouse;* and the same month he arrived at the rue de Douai, where he lived first at No 48, and then in the third étage of No 50, where the Viardots had established themselves. In this very year, 1871, while Turgenev was commencing the purely Parisian period of his life, his rival Dostoevsky, who had just published the answer to *Fathers and Sons*, was returning from his long exile in the West to settle down thankfully in the Russian capital.

Between the publication of *Rudin* in 1855 and that of *Liza* in 1858, Turgenev had written several of his shorter studies including *Faust* and *Acia*, both of which are so far in advance of such earlier stories as *The Jew* and *The Duellist*, and, in many ways, even of *Three Portraits*. Between the publication of *Fathers and Sons* and that of *Smoke*, he had written, among many short sketches, a little study entitled *Enough*, in which his pessimism is formulated as expressively as in *Smoke* itself: "But at the end of all, Nature is inexorable; she has no need to hurry, and sooner or later she takes her own. Unconsciously and inflexibly obedient to laws, she knows not art, as she knows not freedom, she knows not good; from all ages moving, from all ages changing she suffers nothing immortal, nothing unchanging. . . . Man is her child; but man's work—art—is hostile to her, just because it strives to be unchanging and immortal. Man is the child of Nature; but she is the universal mother and she has no preferences; all that exists in her lap has arisen only at the cost of something else and must in its time yield its place to something else." This fragment, written in 1864, shows the deepening and hardening of the novelist's attitude towards *"cette scélérate de nature"* about whom he had lectured Madame Viardot from Courtavenel.

Between *Smoke* and *Virgin Soil* there was only one novel,

Spring Torrents, during the writing of which Turgenev literally relived his youth in the person of Sanin. There were, in this interval, however, several shorter stories, including *Pounin* and *Babourin*, which contained so many intimate memories of his childhood. But the most significant of all these shorter stories is unquestionably *Lear of the Steppes* at which his enemy Dostoevsky sneered so gloatingly. Not even on the immense canvas of Shakespeare's tragedy does the inner loneliness of man stand out in more formidable starkness than in this Russian rendering of the old story of a broken-hearted father who had trusted his daughters too well. Only it is significant and utterly contrary to the usual tendency of Turgenev that here, for once, there is no redeeming Cordelia. It was written at Weimar in 1870 and the picture of Harlov tearing the roof off his daughters' house is almost as unforgettable as that of Lear alone in the storm:

"On the floor of the garret, in a whirl of dust and rubbish a blackish grey mass was moving to and fro with rapid ungainly action, at one moment shaking the remaining chimney, built of brick, (the other had fallen already) then tearing up the boarding and flinging it down below then clutching at the very rafters. It was Harlov. He struck me as being exactly like a bear at this moment too. The head and back, and shoulders were a bear's, and he put his feet down wide apart without bending the insteps—also like a bear. The bitter wind was blowing upon him from every side, lifting his matted locks. It was horrible to see here and there red patches of bare flesh through the rents in his tattered clothes. It was horrible to hear his wild husky muttering."

Perhaps in all the sombre novels of Turgenev there is no more desolate figure than Harlov. In spite of Dostoevsky's sneer, nowhere is Turgenev's artistry more minutely faithful to life. The story is told as it presents itself to a boy who finds out little by little—through snatches of conversation overheard by chance, through an odd word here and there, let fall in passing—not merely the outer catastrophe of this Russian Lear, but the whole inner torment of his life. The boy discovers the entire household of Harlov; he penetrates to the secret relations, one with another, of the two daughters and the son-in-law. It is only a short tale, but in it we have a fulfilled tragedy and the whole after-lives of two highly complex women projected upon a Meissonier-like canvas. Deeper than that, beyond that we have —just as in Shakespeare's play—man in his relations to the elemental forces which seem almost consciously affronted by his arrogant belief in his little self-will. "He is failing; he is becoming paler and paler," Dostoevsky exulted over this work of art at once biting and delicate as though his own judgment once, as Turgenev himself admitted, so true, had been convulsed by the monstrous creations of *Demons*.

Neither this comment nor the fact that he was caricatured in *Demons* mattered very much to Turgenev as he settled down peacefully in the rue de Douai to enjoy those days, perhaps the best of all, which resemble each other. In the morning he would work on his manuscript; in the afternoon he would go to the Salon or pay visits; in the evening he would accompany his friends to the theatre. Besides, there was always music in his adopted home, music that was worth listening to, as Gustave Flaubert acknowledged. "*Hier soir,*" he wrote to George Sand, "*Madame Viardot nous a chanté de l'Alceste . . . de pareilles émotions consolent de l'existence.*"

As at Baden, Turgenev in spite of his health was almost happy. He had not become by any means gallomane, but, when a compatriot brought the old, singularly foolish charges against the French home, he was instantly on the defensive: "It is the fashion among us to tear the French to pieces on this subject; but I can tell you that the French family has very much more solid foundations than our own." For all that, the French spirit was essentially alien from Turgenev's meditative irony. The personality of Victor Hugo, in particular, grated on him, though he acknowledged him to be the greatest lyric poet in Europe. "Once," he tells us, "while I was at his house we talked about German poetry. Victor Hugo, who does not like anybody to speak in his presence, interrupted me and undertook a portrait of Goethe. 'His best work,' said he, in an Olympian tone, 'is *Wallenstein*.' 'Pardon, dear Master, *Wallenstein* is not by Goethe. It is by Schiller.' 'It is all the same: I have read neither one nor the other; but I know them much better than those who have learned them by heart.'"

Another anecdote, attributed to Turgenev on the subject of the great French poet's vanity, is even more astounding. At one of his evenings, it seems, a disciple assured Victor Hugo that the street in which he lived ought to be called after him. Another admirer maintained that the street was too small and they began to suggest for the honour, street after street until, at last, one of them maintained that "Paris herself should esteem it an honour to bear the name of Hugo." "*Ça viendra, mon cher; ça viendra!*" acquiesced the poet who could not have foreseen that the capital of Turgenev's country would one day be called Leningrad.

Turgenev had little faith in expressions of French admiration either for his own genius, or for the national genius of his country. "The French," he maintained, "recognize no originality whatever in other peoples. The genius of England, of Germany, of Italy is a dead letter, or almost a dead letter to them; as for my own country, do not let us speak of it! . . . Apart from their own affairs, they are interested in nothing, they know nothing." The novelist did not believe in the success of the French translations of his works: "Of what interest are they to the French, our dreams and our distracted heroes! . . . My lovers are neither gay, nor voluptuous! . . . The most insignificant romance of Octave Feuillet gives them more pleasure than all mine put together." And, as though to sum up French reactions to Russian literature, he cites the comment of a distinguished Frenchman on one of Pushkin's masterpieces: "*C'est plat, mon cher!*"

Sceptical as he was about the success of his own books in French, Turgenev went out of his way to secure a hearing in

Paris for Count Tolstoy. The *Temps* had already published translations of some of Turgenev's novels and Charles Edmond remarked to him that their mutual friend, Hébrard, would be very glad to publish more of them. Turgenev proposed that they should go at once to his rooms where he assured Edmond that a surprise was waiting for him. On arriving at the house, Turgenev took a bundle of manuscript from a writing-table with these words: "Listen, here is *copy* for your paper of an absolutely first rate kind. This means that I am not its author. The master, for he is a *real* master, is almost unknown; but I assure you upon my souls and conscience . . ." Tolstoy's *Recollections of Sebastopol* began to appear in the *Temps* two days later.

With the same disinterested kindness, he did his best for Zola in Russia. Turgenev was antagonistic to Balzac. *"C'est un ethnographe,"* was his opinion, *"ce n'est pas un artiste."* Naturally, Zola must have appeared to him still less an artist, but it was through his influence that the French realist became Paris correspondent to the *Messager de l'Europe*, a review published in Petersburg. Turgenev, indeed, used to boast of having discovered Zola and on one occasion he invited him to give a reading from his own works. Some ladies, it seems, were curious to see this supposed Bohemian and anticipated a scandal of realism in its most elementary form. Zola, however, appeared in evening clothes and white gloves and seemed quite as presentable as anybody else. But they still hoped to be shocked when he began to read and waited impatiently for that moment. "It arrived at last," narrates Turgenev, "Zola mounted the platform . . . but here he produced a quite unexpected scandal. Zola grew white, grew red, and remained for some seconds dumb, without being able to utter a word. He made a brave attempt to commence the reading, but alas! he himself did not recognize his own voice. His teeth clashed against one another. The book swayed in his hand. He was unable to see. He mumbled something as he looked at the book, but his audience no longer listened to him. The ladies covered their lips with their handker-

chiefs and burst out laughing; the gentlemen made un-
heard-of efforts to remain serious; in short, the scandal
was complete." Zola vowed then and there never to read
in public again and years afterwards he confessed to his
Russian friend: "Even now, when I recall at night that
trifle, I grow hot and cold in turn."

Turgenev himself seems to have been a most sympathetic
reader and Pavlovsky has left this impression of his rendering of the *Tziganes*, of Pushkin: "His figure bent, his face
grew pale. Moved, almost carried away by the subject, he
appeared to have forgotten the audience and everybody
else. He gave himself up without reserve to the wonderful
illusion. The final scene he read with a voice scarcely audible. When he had finished and come down from the
platform his hand was shaking. It seemed to me that he
was weeping, he who never wept." Only a little while before
this he had read a fragment from his own *Annals of a Sportsman* with perfect calmness. Turgenev's kindness was in-
exhaustible; he would even allow himself to be victimized
with his eyes wide open. Once a young woman in distress
borrowed seven hundred and fifty francs from him and the
novelist remarked to a visitor that in his opinion she had
been acting and that she was not separated, as she pretended to be, from her husband. He prophesied that he
had not heard the last of her, and soon afterwards a letter
reached him from Russia in which there was no enclosure
of seven hundred and fifty francs, but many reproaches on
the score that he had wished to rid himself of the writer,
who concluded with a request for a life pension.

On another occasion, a young Russian writer came to
Paris for her health. Turgenev did everything he possibly
could for her, gave her introductions, went from house to
house to look for suitable lodgings and even discovered
doctors whose services, according to his version, were gra-
tuitous. He believed in his young compatriot's talent, but
even more in her self-sacrifice. This girl in her miserable
Russian village had rescued a sick child from her own
neglectful parents. She had taken her to Moscow, paid all

her expenses and finally succeeded in curing her, but at the cost of her own health. This was exactly the kind of life story in which Turgenev delighted. Suspicious as he was of so many established reputations, he would speak with reverence of this poor unknown writer to whom self-sacrifice was merely a matter of routine.

Turgenev was not only discreet, but even humble, almost abashed in his surreptitious kindness. No one knew better than this world-novelist that one must avoid hurting the feelings of proud young people in need of help. If one gave, one must do it stealthily. Sometimes, for no apparent reason, a Parisian editor would commission a translation. Sometimes a manuscript, that had never been even submitted, would be paid for as by magic. In one instance, a young author had received payment in advance, but as his manuscript failed to appear in print he made enquiries. Of course he could get no explanation, for the real explanation was Ivan Turgenev.

Towards the very end of his life, in January 1883, a young Russian girl, who had arrived in Paris too late for registration at the School of Medicine, applied to Turgenev for help. It had become an axiom among Russians in Paris, that looking for work meant looking for Turgenev and the almost dying man undertook immediately the burden of a long correspondence about this would-be medical student. Too ill to approach the authorities himself, he persuaded a friend to do so. Not content with this, the pessimist of *Smoke* anxiously recommended the young girl to wear flannel vests as he had heard that she was delicate. Two weeks later he asked her if she had followed his advice.

On the subjects of impostors, Turgenev was almost clairvoyant in the Dostoevsky sense. "That man," he once observed, "will become a collaborator of Katkov: he will betray the Nihilists with whom he is now associated and will cover them with mud; he will publish his recollections of me after my death, and will pose as my intimate friend. As he has letters from me, people will easily believe in our friendship, and will accept as absolute truth every word that he will put into my mouth." The prophecy proved unerring even in detail; and about another impostor the novelist's predictions were fulfilled equally to the letter.

He continued to give, careless as to whether he was being victimised or not. This kindness is all the more extraordinary because whether in Paris or Russia or England or Carlsbad, his health was torturing him. "My gout is, at least, as bad as the Versailles Assembly," he writes to Flaubert in 1872, "and I believe it'll still be going on when the other has either dissolved itself or been dissolved." The next year, in another letter to his old friend, he observes: "During the past night the ankle of my bad foot suddenly swelled up and now I can neither wear a boot, nor put my foot to the ground." Only the summer before he had written to Flaubert about an invitation to the finest partridge shooting in England, owned by an old General Hall who had left it to his nephew: "Now lo, and behold, the nephew has remembered me and invited me to go and stay with him and kill mountains of partridges, between the 9th and the 14th of September. In spite of my boundless passion for sport, the only pleasure which is left to me, I remembered my promise and gave an evasive answer, all the more so because I don't know if my gout will allow me such escapades. And indeed, there is something shocking in an old greybeard like myself crossing the sea twice in order to pour a lot of lead into a lot of partridges!" It was natural that the author of *The Annals of a Sportsman* should continue to be a sportsman; it was also natural that he should seek again and again that "under the water" tranquillity which so permeated his Russian home. "This isn't the first time I've written to you from here," he observes in a letter to Flaubert, dated Spaskoë, June 1874, "and you know the place, it is green, golden, extensive, monotonous, peaceful, old-fashioned, and there is a terrible stillness about it—a slow, patriarchal, all-persuasive boredom." The next month, in another letter to Flaubert, this time from Moscow, Turgenev's life philosophy expresses itself with a touch of personal bitterness that is rare in his correspondence: "Infirmities, a steady cold disgust at things in general, a painful stirring up of useless memories—there, my dear old boy, is the vista which opens before a man who has passed his fiftieth year and hovering above and beyond it all is resignation—*hideous* resignation. This preparation for death—but enough of this!"

Two or three months later he is still suffering at Bougival but, for all that, he is anxious to keep an appointment with Zola, to whom he gives minute instructions as to the route: "You must start from the Saint Lazare station. The trains leave at thirty-five minutes after every hour. When you get to the station of Rueil, take the American omnibus which will bring you to Bougival (don't take the one which only goes as far as Rueil), and then you'll have five minutes walk from there to Halgan House, which is behind the church."

All through the correspondence with Zola, as with Flaubert, one is conscious of Turgenev's genuine sympathy with his colleagues in literature and of the absence of any sense of puerile rivalry. No matter how he suffered from the production of his own work he could always find time and energy for the affairs of his friends. It was his maxim that no artist could be happy but he detected in unhappiness itself a real sustenance for art.

Once, when he had talked in this vein a despairing friend remarked: "It's all very well to say, 'sit down and write,' when a man has perhaps but one wish, namely to blow out his brains." Not the least disconcerted, Turgenev replied: "Good. What does it matter? Write that too! If all the unhappy artists were to blow their brains out there would be none left, for they are all more or less unhappy; there cannot be artists who are actually happy. Happiness is repose, and repose creates nothing. As for me, I always keep my journal in which I write down everything that interests me. In that journal I am at home; I judge and I reverse judgements, on all men and things." Asked if he ever intended to publish the journal, Turgenev replied: "Never! I have enjoined Madame Viardot to burn it immediately after my death, and she will fulfill my wish religiously."

In 1874 Turgenev had completed his series of sketches, most of which had been written long before and published as *The Annals of a Sportsman*. He had intended to dedicate these *Reliques Vivantes* to George Sand: "I had meant to dedicate the little story to you in this year, but Viardot, whom I consulted about it, advised me to wait till I had written something less insignificant and less unworthy of the great name with which I wanted to adorn it." In actual fact, no one in the world appreciated the power and charm of *The Annals of a Sportsman* more than George Sand who wrote of the book in *Le Temps*, October 1872: "What a master's hand the painting shows! How well one sees, and hears and knows those northern peasants who were still serfs at the time you write of them, and those small squires and nobles, a few moments conversation with whom was sufficient to enable you to draw a picture of them, palpitating with life and colour." This impression was given in the course of her dedication of *Pierre Bonnin* to Turgenev who had become her intimate friend since the war. But before the war Turgenev had appreciated George Sand to whom Flaubert wrote in 1862 after sitting next to Turgenev at one of their dinners: "That man has such an exquisite power of producing impressions, even in conversation, that he has shown me George Sand leaning over a balcony in Madame Viardot's château at Rosay." Writing to her again four years later, Flaubert said: "Apart from you and Turgenev, I do not know a human being with whom I can talk over things which I have really at heart."

With the exception of the Viardots, Flaubert and George Sand were undoubtedly Turgenev's closest friends in France. The Russian who found himself hailed as "*le celébrè Musset russe*" and again as "*le géant des steppes finnoises*", was on terms of varying shades of intimacy with the most distinguished writers in Paris. Zola was particularly attached to him and, one may add, grateful to him. In the opinion of Maupassant, the Russian was an even greater writer than Flaubert. The Goncourts' Journal repeatedly bears witness to the general appreciation of Turgenev. But undoubtedly, apart altogether from that malicious posthumous scandal in regard to Turgenev's inner attitude towards his French friends, the Russian "fitted in" with Flaubert, in a sense that he never "fitted in" perhaps with any of the others.

As an artist he experienced no little of Flaubert's throes in the work of creation, though with him it was not a torment for the sake of the *mot juste*. When writing a book, the Russian would shut himself up in his room and walk up and down groaning "like a lion in a cage." When this stage had passed he would then sit down and write as though with the facility of subconsciousness. Then everything, the physical scald of memories, the salt of old sorrows came to him with the excruciating vividness of hyperesthesia. If this were lacking, if his work became the result of mere will power, it was unstamped by his individual genius. "I must describe her," he writes of one of these images that were as near to him as Balzac's creations were to Balzac, "in her open coffin, when her parents come to kiss her, according to custom. . . . I have taken part in farewells of this kind. There is my day spoilt!" But, when some friend urged that if these tragic endings made him actually ill, it would be better to change them, the novelist answered: "It ends badly, because I wish to unburden myself of a personal memory."

To Flaubert he could reveal every side of his nature, as an artist and as a man, but not even the intimacy of those Magny dinners could make this Slav really at home with the other guests. Their realism was not as his. These ravagers of mystery were inevitably antipathetic to one whose innermost secret was not the flame of passion, but the "*couleur toute particulière*" of love. His revolt was involuntary as of one who refuses to forsake his own inner dream of elusive beauty for the sake of verbal logic. But, at Croisset and at Nohant he was always at home, for both Flaubert and George Sand respected that pleading of his for the *brouillard slave* as a necessity to the Russian. For Russians, Turgenev urged, this mist meant preservation. In a snowstorm one should not think of the cold, for if one thinks of it one will die. "Very well," Turgenev reasoned, "thanks to that mist of which I was just speaking, the Slav in the *chasse-neige* does not think of the cold, and with me in the same way the idea of death effaces itself and soon glides away." Perhaps it was in search of this merciful *brouillard slave* that he so frequently retreated from the boulevards to the Russian plains. But just as in Paris he was perpetually haunted by a vague nostalgia, so in his own country he would feel the want of the stimulus supplied by his foreign friends. In the Goncourts' Journal a tribute is paid to his "*savoir immense et cosmopolite*"; he had translated much of Goethe and Swinburne as well as his own Pushkin. But in reality he remained in the depths of his being a Russian of the Russians like all the other realists of his country. On Sunday, March 5th, 1876, he is quoted in the Journal as expressing once and for all the gulf between the Russian way of thinking and the formulæ of Western thought:

"*Je n'ai jamais si bien vu qu'hier, combien les races sont différentes, ça m'a fort rêvé toute la nuit. Nous sommes cependant, n'est-ce pas tous des gens du même métier, des gens de plume? Eh bien hier, dans* Madame Caverlet *quand le jeune homme a dit à l'amant de sa mère qui allait embrasser sa sœur: 'Je vous défends d'embrasser cette jeune fille,' eh bien, j'ai éprouvé un moment de répulsion, et il y aurait eu cinq cents Russes dans la salle, qu'ils auraient éprouvé le même sentiment . . . et Flaubert, et les gens qui étaient dans la loge, ne l'ont pas éprouvé ce moment de répulsion. . . . J'ai beaucoup réfléchi dans la nuit. . . . Oui, vous êtes bien des latins, il y a chez vous du romain et de sa religion de droit, en un mot vous êtes des hommes de la loi. . . . Nous, nous ne sommes pas ainsi. . . . Comment dire cela? . . . Voyons, supposez chez nous un rond, autour duquel sont tous les vieux Russes, puis derrière, pêle-mêle, les jeunes Russes. Eh bien, les vieux Russes disent oui ou non—auxquels acquiescent ceux qui sont derrière. Alors, figurez-vous que devant ce 'oui ou non' la loi n'est plus, n'existe plus, car la loi chez les Russes ne se cristallise pas comme chez vous. Un exemple, nous sommes voleurs en Russie, et cependant qu'un homme ait commis vingt vols qu'il avoue, mais qu'il soit constaté qu'il y ait eu besoin, qu'il ait faim, il est acquitté.* . . . *Oui, vous êtes des hommes de la loi, de l'honneur, nous tout autocratisés que nous soyons nous sommes des hommes, et comme il cherche son mot, je lui jette 'de l'humanité'. 'Oui, c'est cela' reprend-il, 'nous nous sommes des hommes moins conventionennels, nous sommes des hommes de l'humanité'.''* That is Ivan Turgenev, the Slav guest of Europe, explaining the fluidity of his race which is irreducible to any formula, whether of accepted or rejected experience. It is a message at once complex and simple and this brief monologue at a Parisian dinner party explains the peculiar position of Turgenev among the writers of his own country.

Turgenev understood, none better, both the breadth of mind and the disconcerting naïveté of his fellow countrymen, their emancipation on the one hand and their limitation on the other. Now this synthesis of two apparently contradictory attributes was so inherent in such writers as Tolstoy and Dostoevsky that they were hardly conscious of its existence. Turgenev alone could view the Russians as a Russian and at the same time as a cosmopolitan who could detach himself from his native standpoint. He was able to analyse, as from the outside, what the other two interpreted from the inside. But he shared whole-heartedly the national preference for the Slavonic mist and, like them, he shrank from the generalities of Western crystallization.

The Russian attitude towards truth is instinctively towards her naked figure, while for Western nations she must be always decorously draped, or pruriently undressed. Russian realism of the last century approached her with neither prudery nor pruriency. She was from first to last, its goddess from which the Russian people had too long been severed. These Russian realists were never dumbfounded by the old shibboleths repeated only under compulsion. Far from aiming at compromises, they were unconscious of them in their art; they were temperamentally incapable of dishonesty of intention as well as of that stupidity of intention which underlies so much of the sophisticated art of the West. The Russian realists, above all, were impervious to glamour; they failed to react to the *motif* of prestige whereas in the English fiction of the nineteenth century, as in English life itself, prestige was the very mainspring of action. It was unnecessary to woo the Russian realists to the side of losing causes. They were instinctively with Antigone rather than with Creon and were deaf to Ismene pleading for the smaller truth of safety as opposed to the larger truth of danger. It has been an old reproach against the Russians that they are without principles; of all Russian writers, Turgenev alone realized the justice of the reproach and its futility. He saw his compatriots as too merciful and at the same time too quick to accept any hall-mark of received experience thrust upon them from outside. He understood that revolt with apparent levity against the "everydayness" of dictated conduct. In his day, as now, the Russian mind with its volatile precocity detached itself from what had at no time been accepted with the finality of the West. Then, as now, what appears to Western nations as a dangerous innovation often struck the Russian as merely commonplace.

The explanation of this seeming mental laxity lies in the roots of history. Russian imperialism never accomplished for the Russians what English imperialism has not wholly failed in accomplishing for the English. The inhabitants of this country have been in their own opinion so long part and parcel of the State that the triumphs of the State are their own personal triumphs. In Russia it had been quite otherwise. There the State had not evolved unconsciously from the Russian people but, on the contrary had sought, as an entity separate and detached, to harness the Russians to itself. An Englishman thinks like the State, or, as he would put it "like an Englishman." Under the old régime in Russia, there were no historic reasons for a Russian to think like the State. Fettered in one sense when compared with people of Western nations, the Russians in another sense remained singularly free. Precisely as their national life had never been crystallized by the Tartar invasion, nor by the fetters of an imperialism that was never theirs, so their individual lives were never crystallized by the accepted principles of orthodox civilization.

Now what is peculiarly interesting in the Russia of to-day, in view of Turgenev's analysis of Slav fluidity, is the fact that Russians are self-consciously trying to become *crystallized*. Rigid principles of subversive ethics have been substituted for an unforced humanity. A son, for instance, has quite recently been officially complimented on the betrayal of his father. Repeatedly, the modern Bolshevik novel echoes and amplifies this repellent *motif*. But how far, if at all, has the great mass of the Russian people really assimilated the iron framework of thought, so abruptly thrust upon them? It will be found that Turgenev, more clearly than any other writer of his time, foresaw the real reactions of the Russian peasant to-day as though he were writing under Stalin instead of under Alexander II.

Like Gogol before him, he was a Russian of Russia, but he was penetrated by the sophistication of the West. And, because of the duality of his point of view this enigmatic and ironical observer was able to fling upon his canvasses picture after picture of Russian life racy of the soil, torn from the very heart of the steppe, and yet universal in the Western sense, as was the work of none of his rivals.

CHAPTER XIV

VIRGIN SOIL

FLAUBERT found himself in serious difficulties in 1876, and in one of his letters to his old friend Turgenev, remarks with characteristic sympathy: "Your friends are going to close round you and keep you warm." Only too soon afterwards the author of *Salambo* was cut to the heart by the loss of George Sand. Writing from Spaskoë, "my Patmos," as he calls it in this letter, Turgenev expresses regret for not having sent a telegram of condolence in the name of the Russian public.

"There was no public," he continues, "upon which Madame Sand had more influence than the Russian public, and of course I ought to have said so! Moreover, I had the right to say it—but there! Poor dear Madame Sand! She was very fond of us both—of you especially, as was natural. What a heart of gold she had! What an entire absence there was in her of anything small or mean or false. What a good fellow she was, and what a delightful woman! And now all that she was is buried in that horrible, dull, speechless, insatiable pit which is unconscious even of what it has swallowed up. Ah, well! there's nothing to be done but to live on and try to keep our heads above water."

A few days afterwards he returns to the same subject in another letter to Flaubert: "Yes, I remember little Aurore's eyes; they are astonishing in their depth and goodness and you are quite right in thinking them like her grandmother's; they're almost too good for a child's eyes." He goes on to speak of an article on the dead writer contributed to the *Revue Russe*, by Zola: "The article is very finely written, but a little harsh, they say. Zola could not form a complete judgment of Madame Sand: there was too great a gulf between them." In reality there was a gulf between the Russian novelist and Zola of one of whose works

Turgenev exclaimed spontaneously: "This is not the way."

Once more in the throes of composition, Turgenev alludes to *Virgin Soil* as "my abominable old novel." Some four months later, while he is correcting the proofs, he finds the book "flat and insignificant" in the renewed atmosphere of the rue de Douai. In the December of the same year he is having his usual troubles with "my snake of a publisher." By the end of the next month the first part of *Virgin Soil* had already appeared with a result that might easily have been foreseen by its author. "The first part of my novel," he tells Flaubert, "which has appeared in Russia seems to have pleased my friends very much, and the public very little. The newspapers say I am used up, and worry me to death about my own past work (as they did you about *Madame Bovary*)." He passes on lightly enough to other things, to a meeting with Flaubert's niece Madame Commanville, to Zola's *Assommoir* and to the fact that Maupassant is becoming bald. "He came to see me," he continues, "I gather it's owing to trouble, from what he says. He is still a dear fellow, but exceedingly ugly just at present."

Even to Flaubert, Turgenev would not confess that the reception given to *Virgin Soil* by the Russian critics really hurt him. When Pavlovsky reminded him that he always allowed long intervals to elapse between his works Turgenev answered: "You are right. *Virgin Soil* cost me a great deal of energy. Everybody insults me now. They say that I don't know what I am writing about. It is false. I have studied the subject of *Virgin Soil* to its depths. And, in spite of all the critics, I persist, now as always, in my opinions on the policy to be pursued against the Government." Pavlovsky listened without being convinced. "That was his *dada*," he comments airily. "His conviction that he thoroughly understood our youth was unshakable and our critics could not make him retract." One of these critics, in reference to certain articles on *Virgin Soil* published abroad, observed almost in the manner of one of Turgenev's apostles of liberty:

"Foreigners can devote articles to it; as for us, we've no wish even to spit on it." "What stinginess! Good God!" retorted Turgenev, who had so often lashed that response of Young Russia to all human aspirations—"*crachez la-dessus.*"

But "*crachez la-dessus*" was a childish answer to *Virgin Soil*, which was no hurried, haphazard footnote to the thesis of freedom. Turgenev had weighed well both the realities and the unrealities of the thesis since the publication of *Smoke* had produced the expected outburst of invective. In this book, as in *Fathers and Sons*, a new type of Russian is presented, but whereas Young Russia condescended to imitate Bazarov they hailed Solomin, the factory manager, as "a monster of the deep." Yet Turgenev had, in his own fashion, prepared the way for Solomin. In *The Annals of a Sportsman* he had drawn a series of pictures of the Russians as they actually were in the middle of the nineteenth century. In *Rudin* and *Liza* he had presented the types of mind that were being brought to bear upon the inchoate mass which, without their assistance and co-operation, was dumb and powerless. In *On the Eve*, he had sounded at last the note of heroic expectancy. In *Fathers and Sons* he had presented the type for whom Russians were waiting and of whom Russia had need. *Smoke* followed in protest against those who pushed themselves forward when Russia had no need of them. And now finally came *Virgin Soil* which, though on the surface it seems to reproduce the old negation of pessimism, none the less contains the hint of a reasoned escape. Not only does it contain this hint, but it also points the way; for, though Solomin is an infinitely less heroic figure than Bazarov, Turgenev realized him as the kind of man who would survive until the moment came for reaping the long frustrated harvest from the "virgin soil" of anonymous lives.

Nezhdanov, the illegitimate son of a Russian noble, is a typical Turgenevian hero, a Russian Hamlet who is powerless to cope with the brutality of actuality. Ignorant of the people as he is, this theoretical revolutionary accepts an engagement as a tutor in the country, where his employer, the Russian liberal, Sipyagin, preserves an old-fashioned sympathy for the knout. At his house Nezhdanov meets a young girl, a poor relation who is passionately eager to leave this comfortable, well-ordered home to accomplish something definite for the people. Nezhdanov becomes her ideal just as Rudin became Natalya's; the result is almost as hopeless in the one case as in the other.

For instinctively, the young student realizes that Marianna believes in him too much, that he will never be able to realize in action her dreams of revolt, that the task is beyond his strength and that their love is already petrified at its very source by the anticipation of failure. But, as there are no external circumstances to separate them, as there had been in the case of Rudin and Natalya, Nezhdanov attempts the impossible. He runs away with Marianna and they conceal themselves in a factory, the manager of which is a certain Solomin who has lived for many years in England and has acquired the practical qualities associated with the Anglo-Saxon race.

And now at last, Nezhdanov is brought into direct contact with the Russian peasant. Disguised as a pedlar, the fastidious dreamer distributes leaflets which the moujiks reject as a rule, with jeers. More than this, however, is necessary; the revolutionary authorities are growing impatient. The poet must show himself a leader of men. Nezhdanov starts out in his hideous disguise to prove himself a real leader of the moujiks. He shouts revolutionary sentiments; the peasants merely stare at him drowsily as he lumbers past them in his cart. At last, he catches sight of a group in front of an open barn and jumping down from his cart he approaches them, shouting at the top of his voice: "Freedom! forward! shoulder to shoulder!" and other expressions of energy equally meaningless. The moujiks once more stared and he drives on to the next village, where he is dragged into a tavern by a gigantic peasant. Now he endeavours to become one of the people in deadly earnest and at first vodka is a real bond between them and him. It goes to his head; words rage from his lips as he feels himself at last an apostle of liberty who has penetrated to the very core of the people. But, in the end the peasants become irritated by this abnormal verbosity, handle him roughly and shout at him derisively as he staggers to his cart to drive back to Marianna, a conqueror at last.

But when full consciousness returned to him the glamour had passed into the stale fumes of vodka. Self-deception was no longer possible. He had read the finality of his failure in the brutalized stare of the peasants' eyes. He had meant to come to them as a Slav Mirabeau and they had received him as a drunken clown. He saw himself now in his true relations with the Russian people. The last film of illusion had been torn from him. He knew that he and such as he were as so many flies to be flicked aside by the contented monster who accepted their sacrifice as a mere irritation. The isolated group of dreamers had read only their own aspirations into the Russian people, only their own revolt. It was all a mistake. From the beginning it had been a mistake, a mistake which had stamped upon many a noble life a martyrdom devoid of result and only too often devoid of conviction.

Marianna believed still in the movement; but it was impossible for her to believe any longer in her hero. It was for her to survive and perhaps eventually to succeed where he and such as he had failed and would always fail. It was for Solomin, who understood the practical, to continue in an indirect and cautious fashion the work over which the young student had so hideously blundered. But Nezhdanov could not even pretend to believe now. His personal equation was already solved; for him the masquerade was over. Nezhdanov thrust something into his pocket, went out of doors and stood meditatively under an old apple tree. Except for the muffled pulsation of the factory, all around him was still, like the life of the Russian people: "Nezhdanov gazed up through the crooked branches of the tree under which he was standing at the grey, cloudy sky looking down upon him so unfeelingly. He yawned and lay down. 'There's nothing else to be done. I can't go back to St Petersburg, to prison,' he thought. A kind of pleasant heaviness spread all over his body. . . . He threw away his cap, took up the revolver and pulled the trigger."

But in this, the last of Turgenev's national novels, Nezhdanov the dreamer is not the only victim of the irresponsive silence of the steppes. Markelov, the taciturn soldier type, has been equally deceived. He, too, had gone to the peasants with a message of liberty upon his lips. He, at least had been definite and articulate in his incitation to revolution, with the result that the moujiks seized him, bound him and handed him over to the Governor to be thrown into prison. Poor Markelov had understood the Russian peasant as little as Nezhdanov himself. It is the dwarf Paklin, the intelligent chorus of the book, who really understands. And through his lips Turgenev utters an analysis of the Russian people, that is by no means out of date to-day: "The Russian peasant can never be induced to revolt except by taking advantage of that devotion of his to some high authority, some tzar. Some sort of legend must be invented—you remember Dmitrius the pretender—some sort of royal sign must be shown him, branded on the breast." The authorities in Russia to-day well understood the truth of this when they gave that legendary significance to Lenin's tomb, when no legendary figure was forthcoming to take the place of him who was for the great mass of the peasants a new sort of tzar.

In the nineteenth century the background of Russia cast a long, long shadow. Clever young people cannot deflect the gnarled roots of history. Social upheaval itself obeys the laws of national temperament. Revolution during the Smuta did not resemble revolutions in the West. The servants had looked then for the hereditary Master. Late in the nineteenth century, given the same conditions, the point of view would have been instinctively the same. For, in spite of the emancipation of the serfs time had practically stood still for the moujiks in their relations with the State. They were still faithful to those medieval traditions of the "born Tsar," the "Little Father" who could do no wrong. If he were deposed they would see to it, as their ancestors during the Smuta had seen to it, that another "born" Master should take his place. The miracle, indeed, could be accomplished neither by courage, nor even by genius, but only by craft.

Solomin was precisely the type who might at the right moment attempt it on the right lines. Paklin realized the value of the factory manager when he sums up the confusion of Russian educated opinion for the benefit of Nezhdanov's revolutionary comrade: "It's of no consequence that Russia is now full of all sorts of queer people, fanatics, officials, generals, plain and decorated, epicureans, imitators, all manner of cranks. I once knew a lady, a certain Havrona Prishtekov, who, one fine day, suddenly turned a legitimist and assured everybody that when she died they had only to open her body and the name of Henry V would be found engraven on her heart! All these people do not count, my dear lady; our true salvation lies with the Solomins, the dull, plain, but wise Solomins! Remember that I say this to you in the winter of 1870, when Germany is preparing to crush France. . . ."

Solomin is at his best when inspecting the factory that has been recently started by Nezhdanov's employer, Sipyagin. His point of view, wholly unawed and quietly expressed, cuts through the padding of social politeness just as easily as the more overwhelming roughness of Bazarov broke through the reserve of the old school of Russian gentlemen. Bluntly, he told Sipyagin that the aristocracy was unsuited to industrial enterprises. Asked what he meant by this, he replied with a calmness of which Bazarov was incapable: "I only meant that the gentry are not used to that kind of business. A knowledge of commerce is needed for that; everything has to be put on a different footing, you want technical training for it. The gentry don't understand this. We see them starting woollen, cotton and other factories all over the place, but they nearly always fall into the hands of the merchants in the end. It's a pity because the merchants are even worse sweaters. But it can't be helped, I suppose." One of Sipyagin's land-owning neighbours protested against the insinuation that matters of finance were above the heads of Russian nobles. Solomin's answer stabs at a system which would have horrified the elder generation of *Fathers and Sons*, almost as much as the younger: "Oh, no! On the other hand, the nobility are masters at it. For getting concessions for railways, founding banks, exempting themselves from some tax, or anything like that, there is no one to beat them! They make huge fortunes, I hinted at that just now, but it seemed to offend you. I had regular industrial enterprises in my mind when I spoke; I say *regular*, because founding private public-houses, petty little grocers' shops, or lending peasants corn or money at a hundred or a hundred and fifty per cent, as many landed gentry are doing now, I cannot consider as genuine financial enterprises."

Sipyagin observed that this comment applied to the nobles of the past, rather than to those of the present. "Why shouldn't they be able," he urged, "to understand what is understood by a simple illiterate merchant? They are not suffering from a lack of education and one might even claim without any exaggeration, that they are, in a certain sense, the representatives of enlightenment and progress." The manager was not in the least impressed. "The nobility cannot manage these things," he maintained, and he went on to give his reasons, which lay in the simple fact that Russian landowners had become bureaucrats: "I think that every bureaucrat is an outsider and was always such. The nobility have now become 'outsiders'." Such is the verdict of Solomin, the Russian who was yet to be. He was not merely inspecting a new factory; he was inspecting, with the irony of Gogol's famous comedy in his heart, the landed gentry of Russia many years after the Emancipation of the serfs.

Without enthusiasm, Solomin is equally without cynicism. People like himself are, he believes, necessary to Russia and they should keep themselves alive if only for the sake of their country. Turgenev defended the cunning of this new type as the only quality by which a revolutionary could avoid Siberia, while waiting for the moment to strike. As usual in his work it is in the heroine in whom the fire of the race, the idealism, the limitless capacity for self-dedication, find expression. His political pessimism had deepened during the last twenty-two years, but Marianna is still the sister of Natalya and Liza, while waiting to emulate Elena.

But in the man Solomin, Turgenev read unerringly the future of Russia. In the twentieth century people like Solomin are still necessary to Russia who withers without them. The dreamers have been swept ruthlessly to the "little wall" but the Solomins must persist if any five year—ten year—twenty year plan is to have any meaning whatsoever. Again Turgenev was prophetic in reading the reactions of the peasants. To-day the great stumbling block to the bed of Procustes of the Russian oligarchy is precisely the peasant. The moujik accepted Bolshevism eagerly because it meant the land for himself, but he resists stubbornly and will continue to resist being turned into a unit of agrarian collectivism. The kulaks had been harried into exile in hosts, but even before the War thousands were restored to the rights of citizenship. Why? Simply because there is no power in Bolshevik Russia strong enough to cope with the *vis inertiae* of the Russian peasant. Though the powers that be may dragoon and manipulate the proletariat, now letting out the rope and now drawing it in, they have had to come hat in hand to the kulak, that is to say, to the most obvious obstacle of all their Marxist dreams. Turgenev in *Virgin Soil* was a more subtle prophet than Maxim Gorky was in *The Mother*.

Young Russia, however, cared little for either his new hero or his old heroine, his prophecies or his despairs; like his gout they continued to torment him, but the gout was the more important enemy. "I have had a relapse since I last wrote," he informs Flaubert, at the end of this year. "I am in no pain, but I begin to wonder how people use their legs, folk who walk with crutches even seem to me giants and heroes. I believe I am in this state, so as to feel in harmony with poor France, who, like myself, can move neither hand nor foot."

The year 1878 found him in England as well as Russia, but he could not rid himself of this sustained mood of ironic depression. In the winter, Flaubert was still in difficulties; Maupassant had aged; Goncourt had become thin. Turgenev was feeling every hour of his sixty years. "It's the beginning of the end of life," he assured Flaubert. "A Spanish proverb says, 'The tail is the hardest part of all to skin,' and yet it is the part which promises the least pleasure and the least profit. Life becomes a purely personal matter, only occupied in defending itself from death. And this intensifying of the personal note drains life of all interest, even for the individual concerned."

The sense of age becomes more and more insistent in the correspondence: Turgenev's inner circle, except Zola, who looked "fat and jolly" were all feeling it. "Our poor dinners," he notes in another letter to Flaubert early in 1879, "are collapsing dreadfully. I have received a letter from Daudet, who is suffering greatly from rheumatism in his right arm." That same month, Turgenev lost his brother Nicholas, whose youth had experienced the crushing tyranny of his mother, but who was in possession of some two hundred thousand pounds when he died. Turgenev intended to leave for Russia at once, but postponed the journey.

So for the present his relations with French friends continued on the same cordial footing. The Russian novelist had noticed Flaubert's life-long habit of avoiding any form of physical activity. "It exasperated him," notes Maupassant, "to see people walking or moving about him, and he declared in his mordant, sonorous, always rather theatrical voice, that it was not philosophic. 'One can only write and think seated,' he said." Turgenev, however, tried to affect a change in his old friend: "You are not fond of walking, but you must force yourself to do it. I was once in prison (in solitary confinement) for more than a month. My room was a small one and the heat was intense. Twice a day I carried 104 cards (two packs) one by one from one end of the room to the other. That made 208 turns, equal to 416 in the day; each turn took eight steps, which made it come to more than 3,300, nearly two kilometers! If by chance I missed my walk, I had all the blood in my body concentrated in my head that day."

But though Turgenev, either from the rue de Douai, or from his villa at Bougival, might endeavour to cheer up his old friend, his own serenity was now only a mask of stoicism. His daughter had been married for years and he was free from all anxiety about her; his relations with the Viardots remained always unchanged; his Parisian friendships had stood the test of time, and it was impossible for him to foresee that mischief-making episode which was to make him appear in the eyes of posterity an ungrateful guest to the Parisians who had taken him to their hearts. In a sense all was well with him in Paris, but more and more, as the years encroached, the tranquillity of Spaskoë became a physical necessity to him.

For there he could relive those early boyish impressions when from the garden he had caught the wonder and regret of youth and love. Everything in that garden which contained his youth, which lived in *Spring Torrents*, in *Pounin and Babourin*, which insinuates its pervading freshness through every work ever written by Ivan Turgenev. But as the years passed Spaskoë itself became depressing. The property appeared more and more dilapidated at each visit. Still, Turgenev would insist on his Russian friends conforming to Western habits of living. He had remained himself, however, a genuine Slav in his forgetfulness of dates and a guest's arrival always came to him as an agreeable surprise.

And just as in Paris he would speak constantly of Russia, of Russian literature, of Russian women, of the untranslatable Slavonic spirit, so at Spaskoë, on the contrary, he was inclined to dwell on the peculiarities of foreign nations. His listeners were slightly shocked by what they took for the corruption of French morals, but Turgenev would pass

on to the racial differences between the compatriots of
Goethe and the compatriots of Hugo, after which he would
comment on the gulf which separates the English from every
other nation in Europe, including Russia herself. The
English seemed to him a nation of originals. He had visited
many of their celebrities and had approached Carlyle with
the same respectful irony that he had preserved in the
presence of Victor Hugo. "I was at Carlyle's house," he
tells his Russian friends. "I never saw anyone with whose
originality I was more struck. According to him the greatest
quality in man was blind obedience. And he assured me
that every nation that obeys its sovereign blindly is happier
than free England with her constitution. When I asked him
who was the greatest English poet, he mentioned a mediocrity at the end of the eighteenth century. As for Byron,
he considered him beneath criticism. Then, he assured me
that Dickens had no weight with the English, and that he
was esteemed only abroad. In a word, he retailed to me a
great many stupidities of the same kind." On another
occasion, Turgenev happened to tell Carlyle that he
suffered from motes in the eyes and that once when he was
out shooting he had raised his gun to fire at a hare, but had
been seized by the suspicion that what he took for a hare
was perhaps only a black spot: "Carlyle listened to me
attentively, remained for a moment thoughtful, and then
burst into a noisy and inextinguishable laugh. I could not
understand what had put him into such a good humour;
I saw nothing comic in the incident that I had just related.
'Ha! ha! ha!' he exclaimed at last, still bursting with
laughter: 'to fire at one's own mote in the eyes—Ha! ha!
ha! To fire at a spot. Ha! ha! ha!' Then I understood the
cause of the hilarity; a Frenchman, or a Russian would
have found nothing laughable in my story."

And Turgenev sums up mildly his impressions of *l'humour
britannique:* "For the same reason an actor who makes
grimaces, and who in France would be hissed off the stage
to the accompaniment of baked apples, will amuse the
English public and make it laugh." Even the sophisticated

author of *Vanity Fair* put the Russian out of countenance by greeting with roars of laughter, a fragment from Pushkin.

Thackeray's daughter, Lady Ritchie, has included in her charming *Blackstick Papers* some reminiscences of Turgenev whom she saw for the first time in the drawing-room in Onslow Square when she was a child. Years afterwards she was struck by a certain likeness between the Russian novelist and her father: "It was one of those moments which count in life. Pauline Viardot's singing stirred up unknown perceptions and feelings in us all, her beautiful eyes were alight, she almost whispered the last words. Just then my glance fell upon Tourguenieff leaning against the door-post at the far end of the room, and as I looked I was struck, being short-sighted, by a certain resemblance to my father, which I tried to realize to myself. He was very tall, his hair was grey and abundant, his attitude was quiet and reposeful; I looked again and again, while I pictured to myself the likeness." When the music had finished Turgenev approached Thackeray's daughter and promised to call on her and her sister the following day. He failed, however, to put in an appearance and when Miss Thackeray met him two days later at the house of a mutual friend, he came straight up to her at once and made this characteristic apology: "I was so sorry that I could not come to see you, so very sorry, but I was prevented. Look at my thumbs! See how small they are, people with such little thumbs can never do what they intend to do, they always let themselves be prevented."

Here is another delightful glimpse of the Russian novelist in London. "An old friend," writes Lady Ritchie, "who did not herself care for conventions, told me that she went one day with her daughter to call upon Madame Viardot, to take leave of her just before she returned to Paris, after that enforced residence in England in the winter of 1871. It was in the Wimpole Street region, and as they were reaching the door they saw a figure advancing, half-hidden by countless white frills rising one above the other. It was Tourguénieff carrying a clothes'-basket full of freshly-ironed dresses straight from some foreign laundry. The house was in confusion, he explained, the frocks were absolutely needed by the ladies, and as no one else could go, he himself had been to fetch them home;—so much for a born gentleman's simplicity and natural dignity."

Writing to Madame Commanville, from Bougival in August 1879, Turgenev thanks her for congratulating him on being made an "Officer of Public Instruction," but confesses that he doesn't quite understand the nature of such an appointment. "It appears," he continues, "that it carries with it the right to wear a purple ribbon—purple, not red. I shall fasten it on to my Oxford Doctor's gown, which is a very bright red; the colours will go perfectly together." Àpropos of this radiant hood, Lady Ritchie cites an interesting account of the impression produced by Turgenev when he received his honorary degree at Oxford: "He was entertained on the eve of the ceremony at Pembroke College; the well-known Master of the College being at that time Vice-Chancellor of the University, and it is from his hostess on that occasion, who did so much to make Oxford agreeable to the visitors of those days, that I have received a vivid picture of Tourguénieff. The presence of the tall Russian amongst the University guests, his whole personality, made a great and sudden impression even on those to whom he was but a name. He spoke readily and with great cordiality; his English was exceedingly good, and the amenity of the foreign guest was felt by all. The company that was assembled at the Vice-Chancellor's, the names of those who were to receive their degrees on the following day, and all the circumstances of that commemoration have passed away from Mrs Evans's recollection. Only Tourguénieff remains, his look of power, and especially his wonderful eyes, which flashed as he spoke; these stay and cannot fade from the memory of anyone who conversed with him."

The charm of Turgenev indeed made itself felt in England as in France, and he was welcomed from time to time by his London friends just as heartily as by the Parisians. Here in Spaskoë, "under the water," he would talk them

all over with his compatriots. But he was never too pre-
occupied with the gossip of capitals to be unmindful of the
interests of the moujik. Unfortunately, the improvements
on his estate hung fire for years, just as in the novels. The
infirmary, the hospital and the school grew very slowly.
Close to his village, in spite of all his precautions, a tavern
was established on the property of a neighbouring prince.
Turgenev himself, in spite of his desire to suppress drunkenness, would give fêtes in which among the men at least,
drunkenness was the chief entertainment exactly as in the
days of Madame Turgenev. On such occasions ribbons and
fal-lals would be given to the women, while the children
would be appeased by images and sweetmeats. Only
buckets of vodka, however, appealed to the male population
of Spaskoë. After all, it was still the Old Russia, in spite of
what *The Annals of a Sportsman* had accomplished for the
Russians. On each visit the old kindly relations between
Turgenev and his dependants would renew themselves
automatically, and on fête days the peasants would swarm
into their master's garden, but with no intention of hanging
him. In the evening the women would sing their sombre
songs in front of the terrace, while their husbands and
brothers solaced themselves in the background with bounti-
ful supplies of vodka.

"You wish, then, to learn to read?" one of the guests
once asked a group of little girls. "We? we? Not at all.
God preserves us from it," came the unhesitating reply of
the youth of this Russia, which was still so old. Towards
eleven o'clock the guests on these occasions would wander
back to the village, the men rather uncertainly, but having
been very polite in their thanks for a festivity, marred only
by the mildness of the vodka. Then, on the terrace with his
house party, Turgenev would discuss, quite in the manner
of the heroes of his novels, the progress of the Russian
people since the Emancipation.

These gala evenings were always towards the end of his
visit when autumn was at hand and he was beginning to
think of the boulevards and of that "European nest" in the

rue de Douai. His gout was always at its worst at this time of year, and he would begin to examine his own life with the same ruthless analysis that he applied to the progress of the moujiks. He was only too sensitive to something sombre and menacing in the Russian autumn; his efforts on behalf of the peasants would seem to him as hopeless and quixotic as those of any one of his Hamlets of the steppe. The very disillusion of his art would fasten upon his life; it would seem to him that he and his friends were merely indulging in Russian talks, the talks of Rudin and all the rest of them, the talks that fade away like puffs of smoke.

In such moments his art and his life would seem to merge in that ultimate pessimism which, in 1877, he expressed in a letter to Polonsky: "I am again in front of a table, and in my soul there is a darkness blacker than night. The day passes like an instant, empty, aimless, colourless. There is just time to cast a glance round, and then one must take to one's bed again. One has no more right to life, no more desire to live. . . . You speak of rays of glory and of enchanting sound. . . . Oh, my friend, we are the vibrations of a vase, broken long ago." As the years stole on, his moods would become blacker and blacker and, at the end of these Russian visits, he would hurry back to the sanctuary of his "European nest" to warm himself in the sympathy of the Viardots and to renew the intellectual stimulus of the Magny dinners.

CHAPTER XV

AT YASNAYA POLYANA

TURGENEV had long been treated coldly, both in Petersburg and Moscow, but when, in 1879, he visited the older capital for the inauguration of the statue of Pushkin he received, to his astonishment, a series of ovations which were pale, however, in comparison with those received on the same occasion by his rival and enemy, Dostoevsky. Turgenev was wholly devoid of jealousy and so this fact did not trouble him in the least, gratified as he was by his own reception which was sustained every evening when he read aloud from *The Annals of a Sportsman*. Even in the public streets of Moscow, he was greeted with enthusiasm and the same change of attitude towards him was now visible in Petersburg.

He had long been on quite good terms with Count Tolstoy and the Committee had requested him to persuade the author of *War and Peace* to be present at the unveiling of the Pushkin monument. With this object, Turgenev had visited Yasnaya Polyana, but without success. The two great authors went for a walk together to discuss the matter and Countess Tolstoy has given this record of the discussion: "The dinner-bell had sounded. All had assembled, but neither Tourguénieff, nor Leo Nikolayvitch appeared. At last after long waiting, I guessed where to look for them. Not far from the house, in the wood among the old oaks, stood a small hut Leo Nikolayvitch had built for himself in order, in summer, to have solitude for his work and to escape from flies, children and visitors. I ran to that hut, which was built on four pillars, and ascended the steps, and through the open door saw the two writers hotly disputing." Tolstoy's views on the subject of paying honours to artists have been only too clearly stated in *What is Art?*; it is not surprising that even the persuasive Turgenev failed to induce him to take part in such a ceremony. In other respects, the visit was very pleasant and a woodcock shooting expedition was arranged for the occasion. "In the dusk of the spring evening," writes Mr Aylmer Maude, in his biography of Tolstoy, "the Countess stood beside him awaiting the flight of the birds. While he was getting his gun ready, she asked him : 'Why have you not written anything for so long ?' Tourguénieff glanced round, and in his touchingly frank way, with a guilty smile, said : 'Are we out of hearing? Well, I will tell you. . . . Every time I planned anything, I was shaken by the fever of love! Now that is all over : I am old, and can no longer either love or write.'"

Turgenev spoke to Tolstoy also on this loss of his power to be absorbed in love. "I had an affair the other day," he observed, "and, will you believe it? I found it dull!" To this the moralist responded by this disconcerting footnote to Aristotle's conception of virtue : "Ah! if only I were like that!" Turgenev failed to appreciate the spiritual change that had come over the Count. Towards the end of 1880, he wrote to Polonsky : "I am very sorry for Tolstoy . . . however, as the French say, *Chacun à sa manière de tuer ses puces.*" A few months later he reverted to the same topic : "It is an unpardonable sin that Leo Tolstoy has stopped writing—he is a man who could be extraordinarily useful, but what can one do with him? He does not utter a word and worst than that, he has plunged into mysticism. Such an artist, such a first-class talent, we have never had nor now have among us. I, for instance, am considered an artist, but what am I worth compared to him? In contemporary European literature he has no equal."

Tolstoy paid Turgenev a return visit to Spaskoë. Owing to his driver having lost his way in the dark, he did not reach the house until one o'clock in the morning. Neither his host nor Polonsky, who was staying with him, had retired and the poet, hearing the horses outside, went into the hall and saw what seemed to be a peasant in a blouse, and wearing a leather belt, who was in the act of paying the driver. "Is that you, Polonsky?" the Count asked at last, seeing that the poet still failed to recognize him. A long Russian talk followed during which Tolstoy listened to Turgenev's views without showing the slightest resentment. The next day an hour before dinner time Turgenev's cook was discovered drunk. In despair the novelist determined to cook the dinner himself and set off for the kitchen to execute his purpose. "That's not your business," exclaimed one of the servants. . . . "Go away and God be with you!" On the subject of this visit, there is a characteristic note in Tolstoy's Diary: "At Tourgénef's. Kindly Polonsky, quietly occupied with art and literature, not judging others and poor, was tranquil. Tourgénef fears the name of God, but acknowledges Him. He, too, is naïvely tranquil, living in luxury and idleness of life."

A little later, Turgenev paid another visit to Yasnaya Polyana during which, according to the Countess's record, he seems to have been the life of the party: "In the evening my children and nieces got up a quadrille. The children's merriment infected Tourgénef. He danced in the quadrille with my niece and then took off his coat, and sticking his thumbs into his waistcoat, to the children's great delight, began to perform strange figures with his legs. 'That's how they dance the *can-can* in Paris.' He was very merry that evening, praising everything and everybody. Looking at me kindly, he said to Leo Nikolayevitch, 'How well you did, my dear, to choose such a wife!'" Tolstoy's own view of the evening was rather different as this brief entry in his diary shows: "Tourgénef, *can-can:* It is sad. Meeting peasants on the road was joyful."

Tolstoy sent Turgenev a copy of his *Confession*, and having read the book he wrote to Grigorovitch in October 1882: "A few days ago I received, through a very charming Moscow lady, that *Confession* of Leo Tolstoy's which the censor has forbidden. I read it with the greatest interest. It is remarkable for its sincerity, truth and strength of conviction. But it is built on false premises and ultimately leads to the most sombre denial of all human life. . . . This too, is, in its way, a kind of Nihilism. . . . Yet all the same, he is perhaps the most remarkable man in contemporary Russia." The following year the author of *Smoke* was to write from his death-bed that last appeal to the author of *War and Peace* to return to literature: "My friend—great writer of our Russian land—listen to my request! Let me know you have received this scrap of paper, and allow me yet once more cordially to embrace you, your wife and all yours. . . . I can write no more. . . . I am tired." Unfortunately, Tolstoy neglected answering this letter until it was too late, but shortly after Turgenev's death, while he was preparing a paper on his dead rival to be read before the Society of Lovers of Russian Literature, he wrote to his wife: "I am always thinking about Tourgénef. I love him terribly, pity him, and am always reading him. I am living with him all the time: I certainly will either myself read, or will write something about him and give it to be read. . . . I have just read his *Enough*. Read it—it is charming."

Tolstoy became absorbed in this tribute to the great dead writer. In a letter to her sister, dated October 1883, the Countess says: "On 34 October Lyovotchka will give a public lecture about Tourgénef. It already agitates all Moscow and there will be a tremendous crowd in the University Hall. They have reserved four seats of honour for me in the very middle of the first row." Her next letter, however, is in a very different vein: "Dear Tanya—As you have no doubt already seen from the papers and know by rumour, the lecture in memory of Tourgénef has been forbidden from your disgusting Petersburg. It is said that Tolstoy (the Minister) forbade it; and what could one expect from him except tactless and awkward freaks? Just fancy, the lecture was to have been quite innocent and most peaceful. No one thought of letting off any kind of Liberal squibs. . . . Everyone is tremendously surprised. . . . What danger to the Government could there have been? Now, of course people imagine anything. . . . Everyone without exception is angry about it, except Lyovotchka, who is even glad to be excused from appearing in public—

a thing he is so unaccustomed to. He is always writing, but will not be allowed to print it." It is as though the clock had moved back to those days when Turgenev himself was put in prison for having called Gogol a great man. Pleading his cause then with a senator, a lady of the highest nobility was reminded that Turgenev had actually called the author of *Dead Souls*, a great man. "Ah," she exclaimed, "if that is so I have no more to say." Tolstoy, however, had more to say on the subject of Ivan Turgenev. When talking to a friend he gave what may be accepted as his final estimate of Turgenev, as an artist and as a man: "He was to the end of his life an independent, inquiring spirit. . . . He was a genuine, self-reliant artist, never lowering himself consciously to serve the passing demand of the moment. He may have gone astray, but even in his errors he was sincere."

But after the inauguration of the Pushkin Memorial there remained four years of painful life to Ivan Turgenev. A large part of this difficult period was occupied, curiously enough, in carrying out an idea which came to him from this same Tolstoy whom he was persuading to return to literature. Tolstoy had written a fragment in the form of a prose poem, which he had sent to a Russian paper signed in the name of an old servant. The manuscript was declined with thanks as, in the Editor's opinion, its author was "not yet sufficiently expert in expression!" Tolstoy handed on the idea of such a volume of fragments to Turgenev; to this we owe those exquisite *Poems in Prose*, in which the first fresh savour of life seems to blend caressingly with the regret of age, menaced by the ever encroaching grimace of death.

CHAPTER XVI

THE LAST DAYS

In the meantime, Flaubert's financial position had been going from bad to worse. Turgenev was anxious to secure for him the post of Custodian at the Mazarin Library. The post, it seems, had been promised by Gambetta to someone else, but Turgenev enlisted the sympathies of Madame Adam, at whose house the Tribune was a frequent visitor. Madame Adam said what she could in support of Flaubert, but Gambetta is quoted as having replied somewhat impatiently: "Pray do not press the matter any further—it is impossible." His hostess then brought Turgenev up to him; according to rumour the Russian was very coldly received. As a matter of fact, Gambetta remained seated at the time not out of discourtesy, but because Turgenev approached him on the side of his glass eye and was consequently invisible.

Fortunately, the affair was carried through satisfactorily in the end, as this note in the Goncourt Journal, dated June 8th, 1879, shows: "He (Flaubert) tells me that his affair is settled. He is appointed Custodian (ex-officio) at the Mazarin, at a salary of 3,000 francs, which will be raised in a few months' time. He added that he had genuinely suffered through accepting the money, and that, moreover, he had already made arrangements for its repayment to the State some day. His brother who is very rich and dying into the bargain, is to give him an allowance of 3,000 francs; with that and his appointment, and what he makes by his literary work, he'll be almost on his feet again."

But the great French writer was not to remain for any length of time Custodian of the Mazarin Library. Opening a newspaper one day at Spaskoë, Turgenev was horrified by a paragraph stating that his old friend had died at Croisset on May 8, 1880. In a letter of condolence to Madame Commanville he wrote from his heart: "Your uncle's death has been one of the greatest sorrows I have ever experienced in my life, and I cannot get used to the thought that I shall never see him again."

The death of Flaubert, indeed, was a turning point in Turgenev's old age. The Parisian dinners lost all savour for him. The Slavonic mist could no longer conceal the phantom that was becoming the one reality at these gatherings which the Russian had so often charmed by his evocations of the steppes, by his alien yet persuasive genius, by his sympathy and by his very nostalgia. "*Le dîner*," runs a typical note of the Journal, "*commence gaiement, mais voilà que Tourguénief parle d'une constriction du coeur, survenue de nuit, constriction mêlée à une grande tache brune sur le mur en face de son lit, et qui, dans un cauchemar ou il se trouvait moitié éveillé, moitié dormant, était la mort.*"

His health became worse and worse; his doctor called his malady gouty Angina pectoris. "It is the term we use," Charcot observed to Alphonse Daudet, "when we do not know what to say." But, even in the mist of the most lacerating pain, the Russian preserved his instinct for analysing every phase of human experience. "During the operation," he confided to Daudet, "I thought of our dinners, and I searched for words to convey a just impression of steel piercing my flesh as though it were a knife cutting a banana."

In Paris the flavour of life had gone for him and in his own country he was to meet with the last stab of disillusion. He was cordially welcomed in Petersburg in 1881; it seemed as if the old grudges were forgiven and forgotten. He even considered the question of living permanently in Russia and, in spite of his feeble health, working in the cause of freedom shoulder to shoulder with the younger generation at last. But the reaction came only too quickly. The older generation ridiculed him as a "*vieille coquette*" for seeking to please the "*petits jeunes*" of his native land. And when he endeavoured to collect subscriptions in Russia for a monument to Flaubert at Rouen, each generation rejected him as scornfully as when he had presented them with the book which seemed to be casting ridicule on them both. Turgenev on his side was angry, but considered it useless to defend himself in the Russian newspapers. Then a lady wrote to him from Odessa, asking why he troubled himself about a monument to Flaubert while Gogol was still waiting for one, and reminded him at the same time that the Russian people were hungry; Turgenev answered her letter. Flaubert, he maintained, had but little popularity in his own country and no Frenchman would be particularly grateful to him for his trouble. As for the people who exclaim "Our own poor first," he urged that they were precisely those who gave nothing to anybody at all. Seeing that his correspondent had attacked him for his long sojourn in France, he reminded her that in that country he was never subjected to senseless insults: "It would be best, however, to blush for his country and be silent."

But all the time he continued to work and though he was indeed beginning to lose something of his spell in recalling the first ecstasies of passion, with its aftermath of remembered regret, ghosts still came to him and with a new and more mysterious menace in those *Dream Tales and Prose Poems*. Many of them had been written before Tolstoy's suggestion in 1879; but it was certainly that suggestion which induced Turgenev to continue the series and collect them for publication in book form. He had nothing to add to his final political message to Russia, the message of *Virgin Soil*. He had nothing to add to his reading of the two generations in their relations with each other as presented in *Fathers and Sons*. There was left to Turgenev only his personal magic of illusion. He must woe back those dear ghosts of his; he must stifle the haunting recognition of the fact, that though he had charmed others by his interpretation of deep, quiet love he had never since his boyhood experienced it in his own heart. The *frou-frou* of no *mondaine's* skirts, the fluttering of no perfumed handkerchief could absorb him now to the exclusion of that soul-less prowling of death. He has been hurrying in front of it for so long, snatching from its blind gluttony year after year each one of which had seemed to be the last. Sometimes, in spite of the doctors, he has been able to laugh at it for he remains faithful to that Slavonic mist. No, he would not think of the cold lest he should die of it.

His stoical serenity continued to preserve its outer mask, but in a short story entitled *A Desperate Character*, he depicted something of that extravagant revolt against life, which is so conspicuous in Dostoevsky's heroes, while it is occasionally to be found in Tolstoy's. "*La plupart*," writes Monsieur de Vogüé, "*de ces natures peuvent se ramener à un type commun; l'excès d'impulsion, l'otchaianie, cet état de cœur et de l'esprit pour lequel je m' efforce vainement de trouver un équivalent dans notre langue.*" In the analysis of Dostoevsky who best of all understood it, "this is the sensation of a man who, from the summit of a high tower, leans over the yawning abyss and experiences a shudder of pleasure at the idea that he may hurl himself from it headlong. 'Faster, and let us end it!' Sometimes the people who think like this are very peaceable, very ordinary individuals. . . . The man who finds a delight in the horror that he inspires in others. . . . He strains his whole soul in frantic hopelessness, and in his desperation calls out for punishment as a solution, as something that will decide for him."

This *otchaianie*, so familar to us in *Demons* and *The Brothers Karamazov*, finds a much gentler interpretation in this story of Turgenev's written the year after Flaubert's death. Here, it is rather the Russian sense of brotherhood that is really dominant: "This is my company, my army," exclaims the desperate hero, "all beggars, God's people, friends of my heart. Every one of them, thanks to you, has had a glass; and now we are all rejoicing and making merry! . . . Uncle! Do you know it's only with beggars, God's people, that one can live in the world . . . by God it is!" Exactly this sense of brotherhood permeates the whole atmosphere of these prose poems. In *The Beggar*, the mendicant is thankful not for alms, but for a human hand-clasp. Nor is he the only one to experience gratitude, for Turgenev adds, "I felt that I, too, had received a gift from my brother." In

Masha, a peasant sledge driver shows his sorrow in his face:
"'What is it brother?' I asked him; 'Why aren't you cheerful? Have you some trouble?'" Then the driver tells his fare, as brother to brother, the deep hurt of his life. Again, in *On the Sea*, Turgenev describes a passage from Hamburg to London, in which the only passengers were himself and a little monkey: "We are all children, and I was glad that the poor little beast was soothed and nestled so confidingly up to me, as to a brother."

Echoes of youth return to him avidly in that fragment on the line of a song—"How lovely and fresh those roses were" —in which as in the song itself, the ghosts of the might-have-been are recaptured in a moment of breathless happiness. Another such moment came to him in *A Visit*, when he recognizes the "Bird-woman" of his youth: "I know thee, Goddess of Fantasy! Thou didst pay me a random visit by the way; thou hast flown on to the young poets. Oh, Poesy! Youth! Virginal beauty of woman! Thou couldst shine for me, but for a moment in the early dawn of early spring!" Russian scenes, scenes of his early home life, glimpses of forest and steppe, peaceful places lost in the quietude of Russia—these, too, were evoked wistfully under the grimace of his octopus-like pursuer. Repeatedly the *motif* of death ruffles the dream of beauty. Even when he fringes upon the borderland of the occult, his pessimism remains unchanged.

Typical of his whole attitude towards life, now that he is on the verge of death, is that dialogue between the Jungfrau and Finsteraarhorn. Here the Alpine mountains, after cycles of centuries during which the little race of man dwindles and fades, peer out at the world. "Now it is well," comments the Finsteraarhorn, "it is clean everywhere, quite white, wherever you look. . . . Everywhere is our snow, unbroken snow and ice. Everything is frozen. It is well now. It is quiet." In *The Dog*, the obsessing *motif* of death reappears; in *My Opponent*, the ghost of a dead man returns to earth, but refuses to tell his comrade anything whatsoever concerning human destiny. A note of reconciliation through death is sounded in *The Last Meeting*, but in

Love and Hunger, we have once more an attitude of frank irony towards any merciful solution of the all-engulfing mystery: "Love and Hunger—their aim is the same—preservation of life, of one's own life and the life of others—the life of all." In another sombre fragment he utters the hopeless warning "Stop!" to youth as it hurries passionately forward to old age and death.

All his old charm permeates the dream of *A Free Russian Village,* but in *The Labourer and the Man with the White Hand,* bitter memories of the old futility that he had lashed in so many masterpieces, come back to him. An idealist gives his whole life to the cause of liberty and foolishly, uselessly pays to it the last sacrifice. When this has been paid one of the real people exclaims to his comrade: "Don't you suppose we could get a bit of the rope he's hanged with?"

But whether it were an echo from *Spring Torrents* or an echo from *Rudin* that returned to him, the presentiment of death is rarely far away. It was becoming a veritable obsession. One evening at Magny, the younger Goncourt, who was lying as usual on the sofa, declared that he experienced already the sensation of being actually dead "With me," observed Turgenev, "it is rather different. You know how sometimes there is in a room an imperceptible perfume of musk that one cannot get rid of? Very well: there is around me something like the odour of death, of dissolution."

And now that the élan and rapture of youth, the aspirations national and personal of manhood, had all alike receded Turgenev was imperceptibly propelled towards those veiled portals of imagination beyond the frontiers of human reason. He faced the supreme mystery neither with the supplication of the tardy convert, nor yet with the arrogant curiosity of a later Faust. None the less, he, the fashioner of so many realized figures of flesh and blood, was swept into an unchartered world of phantoms. But even in this world his art did not forsake him; while dealing with unrealities he remained a realist. The sub-title of his last work, *Clara Militch,* is "After Death"; in it he reverts to these two distinct themes—the obsession of death with the shadowy suggestion of a personal survival, and to that lost youth of his which seems to him now as near as death itself.

Aratof is attracted by Clara Militch, but is doubtful about her sentiments towards him. She had been an actress and it occurs to him that out of his love she has been weaving a cruel comedy of her own. Suddenly he learns of her death through a newspaper; from that moment he is permeated by her as he had never been while she was alive. He determines, even now that it is too late, to discover the soul of this woman. He enters the house in which she had died and returns with her photograph and a fragment from her private diary. Clara had died, it seemed, for his sake. But it is neither love nor remorse that masters him now, it is the sense of being absolutely in the power of this unknown dead woman. He seems to see her, to hear her: "Unseen fingers ran light arpeggios up and down the keys of the piano . . . then the voice began again. More prolonged sounds were audible . . . as it were moans . . . always the same over again and over again. Then apart from the rest, the words began to stand out. . . . 'Roses . . . roses . . . roses . . .'"
She comes to him wreathed with roses, and gradually the love that he had denied the living woman is given eagerly to the dead. He is willing even to follow her across the dreaded frontier. And in an ecstasy of anticipation, remote and detached from the humdrum routine of life, Aratof continues in the power of the dead girl until the moment when they find him lying dead. In his cold fingers a lock of black hair is clutched and cannot be extricated. On the intent dead face there is stamped an untranslatable rapture, as of one who has veritably discovered in death what he had missed in life.

In spite of the pervading melancholy of his last works, Turgenev's kindness and generosity in the ordinary relations of life remained unchanged. He was as anxious for Maupassant's success in Russia, as he had been for Zola's. "Your name," he wrote to him in the autumn of 1881, "is making a sensation in Russia; they have translated what is translatable, and I have brought with me a great, thumping article on you (from *le Golos*); very well done and very cordial." The same year, when on a visit to Tolstoy, he took from a portmanteau a copy of *La Maison Tellier* and handed it to the Count. "It's by a young French writer," he said. "You'll see it's not at all bad. As a man he reminds me of Droujinine: like him he is an excellent son, an excellent friend, a man to be trusted, and, moreover, he is in touch with working men—advises them and helps them." On his side, Maupassant was equally appreciative of the great Russian whom, as we have seen, he placed even above his master, Flaubert.

He was anxious to include Turgenev in a series of foreign writers whom he wished to introduce to the French public, but the author of *Smoke* urged that his country should be represented in the series by Pushkin and Gogol. "Carrying modesty almost to the pitch of humility," Maupassant comments, "he did not wish to be talked about in the newspapers; and more than once he was as much hurt by articles full of praise as he would have been by insults, for he would not allow that anything ought to be written, except literature pure and simple. Even the criticism of works of art struck him as mere useless verbiage; and if ever any details about him and his private life were published by a journalist ápropos of one of his books, he was sensible of a genuine irritation mingled with a sense of shame peculiar to authors whose modesty was almost like that of a young girl." Maupassant, like Flaubert, accepted Turgenev as an infallible critic and always listened respectfully to his advice. "In spite of his age," he says, "and of the fact that his career was almost at an end, he had the most modern and advanced literary ideas, rejecting all forms of the old, obviously mechanical, novel, with its dramatic, ingenious plot, and only asking for life, nothing but life—'slices of life'—without complications or wonderful adventures."

Turgenev's whole life proves his patient devotion to his French friends; of that maliciously exploited posthumous quarrel it is enough to say that the Russian's invariable kindness to every one of them whom, at any time or in any way, it was in his power to help, to console or to advise more than outweighs any chance boutade on literary work which, after all, was in many cases wholly antipathetic to his own views on art. Maupassant became his friend from their very first meeting and when the Russian author's sufferings became unendurable it was from Maupassant, who was to die only too soon afterwards by his own hand, that he begged a revolver with which to end them. A little later he nearly killed Madame Viardot by throwing an ink-stand at her, so enraged was he—just as his mother would have been—at being ceaselessly watched.

Almost to the very end of the end, he persisted in work: "I live still, if living is being unable to stir or to stand up-right . . . that is how oysters live! And there still remain for me distractions that they do not possess." Yet, in this very life in death, his creative energy was so persistent that a visitor to Bougival received the impression that literature would be enriched by another volume of poems in prose. Turgenev had related his tormented dreams and the visitor instantly detected that the old power and charm still lingered. Only three months before his death, he dictated in French that sketch entitled *Fire at Sea*, which was yet another memory of youth snatched from the ironic wind-ings of the years.

Van Gogh, whose actual life established the deep kinship between the artist and the peasant in their common wrestle with nature, was attracted by Daudet's appreciative sketch of Ivan Turgenev. He, if any of the sons of men would have sensed any falsity, any "dressing-up" in the Russian novel-ist had there been any such to find. In those Letters of his, which prove him an artist even if he had never touched a brush, in those Letters which contribute more to the under-standing of art than libraries of art criticism, there are several references to Turgenev whom he places among those great ones who die with the serenity with which they have lived: "Sensitive, subtle, intelligent like women, also sensi-tive to their own suffering, and yet always full of life and self-consciousness, no indifferent stoicism, no contempt for life. I repeat—those fellows, they die like women die. No fixed idea about God, no abstractions, always on the firm ground of life itself, and only attached to that. I repeat—like *the women* who have loved much, pathetic, and like Sylvestre tells about Delacroix: '*Ainsi il mourut presqu'en souriant.*'"

With slight reservations, this analysis comes close to the core of Turgenev who clung to literature as to life itself. To him, as to Flaubert, external incidents in his books were so many petty disturbances. The antics of self-assertion, the over-emphasis of personality had always irritated him. He preferred to interpret the inner life of men and women who yielded quietly to the monotonous onsweep of nature whom, in the final issue, none after all can either hurry or evade. Repeatedly, he would rebel against his own disinclination for action. Close as he was essentially to Hamlet he avowed his preference for Hamlet's antithesis, Don Quixote. His sad irony played impartially upon his fellow human beings and upon himself. Permeated by the culture of the West, he tried to persuade himself that he preferred the aims of utility. A proved friend of the people, he fought against his inalienable distaste for the brutalities inseparable from revolution. He placed Bazarov above each and all of his Russian Hamlets: he not only defended Solomin, but saluted him. Glancing back at his life, the dying man knew well that he had projected creations altogether beyond the prejudice of individual temperament and, to the very last, he was puzzled by those who charged him on the one side with being the romantic of the realists and on the other with being the realist of the romantics. Politically, he had been charged with being the revolutionary of the reactionaries by the one side and with being the reactionary of the revolutionist by the other. Yet it was he, the weary doubter, the pessimist of *Smoke*, who showed up remorselessly the past of Russia in *The Annals of a Sportsman* and pointed in *Virgin Soil* to the escape of the future.

In the nineteenth century, more especially in our own country a circle of "Thinkers" arose whose object it was to subordinate art to ethics. English goodness in literary form

—as distinct from that political goodness at which Rostand *fils* has jibed—was in nineteenth-century England quite literally an article of commerce and particularly an article for export. Turgenev had nothing in common with such goodness; but his irony is utterly free from that boyish flippancy of to-day which the simple-minded accept as the protective colouring of very deep natures. Turgenev's irony came from seeing very clearly what human beings were, or rather what human beings were permitted to be, in sharp contradistinction from what the exploiters of goodness tacitly assumed them to be.

He himself was no exception in the comedy which he refused to whitewash. The son of *le beau Serge* could never take his place among the irreproachables. He had lived and he had loved; he who had sworn the oath of Hannibal had bought a serf; he had quarrelled frequently with unusually quarrelsome people; he had been the slave of a long infatuation; he had known all the moments of ironical repentance that Sanin was to know. But when all is said and done he had been true to the motive force of his life; he was a man of the future. Will the future reject him?

The modern régime in Russia has harnessed even Shakespeare in the great network of propaganda, while Turgenev remains a bourgeois artist of the past. Yet in the hour of their triumph they had Bazarov's Marxian formula on their lips. They fulfilled many predictions of Turgenev and even now are fulfilling others. Why then should the gulf between Turgenev and the present rulers of Russia be greater than that between Turgenev and Imperial Russia? In the end, it is safe to predict, this man who saw so clearly the pitfalls of posterity will not be rejected finally by that posterity.

He was an artist who painted his pictures in his own manner, accepting "*cette scélérate de Nature*" as he found her, but accepting human nature as something different, something on the whole kindly and pitiful. It is not Nature in his view who soothes the cares of those whom she has flung indifferently into life; it is rather they themselves, the quite ordinary men and women, unheroic and undeserving, who cluster humbly together to console each other before this stony mother of their fantasy whose fixed and always averted smile fails more and more to deceive. Yes, she was indeed indifferent alike to the tears of the suppliants and to the rage of the rebels.

But supplication and revolt alike, he realized, were at least evidence of that pathetic idealism which from man's own humanity has projected the symbol of an all-embracing, all merciful Nature who will protect the last and least of her children. For this, among so many other attributes, the race of man should not be scoffed at, but rather revered. Above all, pardon should never be withheld; compassion came of itself. The humble and the weak should on no account be crushed still lower, particularly if they seek to help those who are even weaker and humbler than themselves. But to the Titans who, unawed by the mystery around them, gesticulate before their own mirror believing it to be the mirror of human destiny, Turgenev was constitutionally antipathetic even when he tried hardest to believe in them.

Art remained for him interwoven almost with the last gasp of life. In the very atmosphere of death he recaptured in those dream poems the regret for happiness just missed, happiness that one has stumbled past in the darkness, happiness that has deepened through the sense of loss. Such evocations can never become quite faded. Literature may assume a thousand masks, a thousand movements may repudiate in turn new standards that have become old, but so long as youth itself persists, so long as love leaps unbidden and unbought between men and women, Turgenev will be remembered. His political gospel, or want of gospel, may have lost its meaning to new generations for whom *les jeunes* of his day have ceased to exist. But his pictures of Russian life blending intimately with Russian landscapes will remain things of beauty. The Turgenevian hero may survive merely to annotate a period, but the heroines of Turgenev will continue to touch the human heart so long as it is not hardened even against youth that dedicates carelessly to death its most precious treasures. The impression of passion, the deeper impression of love, the consolation of Nature who has no wish to console, the endurance of lonely man on the verge of an unknowable abyss—these things the pessimist of *Smoke* communicated as few others in the whole world of literature.

It has been said of the *Henriade* that there is not a single blade of grass in it; in the novels of Turgenev there are the plains of Russia.

But of Teutonic sentimentality Turgenev was wholly innocent. Like all his race, he was temperamentally disdainful of the concessions and compromises of that gentle opiate. He rejected its promises, its little rewards and, above all, its theory of comfort as the goal of conduct. With the Russian novelists of the nineteenth century as with their only equals in so many respects, the Ancients, love is almost invariably associated with suffering. Here again the three great heirs of Gogol differ profoundly in their presentation of life. To Tolstoy the fugitive blaze of a young girl's love was always merely the starting-point on the *via dolorosa* of maternity. To Dostoevsky it was essentially an abnormal excitation of the brain, painful whether it led downwards into the depths of atavism or upwards to the loneliest spiritual heights. As for Turgenev, in this as in everything else, he remained primarily an artist, clinging consistently to his delicately merciful analysis of that *couleur toute particulière* with a painter's minute attention to the variations of tone and shade. It was for Tolstoy to tell and re-tell the love story of Andromache; it was for Dostoevsky to reveal again the soul of Phaedra; but only Turgenev could have interpreted the noblest unwritten love story in the world—that of Antigone and Haemon.

But modern criticism, little concerned with love stories old or new, regards the work of this incomparable artist as the outpourings of an aesthete without faith and without force. Yet, exactly from the standpoint of such antiæsthetic criticism, Turgenev may be claimed as a real precursor. Without the powerful range of Tolstoy, he was also without what he himself called the Count's "sick conscience." Without the vivisecting penetration of Dostoevsky he was also without that confused agitation which mars so much of his enemy's greatest work. What he saw, Turgenev saw very clearly. He knew those ridiculed heroes of his far better than those who derided them. He detected something in them which is wholly foreign to peoples of the West, among whom repeatedly intellectuals, in spite of their weakness of will, have been dominated by the wish for power. Turgenev demonstrated, more convincingly than Tchekov, that his compatriots were devoid of this primeval instinct and no less a person than Lenin found it necessary to stress this extraordinary lack. He wrote on the very eve of his historic bid for power: "I continue to believe that any political party—especially a party which represents a progressive class—would lose the right to exist, would be unworthy to be considered a party at all, would count for less than nothing, if it refused power when there was a chance of obtaining it." Now the work of Turgenev, as the work of no other writer, explains, illustrates and analyses minutely this want of a root instinct among the intellectuals of Russia.

And the work of Turgenev, as the work of no other writer, examines the hesitating choice between the West and the East over which the Russia of to-day oscillates as if there had been no revolution at all. Will Russia become the proud leader of Asia, or will she become the humble disciple of Europe? Here the friend of Bakunin, the literary emancipator of the serfs, the man of whom it was said, "to dine with Turgenev is to dine with Europe," made the definite choice as Peter the Great had made it centuries before.

Yes, he had seen more clearly than those who had derided him; his vision had penetrated beyond that of those who deride him now. But that vision was clouded pitifully at last. At one of the Magny dinners, Daudet stated his conviction that Turgenev had gone out of his mind. He had confided to Charcot, it seems, his belief that he was "pursued by Assyrian soldiers, and even wished to hurl at him a fragment from the walls of Nineveh." Yet almost the last articulate words of the dying man were sane and very characteristic: "Live and love others, as I have always loved them." This in itself is a significant reply to those who stress the odium of far-off quarrels, maintaining that Tolstoy, Dostoevsky and Nekrasov came to detest this man who forgave so easily. Turgenev was sane, too, when he wrote that splendid letter to Count Tolstoy, which unhappily was to receive no answer.

On December 3, 1883, his sufferings came to an end. The great artist who, in the words of a modern Russian critic, "merely tolerated his presence" was at his bedside. "For two days," wrote Madame Viardot to an old friend of the Baden days, "he had lost consciousness. He suffered no more, his life ebbed out slowly, and after two convulsions he drew his last breath. We were all beside him. He became handsome again, as he had been always in the past. The first day after his death he had still, between his eyebrows, a deep wrinkle which had been formed under the pressure of convulsions; on the second day his normal expression of kindness reappeared on his face. One almost expected to see him smile."

His journal was burnt faithfully in the garden at Bougival; his corpse was carried to the Gare de l'Est. It was accompanied by the larger part of the Russian colony in Paris. Several distinguished Frenchmen, among whom were Renan and About, paid him a last farewell in the name of literature and of France. The French at least had long realized the significance of this suppressed historian of his race.

Gogol's troïka two years before, with the death of Dostoevsky, had ceased to function. The dreamer of a renewed Byzantium and of an ideal Russian yet to be, had passed. Now Tolstoy, with the gospel of non-resistance on his lips and the deeper gospel of the nihilism of all human life in his heart, was left to advance alone. Neither he nor Dostoevsky had comprehended the thought that germinated under the "idleness" of Turgenev. But in the days to come it was to be tested not by the for and against of verbal logic, but by the reality of holocausts of corpses. It has stood the test. Turgenev illustrated the truth that his contemporaries had not the will to fashion new patterns to reflect themselves. He had proved that Russia was scarcely ripe even for the old patterns which Europe, even to-day, hesitates to discard. Slaves in the past, the heroic Russians before the War accepted slavery under the promise that Europe will follow instead of leading them. The "surplus value" might, however, elude their grasp because they, less than any other people in our old Europe, understand the workings of the one real creator of all values—Nature herself. These cold facts of experience, registered quietly in the works of a bourgeois artist, are known as the novels of Ivan Turgenev.

Petersburg was to follow the lead of Paris. Four days later the dead man's prophecy to Polonsky was fulfilled. "Wait a little," he had said, "and then you will see how they will treat us." His funeral like that of his old enemy, Dostoevsky, was a pageant of mourning. The author of *Smoke* who for so long had been neglected by his compatriots became significant to them in death. Two hundred and eighty-five deputations and an enormous crowd followed him to the cemetery. At last, he had returned to his own country to settle down permanently. Very fittingly, he was buried close to Belinsky who had understood and appreciated him from the first.

Yet even now history was to repeat itself inevitably. Turgenev had been imprisoned for praising the dead author of *Dead Souls;* in his turn Tolstoy was to meet with official censure for wishing to pay public homage to the dead author of *The Annals of a Sportsman.* But the voices of great writers are confined neither by the tomb of death, nor by autocracy which, whether in the undisguised phases of the past, or in the disguised phases of the present, remains eternally the tomb of life.

AUTHOR'S NOTE

Among the works to which the Author of this biographical study is indebted, the following should be especially mentioned:

The Complete Works of Turgenev. Translated by Constance Garnett. (Heinemann)

Ivan Tourguénieff: La Vie et L'Œuvre. Par Emile Haumant. (Librairie Armand Colin)

Souvenirs sur Tourguénieff. Par Isaac Pavlovsky. (Paris. Nouvelle Librairie Parisienne)

Tourguenieff Inconnu. Par Michel Delines. (Paris. La Librairie Illustrée)

Ivan Tourguénieff: Lettres à Madame Viardot. Publiées et annotées par E. Halperine Kaminsky. (Paris. Bibliothèque Charpentier)

A Literary History of Russia. By A. Bruckner. (Fisher Unwin)

A History of Russian Literature. By K. Walizewski. (Heinemann)

La Pensée Russe Contemporaine. By Ivan Strannik. (Paris. Librairie Armand Colin)

Le Roman Russe. Par Vicomte E. M. de Vogüé. (Paris. Librairie Plon)

The Life of Tolstoy—First Fifty Years. By Aylmer Maude. (Constable)

The Life of Tolstoy—Later Years. By Aylmer Maude. (Constable)

Blackstick Papers. By Lady Ritchie. (Smith Elder)

INDEX

225

INDEX

227